Competition Laws, National I s and International Relatio

Most of the competition laws currently enforced by states aim to protect consumer welfare and promote fair competition by regulating against anticompetitive behavior. Yet despite the shared objectives the global community does not have a common global competition law. In exploring the reasons for this, this book takes a unique interdisciplinary approach by using international relations theories to illustrate the relationship between the enforcement of competition laws and international relations through an analysis of competition cases relating to cartels, extraterritoriality, and corporate mergers and acquisitions.

Through an examination of this relationship, this book will consider why the views held by state leaders on the condition of international relations may at times lead them to either arbitrarily over-enforce or disregard their competition laws to the detriment of fair competition and consumer welfare. This book also provides suggestions for global business investors who face competition law issues on how they may accommodate such views.

Ko Unoki has been involved with global marketing, corporate strategy formulation, and strategic alliances while working in the electronics and healthcare industries for several decades, and was also a Senior Fellow at The 21st Century Public Policy Institute of the Federation of Japanese Economic Organizations (Keidanren). He received a Doctor of Business Administration degree from Hitotsubashi University, Japan.

Routledge Research in Competition Law

The Internationalisation of Competition Rules
Brendan J. Sweeney

Antitrust Federalism in the EU and the US
Firat Cengiz

Competition and Regulation in the Airline Industry
Puppets in Chaos
Steven Truxal

Merger Control in Post-Communist Countries
EC Merger Regulation in Small Market Economies
Jurgita Malinauskaite

Merger Control in Europe
The Gap in the ECMR and National Merger Legislations
Ioannis Kokkoris

Harmonising Regulatory and Antitrust Regimes for International Air Transport
Jan Walulik

Collective Redress and EU Competition Law
Eda Sahin

Competition Policy and Network Industries
Structural Separation in the Telecommunications Sector
Pierluigi Congedo

Competition Laws, National Interests and International Relations
Ko Unoki

Competition Laws, National Interests and International Relations

Ko Unoki

Routledge
Taylor & Francis Group
LONDON AND NEW YORK

First published 2020
by Routledge
2 Park Square, Milton Park, Abingdon, Oxon OX14 4RN

and by Routledge
52 Vanderbilt Avenue, New York, NY 10017

Routledge is an imprint of the Taylor & Francis Group, an informa business

First issued in paperback 2021

British Library Cataloguing-in-Publication Data
A catalogue record for this book is available from the British Library

Library of Congress Cataloging-in-Publication Data
Names: Unoki, Ko, author.
Title: Competition laws, national interests and international relations / Ko Unoki.
Description: Abingdon, Oxon ; New York, NY : Routledge, 2019. | Series: Routledge research in competition law | Based on author's thesis (LLM -Hitotsubashi Daigaku. Graduate School of International Corporate Strategy, 2019). | Includes bibliographical references and index.
Identifiers: LCCN 2019037224 (print) | LCCN 2019037225 (ebook)
Subjects: LCSH: Antitrust law--Political aspects. | Competition, International. | Foreign trade regulation. | National interest--Economic aspects.
Classification: LCC K3850 .U56 2019 (print) | LCC K3850 (ebook) | DDC 343.07/21--dc23
LC record available at https://lccn.loc.gov/2019037224
LC ebook record available at https://lccn.loc.gov/2019037225

ISBN: 978-0-367-34611-9 (hbk)
ISBN: 978-1-03-208693-4 (pbk)
ISBN: 978-0-429-32685-1 (ebk)

Typeset in Galliard
by Taylor & Francis Books

Contents

Preface

During my years of working at an internationally renowned electronics company based in Japan, I recall that on many occasions the executive leaders of the company exhorted its employees to show empathy with its customers, provide solutions to their needs, or deliver products that elated them. The ultimate, unwavering objective for those who were involved in sales and marketing such as myself was, however, to sell as many products as possible to our customers wherever they were located at the highest possible price and at the lowest possible cost, which was something easier said than done given the cut-throat nature of competition in the crowded global consumer electronics market. This was somehow to be accomplished through executing various generic marketing strategies that were selected depending on the competitive situation that we were facing, including expanding or using specific distribution channels for our products, entering into new, relatively competition-free markets, increasing our product lineup or offerings, and working with our engineers and product planners to produce and deliver new products to our customers that performed better than those of our competitors.

While we all worked towards achieving our objective of selling and accumulating profit as much as possible, company compliance policy dictated us to also periodically attend various company-sponsored education courses on the basic tenets of competition laws to remind ourselves of, and avoid, what constituted unlawful, anticompetitive behavior such as price fixing or colluding with our industry rivals. And, of course, we made sure to adhere to the principles, laws, and regulations promoting fair competition in our business transactions. However, it goes without saying that for some of us marketers, saleswomen and men, our publicly unstated goal was simple: to corner a market and wipe out our competitors. That is, the unspoken and subconscious aspiration was to be a monopoly, or the dominant supplier in our industry.

A major reason why some of us wanted to be a monopoly was undoubtedly due to a desire to avoid getting into a price war with our competitors and instead to accumulate an ever-higher amount of profits (leading to satisfying the self-interest of many of us in getting fatter bonuses). Which goes to say that we wanted to avoid competition because essentially we did not like to compete. Competition, after all, forces those in business to be constantly on their toes and keeps them awake at night. President Theodore Roosevelt of the United States (US) may have recommended the strenuous life of continuous toil, effort, labor, and strife as a means to achieving success for the individual.[1] Why, however, endure this insufferable situation when, by wiping out competitors, a business or an entrepreneur could at one stroke enjoy monopoly profits, do business at their leisure, and not have to worry about what their competitors were coming out with or for that matter what customers thought of their offering? Indeed, historian Carroll Quigley of Georgetown University claimed that businesses hate to compete and substantiated his assertion through many historical examples of companies becoming monopolies or forming cartels with the implicit purpose of quashing competition.[2] In this regard, economist Joseph Stiglitz further observes that, in their pursuit of becoming a monopoly, businesses were often assisted by political forces that supported lax anticompetition enforcement which he claims is behind the existence of high levels of monopoly profits in today's markets and also reinforces the Marxist view that markets tends towards becoming a monopoly economy.[3] In presenting these views this is not to insinuate, however, that in wanting to become a monopoly we equally wanted to ultimately create a post-capitalist communist utopia as envisioned by Karl Marx where no one competes anymore and everyone does nothing but "hunt in the morning, fish in the afternoon, rear cattle in the evening, and criticize after dinner,"[4] activities which the British news magazine *The Economist* called "loafing about"![5]

In retrospect, it would seem that what some of us may have felt in the dark recesses of our psyche suggested or reflected the coexistence of certain forces with a self-contradictory nature within capitalism, that is, a market-based economic system in which most of the means of production are privately owned and the supply of goods and services is guided by demand from markets. One such force is competition. It is competition that motivates businesses to innovate and challenge one another in developing better technologies and products for consumers. On the other hand, it is also due to competition that weaker businesses are eliminated from markets leading to the possibility of fewer competitors in the market and ironically lesser competition.

The other force within capitalism which is closely intertwined with competition is self-interest. The economist Adam Smith had pointed out that it is not out of any feelings of benevolence that companies and entrepreneurs compete to outsell their products to consumers. Rather, they compete out of self-interest and/or self-love to create advantages for themselves in the form of obtaining higher levels of profits and other financial rewards.[6] While Smith had argued that this pursuit of self-interest ultimately led to greater overall prosperity of society,[7] if not checked, it may also encourage businesses to compete with each other with the intent of becoming a monopoly not only to maximize profits, but also because being a monopoly is arguably the only way to ensure the long-term survival of a business, thus fulfilling the most basic self-interest of all businesses.

If the end goal of business is to become a monopoly by ironically quashing competition through competition, could capitalism continue in a situation where monopolies dominate markets? Or, could monopolies last indefinitely under capitalism? And to begin with, is having a monopoly bad for capitalism? No one has ever satisfyingly answered these questions. Marx on his part offered a double-edged perspective on the impact of monopoly on a capitalist system. On the one hand, he predicted a crisis of capitalism and social instability as successful capitalists drive their weaker rivals out of business leading to a concentration of capital, monopoly rents, and greater disparities of wealth as workers who have no alternative places to work face lower wages. In the same breath, however, he admitted that the very concentration of capital had helped to realize technological progress and industrial development. As he saw it, for example, the rapid development of railroads would not have been possible in a situation if the ownership of capital had been decentralized and there had instead been many small railway companies which on their own would not have had an adequate accumulation of capital to make the large-scale investments necessary for expanding their railway lines or for large-scale railroad infrastructure development.

Be that as it may, despite the possible benefits of having monopolies as pointed out by Marx, it would seem most capitalist economies do not want to take any chances on what would happen if competition was completely unregulated. This is perhaps made most apparent by the fact that up to 2019 over 130 states in the world have legislated competition laws (a.k.a. antitrust laws) for the purposes of protecting competition and the welfare of consumers by banning, for example, monopolization or the abuses by a monopoly arising from its dominant position in the market, as well as by prohibiting cartels and acts associated with restraining commercial trade such as horizontal price fixing or the restriction of production output.

Notwithstanding the commonality of objectives shared by most of the competition laws currently in existence and the interest of businesses in seeing uniformity, consistency, and transparency in their application, the international community has not, however, been able to come to an agreement on a global competition law or policy. The signing of the Paris Peace Pact (a.k.a. Kellogg Briand Pact) in 1928 shows that it was possible to surmount the undeniably high hurdle of outlawing war. One would think that if the international community could again put aside their differences and consider the welfare of all peoples, then introducing a law that would at least state some basic principles endorsing the need of protecting competition or consumer welfare would appear to be simple. Alas, history has shown that it would not be, although ever since President Franklin D. Roosevelt of the United States (US) had proposed that the international community outlaw cartels there have been various attempts at creating a global competition law.

A major objective of this book, accordingly, will be to provide an answer to the question: why does the international community not have, despite the common interest of consumers anywhere of getting the best possible products and services at the lowest possible prices, a global competition law or policy that aims to protect competition and the welfare of consumers? Through focusing on the competition policy-related topics of cartels, the extraterritorial application of competition laws, and mergers and acquisitions, I will attempt to answer this question by working from the hypothesis that as the main objective of states is to defend and pursue their national interests, states will not agree to a global competition law that may entail sacrificing their national interests in favor of promoting the global welfare of consumers. As to what those national interests are (aside from protecting national sovereignty) and to what extent state leaders are willing to sacrifice them will depend in turn on how state leaders view the condition of international relations. This interrelationship between competition laws and national interests, as well as the globalization of international business which has been facilitated to a large extent by the spread and use of the Internet, suggests that the study of competition laws or policy should be done not within the isolated vertical silo of legal studies or legal history, but rather in an interdisciplinary format in combination with studies of International Relations (IR) and, in particular, the theories of IR. Accordingly, for the cases to be examined within the competition topics mentioned earlier, I will use the framework of the IR theories of Realism, Liberalism, and Power Transition in the attempt of providing a possible theory as to why states behave as they do in their implementation of competition policies.

I will also propose some suggestions for businesses that face competition law-related issues in a state on the "pitch" they should make towards state leaders that would accommodate the views that these leaders may have on the condition of international relations and consequently what they consider to be their national interests. In this respect, I hope that the interdisciplinary approach of this book may attract not only readers who have a wide interest in competition law, business history, and IR, but will also be of use for business leaders who would like to know about the practical application of IR theories for managing global business transactions that may face issues of competition law.

This book is structured as follows. In the first introductory chapter I will examine the various definitions of competition, what has been happening recently (until 2019) with competition in certain capitalist economies and examine the reasons as to why it should be protected. In the second chapter, after giving an overview on the competition laws of the US, the European Union (EU), and Japan, I will present some assumptions underlying the current situation pertaining to the enforcement of competition laws and propose a hypothesis that will be a guide for the arguments later presented in this book. In the third chapter, I will give a brief overview on the IR theories of Realism, Liberalism, and Power Transition. This will be followed by the fourth chapter which will look at cartels and focus on how governments have used them to pursue their national interests at the expense of consumer welfare. The fifth chapter will consider various examples of the extraterritorial application of domestic competition laws and how this has led to a clash of national interests. In the sixth chapter I will look at international corporate mergers and acquisitions (M&A) and focus on where, when, and how government leaders have intervened to stall or reject what are essentially private business transactions for purposes that have more to do with promoting national interests than with protecting competition or consumer welfare. In the seventh and final chapter I will review how the decisions of government leaders given in the sample cases regarding cartels, extraterritoriality, and M&A could be explained in the context of IR theories. The chapter will conclude with some proposals on the approach that businesses which face competition law-related issues should take towards state leaders in accommodating their view of international relations and national interests, and on what will be needed for the international community to come to an agreement for the enactment of a common competition law.

Although the idea for this book is largely based on a thesis written while studying for a law degree at the Graduate School of International Corporate Strategy of Hitotsubashi University, a major impetus for writing it comes from not only an interest in the study of IR, but also from an interest in the future of capitalism on which many books have been published as of late. In the past few years, we have seen several markets such as retail, distribution, search, and social networking become dominated by a few Internet platform companies that have gained size and arguably stifled competition partly by aggressively acquiring new market entrants and buying up patents of other companies.[8] Some major industrial and emerging market states are facing shrinking and greying populations leading to the possibility of a decline in innovative activity and economic productivity while some of the societies of these same states have become increasingly intolerant towards immigrants, a potential source of innovation (as history, especially that of the US, has shown). Our global natural environment is being ravaged as a result of what are arguably some of the unintended consequences of capitalism. The dumping of plastic waste products into the oceans continues unabated. Factories and automobiles fill the skies in the congested cities of fast-growing emerging economies with noxious fumes that threaten the health of their inhabitants. Man-made emissions of planet-warming carbon dioxide are increasing to alarming levels in the earth's atmosphere threatening to further accelerate global climate change.[9] The expansion of industry and agriculture is facilitating the deforestation of major forests around the world. In addition, despite efforts to find alternative sources for the energy that drives the major market economies, capitalism remains largely hooked on the finite and polluting energy resources of oil and coal. And finally, despite experiencing two disastrous world wars, we continue to face a world in which international politics is still, to quote the IR theorist Hans Morgenthau, a competitive struggle by states for power[10] which has not only manifested in states pursuing mercantilist trade policies that seem to be designed to protect certain industry sectors rather than promoting consumer welfare and protecting competition, but also leaves open to the possibility of capitalism and human society finishing itself off without the need of Mother Nature to do the job.

This is my third book. My first book dealt with mergers and acquisitions and how the cultural factor of tolerance has an impact on the outcome of such transactions, whether it be between companies or between states. My second book looked at the outbreak of the Pacific War and explored its origins using the framework of IR theories. If there is a common, underlying theme that is being highlighted in the previous two books and this latest work, it is that of the importance of maintaining a balance in whatever we do. Despite the signs of its impending doom that I have mentioned, history suggests an ability of the capitalist system driven by competition and what the Moravian-born American economist Joseph Schumpeter called the perennial "gale of creative destruction" to revitalize itself by weeding out old and outdated methods of production and inefficient enterprises in favor of newer technologies and entrepreneurs.[11] And to this end, as we have mentioned, states have enacted competition laws to ensure that competition prevails. If states, however, are lax in their enforcement of competition laws, this may lead to a situation of monopolies or oligopolies forming in certain markets or industries which may hamper competition and innovation. On the other hand, over-enforcement may lead to too much decentralization of an economy leading to the unavailability of large amounts of capital that would be necessary for large-scale technology development or investment such as for, to cite a recent example, 5G wireless communications infrastructure. Furthermore, either under- or over-enforcement of competition laws may lead to friction or a conflict of interests between states. Which goes to say that in the absence (so far) of a global competition law, enforcement of the many state-based competition laws should also be undertaken while taking into consideration the importance of maintaining a fine balance between defending the interests of global consumer welfare, promoting national interests, and protecting innovation-creating competition.

Notes

1 Roosevelt, Theodore, The Strenuous Life, Bartleby.com, April 10, 1899, Online. Available https://www.bartleby.com/58/1.html (accessed June 15, 2019).
2 Quigley, Carroll, *Tragedy and Hope*, The Macmillan Company, 1966, p.452.
3 Stiglitz, Joseph, Are Markets Efficient, or do they Tend Towards Monopoly?, World Economic Forum, May 18, 2016, Online. Available https://www.weforum.org/agenda/2016/05/joseph-stiglitz-are-markets-efficient-or-do-they-tend-towards-monopoly-the-verdict-is-in/ (accessed June 15, 2019).
4 Kamenka, Eugene, *The Portable Karl Marx*, Viking Penguin Inc., 1983, p.177.
5 *The Economist*, Second Time Farce: Rulers of the world: read Karl Marx!, May 3, 2018.
6 Smith, Adam, *An Inquiry into the Cause of the Wealth of Nations*, Book II, Chapter 2, Encyclopedia Britannica Inc., 1982, p.142.
7 Ibid., p.194.
8 Nocera, Joe, The Easiest Way to Fix Facebook? Break it Up, *Japan Times*, November 28, 2018; *The Economist*, op.cit. Some recent examples would be the Internet social media platform Facebook Inc.'s acquisition of rivals Instagram in 2012 and WhatsApp in 2014. As stated in Nocera, as marketing professor Scott Galloway sees it, Facebook, along with the other Internet platform companies of Amazon, Apple, and Alphabet (Google) has through acquisitions "aggregated more economic value and influence" than almost any other commercial enterprise in history. This development has led to a situation, as noted by Noah Smith of Bloomberg (also taken from Nocera), that potential startups may be unable to get funding from venture capitalists who may think that they would end up as "Facebook's kill zone."
9 *Japan Times*, CO_2 Levels Hit Record-High 415.26ppm, Raising Alarm, May 15, 2019.
10 Morgenthau, Hans J., *Politics Among Nations*, McGraw Hill, 1985, p.31.
11 Schumpeter, Joseph A., *Capitalism, Socialism and Democracy*, Harper Touch Books, 1975, p.84.

Acknowledgements

Winston Churchill was reported to have said that writing a book is an adventure. Indeed, in looking back on what I had experienced after putting the final touches to this work which has become my third published book, it has been an adventure for me as well, but one that was not undertaken alone but instead accomplished with the support and encouragement of my professors, work colleagues, relatives, and friends. This book, which has as its origin a thesis on competition laws that I submitted to the Graduate School of International Corporate Strategy of Hitotsubashi University, would not have come to fruition without the kind support of the school and in particular my thesis adviser, Business Law Professor Vicki Beyer of the Hitotsubashi University Graduate School of Law, who provided me with insightful advice, suggestions, and guidance in fortifying the arguments of my thesis and gave me much-needed encouragement to complete what I thought to be the daunting task of attending law classes in the evenings after a full day of work at my office and writing the thesis while at the same time laying the foundations for expanding it into a book. I am much indebted to Routledge Editor of Business and Economics, Lam Yong Ling, who, as with the publication of my first book by Taylor & Francis, *Mergers, Acquisitions, and Global Empires* (2012), saw value and worthiness in having this work also published by Routledge. And as to the other members of the Routledge team, my sincere thanks and feelings of appreciation go to Routledge Senior Editorial Assistant Samantha Phua, and Editorial Intern Felicia Hor, for assisting me throughout the publication process. Many thanks also to Senior Production Editor at Taylor & Francis Group, Cathy Hurren, and to Dr. Kathrin Luddecke for the marvellous work on copyediting my text. Appreciation and gratitude also go to my parents Takako and Hajime who nurtured my lifelong love of reading books and studying. A word of appreciation is also due to my colleagues at work who were tolerant and understanding enough to allow me to leave work early to attend graduate school courses in the evenings. Finally, and, last but not least, my thanks go to my wife Ritsuko for supporting my endeavors in getting a law degree at a relatively late stage in life and for tolerating my time away in writing this book at my PC.

1 Introduction

What is competition?

In the opening section of his epic motion picture *2001: A Space Odyssey*, titled The Dawn of Man, producer and director Stanley Kubrick takes us to the Paleolithic Era where we see a group of proto-humans eke out a precarious hand-to-mouth existence in an African savanna. They live in a hostile, drought-stricken environment where they feed on shrubs, berries, and lice. They have no weapons to defend themselves against more powerful carnivorous predators. In this bleak setting, two tribes of proto-humans fight over a muddy water hole. Instead of sharing, one tribe and its leader are defending the monopoly they already have over this precious source of water against another intruding tribe that is attempting to gain access to it. The proto-humans scream at each other, make threatening faces, thump their chests, and flail their arms, but they do not engage in any acts of physical violence. One day, the leader of the tribe that has control over the water hole has (with some help from a presumably extraterrestrial intelligence) an epiphany and discovers that a hand-held bone could be used as a tool and weapon. To the strain of the exhilarating opening fanfare of composer Richard Strauss' tone poem, *Thus Spoke Zarathustra*, the leader begins shattering the bones of dead animals scattered about on the drought-hardened ground, smashes the head of an unsuspecting tapir with a bone, and realizes the joy of eating fresh meat. The proto-human later uses this newly found weapon to pummel to death the alpha member of the rival tribe and triumphantly throws the bone into the air. The first proto-human tribe's monopoly over the water hole is now undisputed and the first evolutionary steps towards becoming modern humans has been taken.

Although the above sequences of events in the movie sprang from the imagination of Kubrick and the science fiction writer Arthur C. Clarke, sociologists and anthropologists believe that certain basic traits of behavior of the proto-humans depicted in Kubrick's film, such as cooperating with each other and organizing into groups, forming hierarchies, and exhibiting hostility towards people who are viewed as being different from themselves,[1] have been hardwired within the genus Homo Sapiens over the course of several million years of evolution from a common hominid ancestor shared with chimpanzees and bonobos.[2] The activity of competing against one another, or competition, whether it be over a muddy water hole, food, territory, or a mate, has also been a phenomenon that has arguably been ever present within the context of the social, political, and economic development of modern humans ever since they first appeared in Africa around 200,000 years ago. Indeed, some scholars have argued that "competitiveness" is a biological trait associated with natural selection that evolved along with the basic need for human survival.[3] In certain societies children compete for better grades or for being accepted into a good school from an early age. University graduates compete with one another in finding a job or getting into graduate school. Company employees compete over getting a promotion or a salary raise. Businesses and entrepreneurs compete for customers, market share, and profits. Although for many people competitive activity entails the need of coping with a certain amount of physical and mental stress, as the ancient Greek Olympic Games and the prevalence today of sporting events such as soccer matches all over the world attest, humans have, however, also long derived fulfillment or a sense of self-actualization in organizing and participating in activities that promote competition. As noted by sociologist Sander van der Linden, most people have at one point or another enjoyed being part of a competitive event or a situation which tends to be more fun and satisfying if you or your side win.[4]

On what the nature of competition is or on what it means to compete, the British economist John Vickers noted that the concept of competition had "taken on a number of interpretations and meanings, many of them vague."[5] While it was in 2010 that the United Nations Conference on Trade and Development (UNCTAD) had defined competition as being simply "rivalry among firms in the marketplace" that also "extends to envisaged or potential rivalry,"[6] over the centuries several prominent thinkers have attempted to define, or at least describe, what competition is.

In the 17th century English philosopher Thomas Hobbes in his political treatise *Leviathan* made the bleak assessment based on his analysis of human nature that competition, along with diffidence and the pursuit of glory, was one of the principal causes of quarrels among individuals. According to Hobbes, competition induced people to use violent means for the purposes of gain and for making them "masters of other men's persons, wives, children, and cattle."[7] Later on in the 18th century the Scottish economist Adam Smith viewed competition primarily as an activity or process that is undertaken by multiple businesses and laborers.[8] In his *An Inquiry Into the Nature and Causes of The Wealth of Nations*, Smith states that because of "free competition," those involved in the banking business are obliged, due to the "multiplication" of banking companies in the United Kingdom, "to be more liberal in their dealings with their customers, lest their rivals should carry them away" and that the more freer and more general competition is in "any branch of trade, or any division of labor," the more advantageous it is to the public.[9] That is, it is competition that determines the level of economic activity and its impact on the public. The more competition there is, the more advantages there will be for customers since those who are competing for their hearts and minds will race to produce better and more products and services.

As to *why* a banker or people of various trades compete, Adam Smith offers an abstract explanation that people compete for promoting their self-interest. As he put it, "it is not from the benevolence of the butcher, the brewer, or the baker that we expect our dinner, but from their regard to their own interest."[10] People, in short, compete not to benefit others but to create more advantages for themselves, a sentiment that comes from self-love. What prevents the pursuit of self-interest to the extreme leading to abusive behavior in the marketplace such as price gouging, however, is none other than competition from other butchers, bakers, or brewers. In short, competition, as inferred by Adam Smith, is also a regulator of economic activity that restrains the ability of anyone to take advantage of others.

In the 19th century Karl Marx stated that "conceptually competition is nothing other than the inner nature of capital, its essential character, appearing in and realized as the reciprocal interaction of many capitals,"[11] a process which would result in larger capitals beating smaller, weaker capitals. For Marx, competition is what drives competing capitalists in their struggle to survive in a commodity world where the buying and selling of labor and products is the basis of competition among capitals. Indeed, in the latter half of the 19th century it was perceived in the industrialized nations of Europe that competition in the economic sphere implied what the scientist Charles Darwin declared as a biological law of nature: the survival of the stronger at the expense of the weaker. Thus, it was considered natural that the large-scale producer or trader would terminate the existence of the weaker competitor through competition, and that this was to the benefit of the progress and welfare of the community. As the French economist Frederic Bastiat put it in his work *Les Harmonies Économiques*, competition was the "humanitarian force" that "continuously wrests progress from the hands of the individual to make it the common heritage of the great human family."[12]

In Japan in the second half of the 19th century, the Japanese Meiji era scholar Fukuzawa Yukichi (1835–1901) mentioned in his autobiography that, while translating the text of W. and R. Chambers on political economy, he realized the need to invent a corresponding Japanese term for the English word "competition" for which there was no equivalent in the Japanese language at the time. Accordingly, Fukuzawa chose two Chinese written characters, *kyo-so*, which literally meant "race-fight." When questioned about the meaning of this newly created compound term by a government official, Fukuzawa elaborated that this was nothing new, that "all merchants 'race and fight' and that is the way values are fixed."[13] As an example, Fukuzawa mentioned that if one merchant began to sell a product cheaply, his neighbor would try to sell a similar product at an even cheaper price.[14]

Moving into the 20th century, one of the most famous views of competition was provided by the Moravian-born American economist and sociologist Joseph Schumpeter who viewed competition as a "perennial gale of creative destruction" that resulted in the incessant opening up of new markets and "industrial mutation" leading to the constant reinvigoration of the economic structure of capitalism.[15] For Schumpeter, competition, in the context of a capitalist economic structure, is essentially an endless process of innovation that leads to the displacement of older technologies by newer ones and the replacement of incumbent companies in the market by newer and more innovative players. So long as this competitive process of "creative destruction" is maintained in perpetuity, the "capitalist engine" is kept in motion and economic growth continues.[16]

While space does not allow this book to give more than just a short sample of the various interpretations of what competition is that have been provided by scholars over several centuries, the above various views from Hobbes, Smith, Marx, Bastiat, Fukuzawa, up to Schumpeter, seem to suggest that competition is essentially an activity among rival parties, whether it be entrepreneurs, businesses, marathon runners, etc., that often leads to a winner or someone coming out on top and a loser or someone coming in second. That is, it seems that a by-product of a competitive event or situation is the creation of a hierarchy.

The role of competition

As for the role of competition, the United States (US) Supreme Court had stated its views in several cases brought before it. In Northern Pacific Railway Co. v. United States (1958) the court viewed competition as essential not only in ensuring the optimum allocation of economic resources, the lowest prices for consumers, and "the greatest material progress," but also for providing an environment "conductive to the preservation of...democratic political and social institutions."[17] In National Society of Professional Engineers v. United States (1978), the court observed that competition is "the best method of allocating resources in a free market," and "that all elements of a bargain – quality, service, safety, and durability...are favorably affected by the free opportunity to select among alternative offers."[18] The views of the Supreme Court stated in these cases on the role and importance of competition may have been influenced by the thinking of the so-called "Harvard School," legal scholars at Harvard University such as Donald F. Turner and Phillip Areeda who argued that, as companies were more likely to engage in anticompetitive conduct when markets were concentrated, and as they saw political and economic freedom being threatened by market concentration, it was therefore vital to oppose any movement that may lead to market concentration even when it may lead to lower costs and benefit consumers. Accordingly, under the Harvard School approach, US courts and government agencies in the 1960s and 1970s generally took the stance of assuming the per se illegality (i.e., inherently illegal nature) of any mergers, joint ventures, or agreements that would allow companies to obtain or exercise market power regardless of any potential benefits such as lower prices for consumers.[19]

Outside of the Supreme Court, Schumpeter as mentioned earlier claimed that the role of competition was to constantly reinvigorate capitalism and keep its engine in motion through the process of innovation.[20] Business scholar Michael Porter of the Harvard Business School also sees competition as a driver of innovation leading to productivity growth which is the core factor in determining the welfare of consumers and ultimately in a nation's standard of living.[21] For Porter, it is competition within a market economy that motivates and drives entrepreneurs and companies to race each other to innovate and develop better products and services for consumers and cultivate new business sources of profits.

In summarizing the above views on the definition and role of competition, I wish to propose the following definition of and assumptions about competition: competition within the context of business is an activity or process that entails rivalry among entrepreneurs and enterprises who compete, out of promoting their self-interests, in producing ever superior products and services that are able to win the hearts and minds of consumers. It is a core, essential element of a capitalist, free market economic system where enterprises and entrepreneurs are able to enter a market without having to face major barriers to entry and consumers are generally free to choose to purchase products from whoever is offering them. In providing material benefits to consumers through the production of superior products and services, competition's role is to further drive innovation and realize the optimal allocation of economic resources in an economy. In a business environment where enterprises are able to freely compete without government interference and new companies are able to enter a market without having to face any major entry barriers, we can thus arguably expect to see: constantly better quality products and services at lower prices leading to a higher standard of living, higher productivity arising from greater efficiency in the allocation of resources leading to higher economic growth rates, greater equality in wealth owing to less concentration of economic power in the hands of a few enterprises, and the dispersion of economic power leading to a lesser likelihood that democratic government and social institutions will be politically hijacked by a small number of powerful enterprises and be unduly under their influence as a result.

The dilemma of competition and capitalism

While the benefit of competition for consumers and society is manifested in the form of greater innovation leading to better products and services for customers, the question arises: do producers or business owners generally *want* to compete? Past business history, with its many examples of companies in various industries attempting to become a monopoly,[22] forming cartels, or engaging in monopolistic behavior, i.e., monopolization,[23] suggests that the answer to this question is most likely no. Indeed, if we take the view of Adam Smith that people work primarily with their self-interests in mind, it can be argued that no business owner would want more competition that may result in lower profits and in some cases their own destruction. As economist Jeremy Rifkin noted, a small number of enterprises in mature industries that have succeeded in cornering much of the market or have established themselves in a position of monopoly or oligopoly[24] "have every interest in blocking further economic progress in order to protect the value" of the capital they had already invested in outdated technology.[25] Polish economist Oskar Lange noted that when the maintenance of the value of their invested capital becomes the chief concern of entrepreneurs, and especially those that enjoy a monopoly position in an industry, it is in their every interest to see that "further economic progress has to stop, or, at least, to slow down considerably."[26]

The achievement of a monopoly position in a market would confer upon a business the ability to realize uncompetitive pricing and earn higher amount of profits than would be expected if it were facing competition from other enterprises.[27] Given that business owners generally want to maximize their revenues and profits, it is perhaps not too outlandish to suggest that most of them would like to carve out for themselves a position of monopoly or oligopoly. Indeed, billionaire and co-founder of PayPal (one of the world's largest online payment systems) Peter Thiel was candid enough (where most other entrepreneurs would most likely vehemently deny this in public) to state that the goal for all companies should be to achieve monopoly through which they can set market prices.[28] Perhaps a way for a person not involved in running any business to appreciate this psychology is to play the board game *Monopoly* where the objective is to win by maximizing your earnings by cornering as much as possible of a fictitious real estate market and wiping out your opponents in the process.

To get to a position of monopoly or oligopoly an entrepreneur must continuously outcompete all other enterprises. To outcompete, the entrepreneur must accumulate enough profits that will allow her/him to reinvest these in activities such as expanding production and producing superior products (in terms of price, quality, and performance) and services. Through this process of competition leading to the accumulation of profits and capital[29] which is imperative for all enterprises, other companies are either absorbed or eliminated. In this respect, it may be argued that unfettered capitalism, within which competition is allowed to naturally run its course (i.e., in a laissez faire situation without any government intervention in the form of laws or rules in effect to regulate it), contains an inherent, self-contradictory or self-destructive nature. Inter-company competition driven by the forces of survival and self-interest may ultimately lead to the decline of competition as smaller companies are either driven out of business or are acquired by larger, more powerful companies resulting in the concentration of capital and a situation of a monopoly or an oligopoly, a tendency which was observed and pointed out by Marx. In his *Capital* he wrote that, in the battle of competition that is fought by the "cheapening of commodities…the larger capitals beat the smaller" and that, as the minimum amount of individual capital necessary to continue business increases with the development of the capitalist mode of production, competition always results in the "ruin of many small capitalists, whose capitals partly pass to the hands of their conquerors"[30] or of one capitalist killing many[31] leading to the centralization of capital and the expansion in the rate of capital accumulation for large-scale enterprises.[32] That is, it is because of competition that enterprises are forced to do what would spell the ruin for many: invest in churning out products more cheaply than their rivals. Consumers may benefit from this, but as the lowering of prices depends on labor productivity and the scale of production, the producers who are able to produce commodities the most cheaply are the ones who are able to accumulate and deploy the largest amount of capital. Apart from this development, an altogether new force emerges with capitalist production: the credit system.[33] Marx goes on to say that "the credit system becomes a new and terrible weapon in the competitive struggle" that transforms itself "into a vast social mechanism for the centralization of capital."[34] Despite this destructive aspect of competition resulting in the centralization of capital, the elimination of small enterprises, and the creation of monopolies, Marx acknowledges the power of the centralization of capital and the resultant innovation in large-scale planning and logistics by observing that, "The world would still be without railroads if it had to wait for accumulation to build up a few capitals to the point where railroad construction could be undertaken. Centralization, on the other hand, accomplished this in a flash by means of the joint stock company."[35] As the number of enterprises diminishes and a few capitalists monopolize production and capital, however, misery, oppression, and exploitation would increase, leading to a crisis of capitalism and a revolt of the working class.[36] For Marx, however, not only did too much competition lead to monopoly and the agony of laborers. As competition compels enterprises to compete by producing lower priced goods which is accomplished by expanding the scale of production, what inevitably occurs is an "epidemic of over-production" leading to "too much industry, too much commerce." Another crisis for capitalism will occur, predicted Marx, in this case originating from its unplanned nature leading to over-production and under-consumption. Faced with diminishing rates of profit, enterprises will attempt to escape from this crisis by conquering new markets and forcing those people to adopt their products, exploiting current markets more thoroughly, or by destroying the means that created the crises of over-production to begin with: the forces of production.[37]

Putting aside the exhortations of Peter Thiel and other would-be monopolists, does Marx's assertion that capitalism has a tendency towards becoming a monopoly economy and his view that the accumulation of capital leads to the centralization or concentration of industry through "the ruin of many small capitalists" at the hands of "larger capitals" hold true today? Various studies suggest that they do. In a study by economists from York, Cornell, and Rice universities, they reach the conclusion that over a 20-year period from 1997 to 2007 more than 75% of industries in the US have experienced an increase in the ratio of market concentration (i.e., the ratio of the combined market share of a given number of companies to the entire market size) with one of the adjoining manifestations being an approximately 50% decline in the number of publicly traded companies.[38] In November 2018 the Open Markets Institute released data that largely corroborated earlier research by showing that the market shares of the two largest companies in more than 15 different US industries have increased from the early 2000s to 2018. The essential message from this data was that big companies have become much more dominant than they were over that time span.[39] Evidence obtained in a study on market concentration undertaken on a more global level by the Organisation for Economic Co-operation and Development (OECD) suggested that between 1997 and 2007 there has been a "moderate increase" in market concentration in at least the US and Japan though not in the European countries.[40]

Aside from the above studies, a survey of the US economy undertaken by *The Economist* suggests that there is an emerging consensus among economists that competition has weakened significantly.[41] This view is based on the following developments: First, the number of new, small companies coming into existence is currently at its lowest level since the 1970s. Second, since the 1990s, two thirds of approximately 900 different industries have become more concentrated. Indeed, according to a survey by the US Census Bureau, all sectors of the US retail industry, such as food and beverage stores, health and personal care stores, general merchandise stores, supermarkets, bookstores, and computer and software stores, have seen a significant increase in the concentration ratio or the percentage of sales for the four largest firms from 1992 to 2007. For example, in the merchandise stores sector, while the industry concentration ratio was 47.3% in 1992, in 2007 it was 73.2%, a ratio that was largely fueled by the chain store Walmart. For bookstores, the concentration ratio in 1992 was 41.3%. In 2007 this had jumped to 71%.[42] Third, half the pool of abnormally high profits was earned by technology companies.[43] Fourth, certain companies, particularly the five Internet platform companies of Alphabet (Google), Amazon, Apple, Facebook, and Microsoft, while admittedly innovative, have behaved in a manner that suggests the possibility of stifling the entry of new players into the market by buying up 519 small, often embryonic rival companies as well as by newly acquiring patents of other companies with huge amounts of money not readily available to new market entrants.[44] A conspicuous example of this would be Facebook's acquisition of a potential rival, Instagram, in 2012, and WhatsApp in 2014.[45] In 2011, Apple, Microsoft, and others acquired through auction some 6,000 patents of the bankrupted telecommunications and data networking equipment manufacturer Nortel, worth US$4.5 billion; Google purchased the American telecommunications company Motorola's subsidiary Motorola Mobility for US$12.5 billion, acquiring in the process 17,000 patents; Microsoft purchased 925 patents from the online service provider and web portal AOL for US$1.1 billion; and Facebook purchased 650 patents from Microsoft for US$550 million.[46] These Internet platform companies have also been behaving, according to *The Economist*, "badly" in general by locking in customers with data and exerting their market power up and down the supply chain.[47] As Columbia University law professor Tim Wu noted, the Internet is increasingly looking "like a Monopoly board" with Alphabet "owning" search, Facebook social networking, Apple dominating online content delivery, Amazon retail, etc.[48] Fifth, the number of listed firms on the New York Stock Exchange has declined from 7,322 in 1996 to 3,671 in 2017 while the value of listed firms has risen from 105% of Gross Domestic Product (GDP) in 1996 to 136% in 2017.[49] To this trend we should perhaps add that, according to the Congressional Budget Office, from 1989 to 2013 the percentage of total US household family wealth (i.e., net worth or the amount of total assets held less liabilities) held by the richest 10% of families in the US had increased from 20% to 51%, suggesting the rise of greater wealth inequality within the US.[50] The fall in the number of initial public offerings (from a yearly average of 300 in the two decades up to 2000 to about 100 a year up to 2016), the availability of venture capital funding outside of the stock exchange, the fear of red tape when listing, and the need for less fixed assets and capital on the part of new technology companies are some of the possible reasons pointed out by *The Economist* as to why the number of listed companies has declined. But some of the decline is also caused by takeovers by other listed companies leading to an overall reduction in the number of competing companies.[51]

Despite the above research that seems to support what Marx had envisioned might happen to capitalism, researchers at the Peterson Institute for International Economics have concluded that while the trend in the US has indeed been towards concentration, concentration ratios at the global level from 2006 to 2014 had declined in most industries, on average by about 4 percentage points. The researchers attribute the decline to growing competition from emerging markets and especially China, leading them to conclude that, while there may be concerns over growing monopoly power in the US or other advanced industrialized countries, competition from China and other emerging market economies[52] would entail that there is vigorous competition on an international level, although, they add, Chinese state-owned companies may distort competition in certain sectors.[53]

As economist Jason Furman noted, if one were to ask about the state of the economy as a whole, one would not have one definitive data source or study to answer the question and would instead need to take into consideration a variety of views, as it indeed seems to the be the case if we were to ask whether Marx was correct or not in his view on the tendencies of capitalism.[54] Be that as it may, in a situation where the number of companies decreases due to competition and a situation of monopoly or oligopoly develops, one possible scenario or outcome is that the need to fiercely compete declines and accordingly so does the need and incentive for innovation. With innovation in decline and the number of companies decreasing, the remaining few companies will have less need for skilled inventors and labor leading to the development of a surplus in the labor pool. Lack of employment options for workers will put downward pressure on wages leading to less disposable income among households. Greater income disparities will exist with a smaller number of people working in the remaining large monopolistic companies holding greater wealth. New companies will be unable to compete owing to monopolistic barriers to entry such as lack of economies of scale or control over key intellectual property rights thrown up by the incumbent monopolies. Sooner or later monopolies will raise prices. Accordingly, if a situation of monopoly was kept unchecked, in this scenario the combination of falling wages, reduced disposable income, increasing income disparity, and decline in innovation may lead to lower productivity growth, economic stagnation, and ultimately create the perfect storm for social upheaval.

While we have stated a worst-case scenario for capitalism where the concentration of capital would lead to the decline in incentives for innovation and economic growth, there is also the contrasting view of the scholars of the so-called "Chicago School" (in recognition of many of its followers coming from the University of Chicago) that economic concentration or the existence of monopolies are not per se bad for capitalism. One of the Chicago School supporters, Richard Posner, an academic who later became a judge, argued that by getting big either through internal means or inorganic growth (i.e., through mergers or acquisitions, i.e., M&A), companies could achieve economies of scale that could benefit consumers.[55] For the Chicago School, the sole goal of competition laws should be to improve economic efficiency and increase consumer welfare.[56] That is to say, the application of competition laws should be to ensure that conduct that restricts output or tends to increase prices is deterred.[57] One prominent legal scholar and jurist who concurred with the views of the Chicago School was appeals court judge and Supreme Court judge candidate Robert Bork. In his *The Antitrust Paradox* published in 1978, Bork argued that the main purpose of antitrust laws was to protect consumer welfare by promoting economic efficiency rather than helping small businesses.[58] Accordingly, competition authorities should avoid blocking M&A that led to vertical integration, that is, a merger of companies in different positions along a distribution value chain (e.g., a merger between a supplier company and a distributor). For Bork, only in those horizontal M&A transactions that led to the reduction in the number of rival companies in direct competition with each other would there be a possibility that a M&A could lessen competition.[59]

Notwithstanding the foregoing views of the Chicago School, however, US courts have for some time in the post-World War II (WWII) period given decisions or opinions that have been favorable to protecting competition and smaller enterprises from monopolistic abuses. In the 1945 case United States v. Aluminum Co. of America (Alcoa), while stating that a business that becomes a monopoly by its "superior skill, foresight and industry" is not guilty of monopolization, judge Learned Hand nevertheless found Alcoa abusing its position of monopoly by attempting to exclude others from entering into the ingot market.[60] In the 1953 case United States v. United Shoe Machinery Corp. the Supreme Court found United Shoe guilty of enhancing its monopoly position by refusing to sell shoe making machines to new industry entrants.[61] In the 1962 case Brown Shoe Co., Inc. v. United States,[62] the Supreme Court rejected the merger of two companies that were both involved in the manufacturing and retailing of shoes citing that it would lead to unhealthy market concentration and therefore be detrimental to competition. In his concluding opinion Chief Justice Earl Warren stated that the legislation of the 1950 Cellar–Kefauver Act (more on this later) by Congress illuminated their concern to protect "competition, not competitors" and that while "the protection of viable, small, locally owned businesses" may lead to the "occasional higher costs and prices" as a result from the "maintenance of fragmented industries and markets," Congress had nevertheless resolved this competing consideration "in favor of decentralization."[63]

Despite the above judgements, the overall general inclination of US courts since the Alcoa case has been towards allowing dominant enterprises greater discretion in choosing strategies even if their specific tactics may eliminate smaller rivals.[64] Legal scholars Ernest Gellhorn and William Kovacic contend that a factor behind this trend was the rise of Japan and Europe as economic rivals in the 1970s which created strong pressure on the US to reexamine its national policies (including antitrust) that impacted the competitiveness of American companies.[65] A noticeable development since the publication of Bork's thesis, is that it can also be argued (as does Tim Wu) that the courts and the US Federal Trade Commission (FTC) have increasingly adopted a far more favorable approach to big business suggesting that the views of the Chicago School had gained ascendency.[66] In an example of what could arguably be considered a decision that clearly reflected the views of the Chicago School, the FTC ruled in the 1980 case E.I. duPont de Nemours & Co. that "[t]he essence of the competitive process" is to make companies more efficient so that they can "pass the benefits of the efficiency along to consumers." Accordingly, even if a situation of monopoly may occur from competition, if antitrust laws were used to block "hard, aggressive competition" that is based solely on efficiency and growth opportunities, that process of passing the benefits of efficiency on to consumers "will be ill-served."[67]

The trends and developments as pointed out by *The Economist* suggest that since the 1980 FTC ruling in E.I. duPont de Nemours & Co. the US has been even more heavily favoring incumbents and that the views of the Chicago School and its belief in the primacy of economic efficiency is dominant within the US government.[68] Indeed, from the publication of *The Antitrust Paradox* in 1978 through to 2016, of the thousands of vertical mergers that occurred during this period only 52 had been challenged by the US government for antitrust reasons, with none of them actually going to trial.[69] During the period of 1970 to 1999 antitrust regulators contested an average of 16 M&A cases annually. This stands in striking contrast to the trend from the period of 2000 to 2014 where the annual number of cases had declined to below three.[70] On June 12, 2018, US District Judge Richard J. Leon gave a ruling that rejected an attempt by the Department of Justice (DoJ) to block the pay television provider and communications company AT&T from acquiring the entertainment and news company Time Warner for US$85.4 billion.[71] While supporters of the Chicago School would arguably not have a problem with this deal, voices of concern have been raised over the possibility that a combined AT&T and Time Warner would lead to the jacking up of rates it would charge other distributors for the entertainment content that it would hold, leading to increasing prices for consumers.[72] Steven C. Salop, Professor of Economics and Law at Georgetown University Law Center, contends that, given the potential market power that this merger would give to AT&T and Time Warner and that the harm arising from this vertical deal would outweigh the benefits, this deal should have been blocked.[73] Of concern for competition is whether this deal may lead to a further round of megamergers and industry consolidation.

Despite the suggested recent tendency of courts to give out decisions favoring monopoly power and growing economic concentration in the US market, a key unanswered question that arises is: Will a situation of monopoly pose a threat to the future of competition and ultimately to capitalism? If Schumpeter is correct that the inherent nature of capitalism is such that the "process of creative destruction" will ensure that competition will continue to exist no matter how much centralization of market power may occur, then we need not worry about attempting to answer this question or about "one capitalist always killing many" other capitalists and a crisis marked by social instability hitting capitalism as predicted by Marx.[74] Ultimately, however, as it was in the late 19th century when popular anger towards monopolies gave way to the birth of the Sherman Act and other antitrust laws, it will be consumers who will have to decide again to what extent they will tolerate what seems to be a situation of increasing economic concentration and growing wealth inequality.

The benefits that competition brings to a capitalist economy or the need for competition do not, however, preclude the possibility that competition has flaws or is not always good for society. Nor does it necessarily entail that competition is something that brings out the better aspects of our nature and makes us altruistic or generous in our thoughts and behavior as Adam Smith had pointed out. Indeed, if competition is an activity that essentially involves individuals racing each other in the pursuit of furthering their self-interests, it may make people in a society less cooperative, and accordingly less willing to make contributions to the formation of public goods and services, leading to a society that overall is worse off. Such a possibility suggests that as with any activity a sense of maintaining balance is important as well as the ability to be able to harness the outcomes of individual competition for the greater good.

In addition to the above tendency of recent court decisions favoring big businesses arguably at the expense of protecting competition, there is the contradictory effect that intellectual property (IP) laws have had on competition since their inception: while on the one hand patent, copyright, and trademark laws arguably provide an incentive for innovation thereby indirectly promoting competition, on the other hand these laws give companies the ability to take advantage of the monopoly power over their own inventions which these laws confer upon them; this may allow then the companies to essentially eliminate their competition. Indeed, in the Supreme Court ruling given in 1902 in E. Bement & Sons v. National Harrow Co., the court opined that the general rule of "absolute freedom in the use or sale of rights under the patent laws…is monopoly… The fact that the conditions in the contracts keep up the monopoly or fix prices does not make them illegal."[75] In response to the claims by the plaintiff Berkey Photo Inc. in Berkey Photo, Inc. v. Eastman Kodak Co. (1979), that Kodak, by failing to disclose before its release a new type of photographic film (that would be compatible only with a new type of Kodak instamatic camera and therefore preventing rival camera manufacturers from preparing cameras with similar designs for sales), had used exclusionary tactics to protect and extent its monopoly position in the photographic film market and had thus violated Section 2 of the Sherman Act, the Second Circuit rejected Berkey's claim and refused to impose a pre-disclosure obligation on Kodak and other monopolists by saying that such a pre-disclosure duty would enable other competitors to free-ride on Kodak's R&D activities and impact the company's incentive to innovate. Furthermore, the court ruled that "any firm, even a monopolist, may generally bring its products to market whenever and however it chooses" even if it makes it more difficult for smaller firms to compete or remain in business.[76] As the American economist Michael Perelman observed, companies could divide up the market and exclude new competitors through patent pools. "In this way intellectual property rights were effective in firming up monopolistic power."[77]

Conclusion

It could be that, while – as some such as Marx argue and as recent trends in the US economy seem to suggest – there may indeed be a structural feature within competition-driven capitalism that promotes capital concentration leading to the creation of a monopoly or oligopoly market, capitalism inherently has self-correcting mechanisms to prevent monopolies from lasting indefinitely and in turn prevent its self-destruction which we have just described in the above hypothetical scenario. Schumpeter as we have mentioned earlier argued, for example, that the process involving the opening up of new markets and "industrial mutation" (leading to the organizational development of craft shops and factories into becoming major economic concerns) arising from competition constantly reinvigorated and revolutionized the economic structure of capitalism thereby making monopolies impermanent. And for Schumpeter it is this process of what he labeled creative destruction that is "the essential fact of capitalism."[78] Indeed, it should perhaps be noted that some of the platform companies mentioned earlier that hold a monopoly or near monopoly position at the moment (in 2019) face issues that may lead to a weakening of their respective business models and eventually an end to their monopoly powers.[79] Marx on his part and despite his pessimistic view of capitalism saw the existence of "counteracting tendencies" within the capitalist system that have a decentralizing effect on the "centralization of existing capitals" thereby limiting the existence of monopolies.[80] What exactly those "counteracting tendencies" are Marx did not elaborate, but as political scientist Brett Christophers of the University of Uppsala argues one of them would be what Marx had not foreseen: competition law.[81]

For a condition of competition to exist in a capitalist economy, business enterprises in principle should have limited or no power to influence the price or terms on which products are sold in the market or to control the distribution or allocation of resources necessary for sustaining a business. To this end states have resorted to enacting laws generally known as "competition law (a.k.a. antitrust law)." According to UNCTAD, competition laws are to be designed so as to counter anticompetitive practices "arising from the acquisition or exercise of undue market power" by companies that result in harming consumers through "higher prices, inferior quality, limited choices, and lack of innovation."[82] That is, the prime objectives of enacting competition laws are to protect the welfare of consumers and to foster the activity of competition among companies, which leads to innovation that ultimately benefits consumers. Although the scope of competition law is wide, in this work it will be defined as being those laws, rules, and regulations that are directed at controlling the competitive behavior of economic entities. As for "competition policy," while there is also no generally agreed upon definition of this term, for the purposes of this work I will refer to the definitions provided by Lawrence J. White of New York University and competition law specialist Martyn Taylor who stated that competition policy can be defined as a set of government policies and instruments that are intended to encourage both competition in markets and the allocative efficiency that generally accompanies competition.[83] Accordingly, in this work competition law will be considered as an instrument and a component of competition policy.

In the next chapter, an overview will be given of some of the major competition laws that are enforced today, after which I will present some assumptions and propose a hypothesis or argument that will guide the development of the sections that follow. Space constraints and the scope of this book will limit the review to the competition laws currently enforced in the three largest industrialized market economies of the US, the EU, and Japan.

Notes

1 Diamond, Jared, BBC, Why All Men are Not Created Equal, July 16, 2012, Online. Available http://www.bbc.com/future/story/20120713-why-all-men-are-not-created-equal (accessed January 7, 2014).
2 Morris, Ian, *War What is it Good for?*, Profile Books, 2015, p.290.
3 Linden, Sander, van der, The Psychology of Competition, *Psychology Today*, June 24, 2015, Online. Available https://www.psychologytoday.com/us/blog/socially-relevant/201506/the-psychology-competition (accessed April 29, 2019); Morris, op.cit., p.294.
4 Ibid.
5 Christophers, Brett, *The Great Leveler*, Harvard University Press, 2016, p.29.
6 UNCTAD Secretariat, The Role of Competition Policy in Promoting Economic Development: The appropriate design and effectiveness of competition law and policy, United Nations, November 2010, p.3.
7 Hobbes, Thomas, *Leviathan*, Encyclopedia Britannica Inc., 1982, p.85.
8 Christophers, op.cit., p.31.
9 Smith, Adam, *An Inquiry into the Causes of the Wealth of Nations*, Book II, Chapter 2, Encyclopedia Britannica Inc., 1982, p.142.
10 Ibid., p.7.
11 Marx, Karl, Grundrisse: Notebook IV-The Chapter on Capital, 1857, Online. Available https://www.marxists.org/archive/marx/works/1857/grundrisse/ch08.htm (accessed May 12, 2019), Barone, Charles A., *Marxist Thought on Imperialism*, M.E. Sharpe Inc., 1985, p.161.
12 Carr, Edward Hallett, *The Twenty Years' Crisis 1919–1939*, Harper Torchbooks, 1964, p.47.
13 Suzumura, Kotaro, *Competition, Welfare, and Competition Policy*, CPRC, December 2005, p.3
14 Ibid.
15 Schumpeter, Joseph A., *Capitalism, Socialism and Democracy*, Harper & Row Publishers, 1975, p.83.
16 Ibid.
17 356 U.S.1; ibid., p163.
18 435 U.S. 679; Stucke, Maurice E., Is Competition Always Good?, *Journal of Antitrust Enforcement*, Vol. 1, No. 1, 2013, p.165.
19 Piraino, Thomas A. Jr., Reconciling the Harvard and Chicago Schools: A New Antitrust Approach for the 21st Century, *Indiana Law Journal*, Vol. 82, No. 2, Article 4, Spring 2007, Online. Available https://www.repository.law.indiana.edu/cgi/viewcontent.cgi?article=1354&context=ilj (accessed June 15, 2019).
20 Schumpeter, op.cit., p.83.
21 Porter, Michael, *Competition and Anti-trust: A Productivity-Based Approach*, Harvard Business School, 2002, p.3.
22 A monopoly is a seller who has a product or service where there are no comparable substitutes and who is thus able to restrict output and raise prices for its customers. This will allow the monopolist to earn higher profits than would otherwise be expected with competition from other sellers, or to maximize profits. Essentially, wealth is transferred from customers to the monopolist.

23 Gellhorn, Ernest, Kovacic, William E., *Antitrust and Economics*, West Group, 1994, p.128. In United States v. Aluminum Co. of America (Alcoa), 1945, 148 F.2d 416, Judge Learned Hand defined monopolization as monopoly power plus conduct to exclude other competitors from the market so as to allow the maintenance of a monopoly.
24 An oligopoly is a market situation where there are a small number of companies producing a similar type of product or service. The automobile industry in certain countries where there are only several large, asset heavy companies is arguably an oligopoly.
25 Rifkin, Jeremy, *The Zero Marginal Cost Society*, Palgrave Macmillan, 2014, p.7.
26 Ibid.
27 Christophers, op.cit., 2016, p.100.
28 Henry, Zoe, Peter Thiel on How to Build a Monopoly, Inc, April 14, 2015, Online. Available https://www.inc.com/zoe-henry/peter-thiel-how-to-build-a-monopoly.html (accessed May 2, 2019).
29 Marx, Karl, *Capital*, Vol. I, Chapter 24, Encyclopedia Britannica, 1980, p.294. For Marx, competition led to the accumulation of capital which was the driver for the growth of capitalism. He writes, ibid., "Accumulate, accumulate! That is Moses and the prophets!"
30 Ibid.
31 Ibid., p.378.
32 Ibid., p.310.
33 Ibid.
34 Ibid.
35 Ibid., p.311.
36 Ibid., p.378.
37 Kamenka, Eugene, *The Portable Karl Marx*, Viking Penguin Inc., 1983, pp.208, 210.
38 Grullon, Gustavo, Larkin, Yelena, Michaely Roni, Are US Industries Becoming More Concentrated? Review of Finance, April 2017, Online. Available https://pdfs.semanticscholar.org/138f/249c43bfec315227a242b305b9764d57a0af.pdf (accessed May 18, 2019). In this study market concentration was measured using the Herfindahl-Hirschman Index (HHI) of market concentration which calculates the square of the market share of each company in the market and sums the resultant figures. Scores can range from near zero to 10,000.
39 Leonhardt, David, The Monopolization of America, *The New York Times International Edition*, November 28, 2018.
40 Pike, Chris, Market Concentration, OECD Secretariat, April 20, 2018. The primary tool in calculating market concentration in this study was the HHI.
41 *The Economist*, Crony Capitalism, April 15, 2017.
42 US Census Bureau, Concentration Ratios, Online. Available https://www.census.gov/econ/concentration.html (accessed June 16, 2019); Foster, John Bellamy, McChesney, Robert W., Jonna, Jamil R., Monopoly and Competition in Twenty-First Century Capitalism, *Monthly Review*, Vol. 62, No. 11, 2011, Online. Available https://monthlyreview.org/2011/04/01/monopoly-and-competition-in-twenty-first-century-capitalism/ (accessed June 16, 2019). The HHI was the primary measure used in the US Census Bureau study for measuring market concentration.
43 *The Economist*, Crony Capitalism, op.cit.
44 Ibid.; Nocera, Joe, The Easiest Way to Fix Facebook? Break it Up, *Japan Times*, November 28, 2018.
45 Nocera, op.cit.
46 Rifkin, op.cit., p.246.
47 *The Economist*, Crony Capitalism, op.cit.
48 Rifkin, op.cit., p.246.
49 *The Economist*, Life in the Public Eye, April 22, 2017.

50 Inequality.Org., Wealth Inequality, Online. Available https://inequality.org/facts/wealth-inequality/ (accessed June 12, 2017).

51 *The Economist*, Life in the Public Eye, op.cit.

52 Freund, Caroline, Sidhu, Dario, Global Competition and the Rise of China, Peterson Institute for International Economics, February, 2017, Online. Available https://piie.com/publications/working-papers/global-competition-and-rise-china (accessed May 18, 2019).

53 Freund, Caroline, Sidhu, Dario, Global Concentration is Declining, Peterson Institute for International Economics, February 28, 2017, Online. Available https://piie.com/research/piie-charts/global-concentration-declining (accessed May 18, 2019).

54 Furman, Jason, Antitrust in a Changing Economy and Changing Economics, Peterson Institute for International Economics, September 13, 2018, Online. Available https://piie.com/commentary/testimonies/antitrust-changing-economy-and-changing-economics (accessed May 18, 2019).

55 *The Economist*, Crony Capitalism, op.cit.

56 Gelber, David J., *Global Competition*, Oxford University Press, 2012, p.143.

57 Ibid. p.141.

58 Stewart, James B., Antitrust Law is Overdue for an Upgrade, *The New York Times International Edition*, June 15, 2018; Matthews, Dylan, Antitrust was Defined by Robert Bork. I Cannot Overstate his Influence, *The Washington Post*, December 20, 2012.

59 Matthews, op.cit.

60 148 F.2d. 416; Gellhorn, Kovacic, op.cit., p.126.

61 258 U.S. 451; Gellhorn, Kovacic, op.cit., p.131.

62 370 U.S. 294.

63 Gellohorn, Kovacic op.cit., p.34; *New York Times*, To Take Down Big Tech, They First Need to Reinvent the Law, June 20, 2019. The case goes back to 1956 when Brown Shoe, a manufacturer and retailer of shoes, merged with another manufacturer and retailer of shoes, G.R. Kinney Co. The US government sued Brown Shoe for the merger on the grounds that it would increase market concentration in the manufacturing and selling of shoes, eliminate a major competitor, and prevent other competitors from having a fair opportunity to compete. In 1959 the U.S. District Court for the Eastern District of Missouri ruled in favor of the government (179 F. Supp.721). This ruling was later affirmed in the Supreme Court decision of 1962.

64 Gellhorn, Kovacic, op.cit., p.130.

65 Ibid., p.36.

66 *The Economist*, Crony Capitalism, op.cit.

67 96 F.T.C. 650; Gellhorn, Kovacic, op.cit., pp.133–134.

68 Mccullagh, Declan, Microsoft Judge Ripped in Court, *Wired*, February 28, 2001, Online. Available https://www.wired.com/2001/02/microsoft-judge-ripped-in-court/ (accessed June 28, 2019), StatCounter, Operating System Market Worldwide, Online. Available http://gs.statcounter.com/os-market-share (accessed July 13, 2019); Mcalinn, Gerald Paul, Rosen, Dan, Stern, John E., *An Introduction to American Law*, Carolina Academic Press, 2010, p.341. A notable exception may be the Department of Justice's (DoJ) case against Microsoft (United States v. Microsoft Corporation, 253 F.3d 34) in which the DoJ accused the latter of engaging in monopolization practices contrary to Sections 1 and 2 of the Sherman Act and to Section 3 of the Clayton Act prohibiting tie-ins (i.e., sales made conditional on the purchase of an additional product from the same supplier) when the company licensed its Windows operating software to third parties on the condition that the licensees take its Internet Explorer browser. Despite the ruling of Judge Thomas Penfield Jackson of the District Court for the District of Columbia who concluded that Microsoft had indeed committed monopolization and the subsequent ordering of the breakup of Microsoft into two separate units by the court on June 7, 2000, the DoJ, however, settled with Microsoft with an agreement that included the requirement for the latter to share its application programming interfaces with third parties after the D.C. Circuit Court of Appeals overturned Judge Jackson's rulings against Microsoft (partly due to accusations raised by the appellate

court of unethical conduct on the part of Judge Jackson for doing news interviews while the Microsoft case was going on) as well as overturning the per se illegality view of tie-ins by holding that the bundling of two products would be allowable if the two products are constituted as integrated products, a ruling that reflected the court's view that a per se rule on bundling may have an impact on innovation. Despite the gravity of the original accusation and the subsequent ruling by Judge Jackson, it can be argued that Microsoft got away with a slap on the wrist. Yet two decades later the ruling did not result in Microsoft continuing to command a monopoly position with its Windows operating software. According to the Internet statistics provider StatCounter, as of May 2017, Microsoft was in second place in the market for operating software usage for all platforms (i.e., desktop personal computers (PCs), mobile phones, tablets) with 37% of the market while the Android software had 39% of the market. On the other hand, for PCs, Microsoft commands an overwhelming market share of 83% with the next player at 12%. On a similar note to the ruling on tie-ins given in the aforementioned Microsoft case, the Supreme Court in the 2007 case Leegin Creative Leather Products, Inc. v. PSKS, Inc., 551 US 877, ruled that vertical price restraints were not necessarily illegal per se, thereby overturning the almost century-old per se ban on vertical price fixing established in the Supreme Court 1911 case Dr. Miles Medical Co. v. John D. Park & Sons Co., 220 US 373.

69 Stewart, op.cit.
70 *The Economist*, Green Light, Amber Warning, June 16, 2018.
71 *The New York Times*, Mr. Trump Gambles and Loses on AT&T, June 15, 2018.
72 Ibid.
73 Stewart, op.cit.
74 Marx, Karl., Chapter 32 of *Capital*, The Historical Tendency of Capitalist Accumulation, p.492, from Kamenka, op.cit.
75 186 U.S. 70; Christophers, op.cit., pp.154–155.
76 603 F.2d 263; Gellhorn, Kovacic, op.cit., pp.132–133, 144.
77 Christophers, op.cit., p.155.
78 Schumpeter, op.cit., p.83; Foster, John Bellamy, McChesney, Robert W., Jonna, Jamil R., Monopoly and Competition in Twenty-First Century Capitalism, *Monthly Review*, Vol. 62, No. 11, 2011, p.21.
79 Hutchinson, Martin, Will America's Internet Giants Prove Toothless, *Japan Times*, April 17, 2018. Facebook, for example, is facing mounting criticism for selling data on private individuals to third parties for a fee as well as for its intention to set up its own "Supreme Court" to monitor hate speech content on its platform website, in effect allowing it the ability to censor content as it sees fit. Amazon, meanwhile, after having been in business for more than 20 years and showing consecutive growth in top line revenues has still not made a profit from its retail business. Alphabet, the parent company of Google, is like Facebook encountering suspicion for its scooping up of consumer information and using it for purposes that are not necessarily clear.
80 Christophers, op.cit., p.85.
81 Ibid., p.90.
82 UNCTAD, The Benefits of Competition Policy for Consumers, United Nations, April 29, 2014, p.2.
83 White, Lawrence J., The Role of Competition Policy in the Promotion of Economic Growth, CPRC Discussion Paper Series, May 2008, p.3; Taylor, Martyn, International Competition Law, Cambridge University Press, 2006, p.28.

2 The development of competition laws and a hypothesis

Pre-modern laws and rules regulating competition

In 2017 there were over 130 states and areas of jurisdiction that had competition laws.[1] While many of these competition laws have largely been enacted since the end of World War II (WWII), political authorities have taken measures since ancient and pre-industrial times to protect consumers from unscrupulous merchants. In the Indian subcontinent, for example, laws were enacted in ancient times to regulate the profits of merchants earned through boycotts.[2] In the Roman Empire, Diocletian's Edict on Maximum Prices enacted in 301 CE and the Constitution of Zeno of 483 CE both imposed fines as well as physical punishment on those who illegally raised the price of food or a commodity.[3] In 737 CE the Tang Court of China promulgated the Tang Code which contains what is arguably the oldest known body of competition laws in history. Article 33 of the miscellaneous provisions of the code prohibited any person selling or buying goods from forcibly creating a barrier to entry in a marketplace, fixing the prices of goods they would buy or sell, or misrepresenting the prices of such goods.[4] During Japan's Warring States Period (1467–1590) the Japanese warlord Oda Nobunaga issued his Regulations for the Township Below Mount Azuchi in 1577 in which he declared that the castle town Azuchi beneath his fortress on Azuchiyama was "to be a free market (rakuichi)." Accordingly, the town was to be immune from all monopolistic guilds, the za (which for hundreds of years since the Heian period held monopoly rights on the production and trade of certain goods in certain territories and were able to restrain competition by being able to block new market entrants), duties (yoku), and taxes (buji).[5] The first reported competition case brought before a law court was the 1603 English case Darcy v. Allein 1603, in which a monopoly granted by the Crown was struck down for violating the Magna Carta of 1215.[6] In 1624, the English Parliament enacted a Statue of Monopolies which deemed that all laws creating monopolies were to be "utterly void" with exceptions made for temporary patents and inventions.[7]

Competition law in Canada and the United States (US)

Modern competition law came into existence with the enactment of a statute regulating competition (The Act for the Prevention and Suppression of

Combinations formed in Restraint of Trade) that came into effect in Canada in 1889. With this piece of legislation (followed later in Canada by antidumping legislation enacted in 1904 and legislation with respect to mergers and monopolization in 1910, misleading advertising in 1914, price discrimination and predatory pricing in 1935, and price maintenance in 1951), Canada became the first industrialized nation in the world to have laws relating to preventing companies from forming agreements that would restrain trade.[8]

Canada was followed by the US where the first federal laws addressing the abuse of monopoly power came about as a result of the growing popular fear and outcry that the so-called "robber barons" of the oil and railroad industries might dominate the economy and manipulate American politics, as well as the belief, according to the competition law scholar Eleanor Fox, of "farmers, shippers, and other suppliers and customers that they were being overcharged and underpaid."[9] Indeed, between 1897 and 1901 more than 2,000 mergers took place in the US in effect reducing the number of companies as well as giving rise to monopolies in various industries such as railroads, sugar refining, and tobacco manufacture that were controlled by a few families such as those led by John D. Rockefeller, J.P. Morgan, and E.H. Harriman who had organized trusts with a board of trustees through which they controlled the stock of all of their acquisitions.[10] Rockefeller, for example, formed huge enterprises by buying out other companies. By 1880 he had merged approximately 100 independent oil refinery companies with his Standard Oil Company enabling him to control about 90% of the oil business in the US.[11] In 1882, Standard Oil became the Standard Oil Trust, an entity that controlled all of the stock of Rockefeller's many acquisitions. Forming a trust speeded up the process of acquisitions, eliminated competitors, amassed monopoly power, thereby allowing the dictation of prices and wages, and most importantly, enabled Rockefeller and other families to hide the fact that they were monopolies.[12]

As public criticism grew towards the trusts along with increasingly vocal calls from so-called "Progressives" who were demanding that the US states pass laws to make cartels and monopolistic practices illegal,[13] in response the US Congress passed the Sherman Act[14] in 1890, the first and arguably the most important of the US antitrust statutes. The bill was viewed by many as a federal enactment of common law prohibitions against the restraint of trade.[15] As the bill's sponsor Ohio Senator John Sherman put it, the Act reflected the intentions of the legislators in Congress to set forth the "rule of the common law" which prevailed in the US and that banned anticompetitive arrangements such as price-fixing cartels.[16] Interestingly, while this legislation prohibits those contracts, combinations, and conspiracies that restrain trade[17]and monopolization,[18] the Act does not contain the word "competition." Nevertheless, it was made clear in the congressional debate that took place in deliberating the Act that Congress sought to preserve and promote competition in the marketplace.[19] As confirmed by the Supreme Court in 1904 in Northern Securities Co. v. U.S.,[20] "Congress has, in effect, recognized the rule of free competition by declaring illegal every combination or conspiracy in restraint of interstate and international commerce."[21]

Violations of the Sherman Act may be prosecuted as civil or criminal offenses. The US Department of Justice (DoJ) has sole responsibility for the criminal enforcement of the Act and criminally prosecutes per se offenses, i.e., horizontal price fixing, customer allocation, bid rigging, or other cartel activities that would also be violations of the law in many other countries. Criminal violations of the Act are punishable by fines and imprisonment. Corporate defendants may be fined up to US$100 million while individual defendants may be fined up to US$1 million and sentenced to up to ten years' imprisonment. In a civil suit, private parties can receive injunctive relief and three times the amount of damages incurred plus attorney's fees as a result of an enterprise violating the Act.[22]

While Section (§) 1 of the Sherman Act was worded to declare that any "combination in the form of trust…or conspiracy" that restrained commercial trade was illegal and abuses of monopoly power were banned in §2, congressional concerns arose that the generality of the Act was not effective in preventing the possibility that businesses might be able to undermine the ban against trade restraints and monopolization.[23] In the 1895 court case United States v. E.C. Knight Co.,[24] for example, the Supreme Court ruled that since under the Sherman Act manufacturing was not "commerce," the Sugar Trust was allowed to keep control of 98% of American sugar refining capacity, in effect suggesting that the Act would tolerate mergers leading to absolute control of an industry's total production capacity.[25] Another case in point was the 1911 ruling from Standard Oil Co. of New Jersey v. United States,[26] in which the Supreme Court stated, according to legal scholars Ernest Gellhorn and William Kovacic, that while the Standard Oil Trust was to be dissolved into 33 companies, the Sherman Act outlawed only those restraints whose character or effect were unreasonably anticompetitive.[27]

To Congress and President Woodrow Wilson such rulings passed by the Supreme Court made it appear that despite the enactment of the Sherman Act, the threat still existed that a monopoly could be created, with the potential to wield excessive competition-restraining market power.[28] Accordingly, to counteract such a possibility, in 1914 Wilson proposed supplementing the Sherman Act with legislation stating specific illegal business practices. In response Congress passed the Clayton Act,[29] which expanded on the general prohibitions of the Sherman Act and addressed anticompetitive acts while in their incipiency.[30] Price discrimination "where the effect…may be to substantially lessen competition or tend to create a monopoly in any line of commerce" was prohibited,[31] and likewise for the same reasons tying, exclusive dealing, and requirements contracts were also made illegal.[32]

Regarding mergers and acquisitions, §7 of the Clayton Act prohibited companies from acquiring stock of another company where the effect would be to substantially lessen competition.[33] The lack of any provision preventing a company from eliminating competition by buying up the physical assets of another company was essentially a loophole that led to the enactment by Congress in 1950 of the Celler–Kefauver Act (a.k.a. the Antimerger Act of 1950),[34] which amended §7 by elaborating that "No person engaged in commerce or in any activity affecting commerce shall acquire, directly or indirectly, the whole or any part of the stock or…assets of another person" who is also engaged in commerce or in any activity affecting commerce, where the consequence of such acquisition "may be substantially to lessen competition, or to tend to create a monopoly."[35]

Along with the Clayton Act, with the backing of Wilson Congress also passed the Federal Trade Commission Act[36] which established the Federal Trade Commission (FTC) for the purpose of taking administrative action against "unfair methods" of competition, "unfair or deceptive acts or practices" affecting commerce,[37] and of taking measures against conduct that violates the Sherman Act as well as anticompetitive practices that do not fall within the scope of either the Sherman or Clayton Acts.[38] While the Act allows the FTC to issue prospective decrees and to seek injunctive relief in a federal court,[39] it does not provide the FTC with the power to impose criminal penalties.[40]

The consecutive passing of several competition laws since the enactment of the Sherman Act, however, still did not curtail US court rulings that were arguably favorable to corporate acquisitions leading to or sustaining monopoly power and ultimately a weakening of competition. Unlike what happened with the breakup of Standard Oil Trust in 1911, in the landmark case of United States v. United States Steel Corporation (US Steel) in 1920,[41] the Supreme Court did not order the dissolution of US Steel. Prosecutors in the case charged the company and its subsidiaries with being a combination of competitors who were, by attempting to monopolize the steel industry and engage in abusive monopolistic behavior, violating the Sherman Act.[42] The Court, however, held another view. It acknowledged that US Steel's growth through acquisitions of complimentary and competing companies (giving it a domestic production share of more than 80%) had the likelihood of illegal intent. Nevertheless, the Court ruled that neither "mere size" nor "the existence of unexerted power" were offenses; a violation of the Sherman Act "requires overt acts."[43] Furthermore, it concluded that the consolidation of companies was necessary and inevitable in order for US Steel to attain benefits from economies of scale.[44] Following this decision, from 1924 to 1928 many large companies went on an acquisition spree, redolent of a similar acquisition wave that had occurred at the beginning of the 20th century. As recounted by Gellhorn and Kovacic, this second wave of acquisition activity led to the creation of oligopolistic markets with strong number two firms in industries that were formally dominated by a single company.[45]

Despite the court rulings favorable to large mergers, Congress, to its credit, did not relent in enacting further legislation protecting competition. As an amendment to the Clayton Act and in the midst of the Great Depression, in 1936 Congress passed the Robinson Patman (RP) Act[46] that banned anticompetitive practices particularly with regard to price discrimination. This was intended to protect small businesses against chain stores which had been growing rapidly in the 1920s and 1930s.[47] The RP Act stipulated that businesses were required to sell their products to anyone within the US whoever they may be at the same price, and that any discrimination in price "between different purchasers of commodities of like grade and quality" which may substantially impact competition or "tend to create a monopoly" or "injure, destroy or prevent competition" was prohibited.[48] The scope of the quantity discount justification for price differences was also limited by allowing the FTC to "fix and establish quantity limits" in those cases where it finds "that available purchasers in greater quantities are so few as to render differentials on account thereof unjustly discriminatory or promotive of monopoly in any line of commerce."[49] Unlike the Sherman and Clayton Acts which arguably sought, by protecting competition, an improvement in consumer welfare, the enactment of the RP Act was aimed at protecting small scale enterprises that were having their businesses eroded on account of the competitive low prices offered by large scale distributors and chain stores.[50]

After the passing of the RP Act, the latest major piece of antitrust legislation that Congress has enacted to date is the Hart–Scott–Rodino Antitrust Improvements Act of 1976.[51] This Act, signed into law by President Gerald Ford, stipulated the requirement for persons to provide notice to the FTC and the Antitrust Division of the DoJ for certain proposed mergers or acquisitions and imposed a waiting period of thirty days during which the FTC and the DoJ would determine if the transaction may infringe any US antitrust laws.[52]

Competition law in Japan and the European Union (EU)

Japan

While the above competition laws in Canada and the US were enacted over a span of close to 90 years starting from the late 1880s, it was not until 1947 that a set of laws specifically aimed at protecting competition and consumer welfare came into effect outside of North America. In 1948 the Act of Prohibition of Private Monopolization and Maintenance of Free Trade (a.k.a. Antimonopoly Act, or AMA) was enacted in Japan making it the third country in the world to have a body of laws that comprehensively and specifically dealt with regulating competition for the purpose of protecting and promoting the interests of consumers.[53] The law was in effect forced upon a defeated Japan by the US after WWII in 1948, based on the belief of the latter that the prewar zaibatsu or combines (of which the four largest were the Mitsui, Mitsubishi, Sumitomo, and Yasuda combines) and wartime control associations were partly responsible for fueling Japanese militarism.[54] Indeed, in the prewar era the zaibatsu was known to have collaborated with the Japanese government in spearheading the development of the Japanese economy including its munitions and armaments industries.

The AMA basically provides a framework that prohibits three types of conduct: monopolization, unfair methods of competition, and unreasonable restraints of trade. The purpose of the AMA is "to promote fair and free competition" as well as to secure the interests of consumers by prohibiting private monopolization, unreasonable restraint of trade and unfair trade practices, preventing the excessive concentration of economic power, and by eliminating unreasonable restraints on production, sale, price, technology, etc., and "all other unjust restrictions on business activity through combinations, agreements, etc."[55]

Enforcing the AMA is the role of the Japan Fair Trade Commission (JFTC), an independent administrative commission that belongs to the Cabinet Office of the Prime Minister, in effect making the Chairperson of the JFTC (who is appointed by the Prime Minister) report directly to the Prime Minister while not being a member of their cabinet. Although entrusted with enforcement, the JFTC cannot take administrative action until it has identified an act in violation of the law nor can it launch any criminal prosecution as this is done by the Prosecutor's Office in the Ministry of Justice.[56]

If a business is found to have committed an "unreasonable restraint of trade" as defined in Article 2(6) of the AMA which includes undertaking horizontal restraints to competition, price fixing and bid rigging, in accordance with Article 7(2) the JFTC will order the offending business to pay the national treasury a surcharge of an amount equivalent to 10% (3% for a retail business, or 2% for a wholesale business) of the amount of sales from the affected goods or services, calculated using a calculation method provided by Cabinet Order.[57] In addition to this penalty, for some categories of violations limited to price fixing and bid rigging, businesses can be charged criminally. Under Article 95 of the AMA companies can be prosecuted and fined up to JP ¥500 million and under Article 89 individuals can be prosecuted as well. If found guilty of violating the provisions of Article 3 of the AMA such that the individual had engaged in monopolization or unreasonable restraint of trade, the individual can be punished by imprisonment with work up to five years or by a fine of less than JP¥5 million.

EU

Europe's first modern competition law was enacted in West Germany in 1957. The German Law against Restraints of Competition contained provisions for protecting competition. In the same year the Treaty of Rome which established the European Economic Community (EEC) came into effect.[58] Although brief, several provisions within the Treaty later provided the foundation for European competition policy regulating competition within the European Single Market.[59] With the transformation of the EEC and its establishment as the EU in 1993, the competition provisions of the Treaty (which were formerly Articles 81–89) were then enshrined in Articles 101–109 of the Treaty on the Functioning of the European Union (TFEU) and in a series of various directives and regulations.

Article 101 of the TFEU covers cartels, collusion, and other anticompetitive practices. Market dominance or the prevention of the abuse of a company's dominant position in a market is covered in Article 102. Mergers are covered under the European Union Merger Regulation (European Commission Regulation No.139 of January 2004 on the control of concentrations between undertakings). As stated by the EU, the purpose of having laws to protect competition is to ensure that companies are encouraged to offer consumers goods and services at the "most favorable terms and services" and also to promote efficiency and reduction in prices.[60]

Competition policies and laws of the EU are enforced by the national competition authorities of the member states in parallel to its enforcement by the European Commission (EC), the executive arm of the EU which is solely responsible for drawing up proposals for new European legislation.[61] When a violation of the TFEU committed by a business is detected, the EC begins an investigation and conducts administrative hearings after issuing its objections to the violations. In 2004 the EU made a decision which required member states to apply EU law rather than national law in major competition law cases.[62] Accordingly, while member states continue to have their own national competition laws, such laws have been revised to achieve harmonization with EU competition laws.[63]

A company that has violated the Article 101 of the TFEU may have to pay a fine. According to the EC, its fining policy is aimed at "punishment and deterrence."[64] The fines reflect the seriousness and length of the infringement and are calculated under the framework of a set of guidelines established by the EC. The starting point for calculating the fine is the percentage of a company's annual sales of the product involved in the infringement of Article 101.[65] This figure is then multiplied by the number of years and months the violation had lasted. In cartel cases, the fine is increased as an additional deterrent by a one-time amount equivalent to 15% to 25% of the value of annual sales of an offending company.[66] The maximum level of a fine is capped at 10% of the company's annual worldwide turnover of the previous year. A major point of distinction of EU competition law is that, unlike the US antitrust laws and the AMA of Japan, there is no criminal penalty of imprisonment and criminal fines.

A summary of what competition laws generally address

As I have briefly shown, the competition laws of the major industrialized economies of the US, EU, and Japan share several common aspects that are viewed as necessary to ensure that competition flourishes and that consumer welfare is protected. They include, for example, provisions designed to prevent competition-inhibiting economic concentration, price fixing, and collusion. Most of the 130 competition laws that are currently in existence globally also address these concerns. Accordingly, as noted by UNCTAD and economist Lawrence J. White of New York University, competition laws that are enacted to protect consumer welfare and competition can be said to generally address the following:

- Agreements between companies in the same market such as cartels that lead to a restraint in competition, leading to price fixing deals, market allocation schemes, or arrangements on product quality and standards.
- Attempts by a large company to abuse its dominant market position by independently and unilaterally taking measures (e.g., predatory pricing) that would significantly enhance its market power with the outcome of driving rivals from a market, monopoly profits, and higher prices for consumers.
- Attempts by companies to merge in order to significantly reduce competition or strengthen their market power.[67]

The search for a global competition policy

The science of economics assumes certain traits of human behavior, including the desire of all humans to obtain or maintain, through rational or maximizing behavior, what the economist Gary Becker identified as "stable preferences."[68] These preferences are for the basic aspects of life such as food, safety, and health. Economics assumes that people everywhere do not differ in these basic wants or needs.[69] Accordingly, it can be deduced from these basic preferences and common behavioral traits that people as consumers, irrespective of their location, have the desire of wanting to buy the highest quality products and services, such as food and safety, at the lowest possible prices.

As mentioned previously many economists and legal scholars have held the view that competition is an activity that spurs innovation which in turn drives economic growth. Given that most competition laws and policies are designed primarily to protect competition and enhance consumer welfare, the question then arises: why is there no common or global competition law or policy? The harmonization of competition policies and laws leading to a global competition policy or law would arguably benefit both businesses and consumers, since a single standard would reduce uncertainty and transaction costs for those engaging in multinational business, thereby allowing them to reduce costs and pass on the savings to consumers. It would also allow companies to increase their efficiency and lower legal costs, particularly regarding the execution of cross-border mergers. Harmonization of competition laws would facilitate the uniform application and enforcement of competition laws extraterritorially, thereby reducing the potential for international disputes over jurisdiction. Harmonization would also encourage states to take a concerted approach in dealing with abusive monopolies and cartels that pose a threat to competition and consumer welfare. Instead of harmonization, however, what we have currently are different views on enforcement, and disparate views on anticompetitive behavior.[70]

The current lack of a global competition policy does not mean, however, that there have been no previous attempts to create it. In 1944, with the belief that the industrial cartels in Nazi Germany such as I.G. Farben were responsible for fueling Nazism, US president Franklin D. Roosevelt suggested that in the postwar era cartel activity be monitored by an international authority such as the United Nations (UN), in effect having private competition regulated by an international organization.[71]

Although Roosevelt did not live to further pursue this line of thought, his idea of regulating anticompetitive behavior on an international basis was taken up in 1945 when the US and the United Kingdom (UK) jointly published a paper, Proposal for the Expansion of World Trade and Employment. This paper viewed anticompetitive behavior as a barrier to the expansion of world trade and posited that there should be some form of international regulation to prevent such behavior.[72] Further, in 1948 the draft of the Charter of the International Trade Organization (ITO) was drawn up by the US and the UK. Along with the International Monetary Fund (IMF) and the International Bank for Reconstruction and Development (later known as the World Bank), the ITO was originally conceived and positioned by the participants of the July 1944 Bretton Woods Conference as one of the three pillars that would support a new postwar economic order based on the principles of open markets and free trade.[73]

The concept of the ITO in particular was put forth jointly by the US, Canada, and the UK with the goal of reconstructing, developing, and maintaining trade, particularly in Europe. The draft Charter of the ITO (generally referred to as the "Havana Charter") contained a section that condemned restrictive business practices such as market allocation, price fixing, and abuse of industrial property rights in effect incorporating to some extent Franklin D. Roosevelt's idea of putting private competition under the supervision of an international authority. Alas, after numerous rounds of negotiations among the 57 countries participating in the discussions on the ITO, the ITO itself, however, was rejected in 1950, becoming a victim of numerous adverse geopolitical developments including the start of the Cold War and a growing rift between the underdeveloped and the advanced industrial countries, as the former were demanding "unequal" treatment while the European countries and especially Britain did not have sympathy with the different levels of economic development there existed in certain nations.[74] The US Senate is reported to have rejected the Havana Charter partly also due to the fears of US companies that limitations placed on restrictive business practices could be used against their commercial interests.[75] That is to say, the US rejected the Charter based on the concern that the Charter's liberal principles would impair its economic interests.

The failure of the ITO, however, did not mean a rejection of the Havana Charter and the concept of an international competition law or policy. In fact, many government leaders at the time accepted the idea of having such a law.[76] A list of restrictive business practices similar to those mentioned in the Havana Charter were incorporated into a UN document in 1952 that also recommended creating a UN body to facilitate international antitrust consultation between states and to investigate complaints between member states. But this recommendation too failed to receive adequate support from UN member states including the US.

Regardless of the unsuccessful outcome of the ITO, what may be considered a few elements of a global competition policy were embedded within some of the Articles of the General Agreement on Tariffs and Trade (GATT) which were originally agreed upon by member states in 1947. In Article I the concept of Most Favored Nation (MFN) treatment is outlined: a trade concession which is granted to one member nation is applied immediately all other member nations.[77] Article III contains the principle of non-discrimination: that member states may not use internal measures to discriminate between products imported from another member state and domestic goods.[78] Finally, Article XI provides that all quantitative trade restrictions and all new trade measures should be in the form of tariffs, presumably for the purpose of ensuring transparency.[79]

In 1995 the World Trade Organization (WTO), which was created as a result of the Uruguay Round of trade negotiations (1986–1993), superseded GATT and incorporated the Articles of GATT as well as agreements on several specialized topics including the Trade-Related Aspects of Intellectual Property Rights (TRIPS). At the 2001 WTO Ministerial Conference in Doha, Qatar, the topic of competition policy was included on the agenda. In the Doha Ministerial Declaration it was stated that a working group of the WTO would do further work to clarify core principles on some key issues of competition policy, including transparency, non-discrimination and procedural fairness, and provisions on hardcore cartels.[80]

Despite this promising development, at subsequent WTO meetings the member states have not been able to reach a consensus on the possible content of a global competition policy and in 2004 the topic of competition policy had been dropped from the Doha agenda. Various reasons have been given as to why the WTO failed to address the issue of creating a global competition policy, including the prevalence of various constitutional and procedural constraints, different interpretations among states as to the meaning of fairness and efficiency, and the difficulty in harmonizing various national regimes into a single standard.[81] Be that as it may, since the Doha Declaration, the adoption of a global competition law or policy has so far continued to elude the international community.

Some assumptions

The failure of the international community in developing a global competition law or policy leads us to attempt to form a hypothesis as to why states so far have not been able to agree upon a common competition law or policy despite the common interest of the many states that have competition laws to protect consumer welfare and competition. What follows is an identification of some assumptions that will provide the basis for the hypothesis to be developed.

American economist Corwin Edwards, after seeing the failed attempts of the international community to create an international competition law, concluded that a "global agreement was impractical because many states used restraints of trade as a weapon against other countries."[82] His conclusion suggests several assumptions. First, there is a link between international trade and competition policies. So-called "voluntary" export restraint agreements or import safeguard measures which distort or restrain competition by restricting the imports from a state leading to an increase in consumer prices or a decrease in consumer choices are some examples where trade policy has an influence on the enforcement of competition law and adversely impacts competition law objectives such as protecting consumer welfare and competition. Second, the use of trade policy as a weapon and its impact on the enforcement of competition law suggests that states, even when they are not engaged in military warfare, nevertheless remain concerned about promoting their perceived national interests and will use trade and competition policies to promote such interests. Third, many states have little or no regard to the welfare of foreign consumers or producers. The main concern of most states is the welfare of their own citizens (assuming of course, that such states are not hostage to politically strong special interest groups). Thus, on matters of trade, states will seek to pursue, if they can, trade arrangements that will allow the maximization of exports and the minimizing of reliance on imports through beggar-thy-neighbor policies. The focus of states on maximizing their respective domestic welfare instead of the global welfare of the international community creates what is known in microeconomic theory an "economic externality," a situation where, for example, an economic spillover effect harms a third party not directly involved in the relevant activity.[83] Fourth, and consequently, international trade liberalization policies such as multilateral and bilateral trade agreements that have the effect of limiting a state's ability to use trade policy as a "weapon" against other states will induce states to use other tools such as competition policies to pursue the same goal of defending their sovereignty and interests, resulting in similar beggar-thy-neighbor consequences for foreign consumers and producers. As legal scholar Bradford Anu put it, states will be expected to apply their domestic competition laws to advance their national interests at the expense of global welfare and will consequently either under-enforce or over-enforce their competition laws depending on trade flows.[84] In a similar vein, competition law scholar Eleanor Fox observed that, as trade barriers fall, businesses and nations will "face perverse incentives to rebuild border barriers for private and nationalistic ends, protecting the newly vulnerable national advantage" and thus setting the stage for "private and hybrid abuses."[85] Disagreement among states regarding approval or rejection of cross-border mergers which I will further examine later on is arguably a byproduct of competition policies or laws used by states as a "weapon." As legal scholars Geoffrey Manne and Seth Weinberger had pointed out, the lack of a common competition policy has led to a situation where states allowed politics to play a major role in the shaping of their competition policies leading to a condition where states confer and deny political favors, raise administrative revenues, send political signals, erect trade barriers, and effect social policy through the operation of their competition laws.[86]

A hypothesis and International Relations (IR) theories as a framework

Given that competition policies and law have been assigned the roles of defending national interests on the one hand and of protecting competition and enhancing consumer welfare on the other, the distinction of competition between companies in the private sphere of economic activity and between states in the public realm of global political competition and international relations has become blurred. But what are those "national interests?" Are they the same with all states?

In attempting to answer this question, the International Relations theory scholar Kenneth Waltz proposed comparing a private company to the state. For Waltz, each company regardless of size pursues its perceived business interest: the maximization of expected returns. How this interest is appropriated in the market is determined by the structure of the market in which the companies compete as well as by the actions and reactions of other companies. Further, companies are in a "self-help situation" in as much as their survival depends on their own efforts within the limits established by laws. So long as they are in this situation, however, the interest of surviving will outrank the interest of maximization of profits as survival is a prerequisite to the achievement of any other interest. Similarly, for a state, while it may have interests such as the maximization of its exports and may act in pursuit of them and respond to the reaction of other states accordingly, survival or the maintenance of its sovereignty is a fundamental goal or interest. Without it the pursuit of other interests would not be possible.[87] What additional interests a state perceives that it has, as IR theorist Robert Gilpin asserts, depends on the view of that state's political leaders on the nature of international relations, the intensity of the pressure on them by powerful interest groups, and the structure of the state's political system and economy.[88]

Accordingly, using the previously mentioned assumptions, this book will argue as follows: states are fundamentally driven in their behavior by their national interests. The values, beliefs, ideologies, and views on the condition of international relations held by their leaders and their citizens help to shape what these national interests are. Consequently, whether or not states cooperate in the international arena on competition law enforcement on in creating a global competition law is largely a political question that will be determined by the extent to which states are able to restrain their pursuit of advancing national self-interests for the broader goal of achieving greater global consumer welfare.

To test the above hypothesis, which is a major objective of this work, I will use the three IR theories of Realism, Liberalism, and Power Transition which I will review in the next chapter. The theoretical frameworks they provide on the condition of international relations will help to identify the various motives of political leaders relating to their enforcement (or under-enforcement) of competition laws and policies. Theories, of course, do not explain everything but they can help facilitate our understanding of certain trends or behavior by clarifying or simplifying cause and effect relationships and therefore help us predict the results of an action taken or a policy decision that has been made. Another reason for using theories is that, as the IR scholar Stephen Walt had noted, since IR theory helps to develop an understanding on what is happening around us, it is invaluable for developing our critical faculties and abilities in seeing the "big picture" of events. Without theory, the most we can do, according to Walt, is to extrapolate from present conditions in attempting to predict future outcomes.[89] Accordingly, I propose the assumption that the theoretical framework employed by states in viewing the condition of international relations will determine, first, what are their "national interests," second, how competition policies may be used by states to promote these national interests, and third, the likelihood of the creation of a global consensus leading to the establishment of a global competition law and its global enforcement.

Notes

1 United States Department of Justice (USDJ), Federal Trade Commission (FTC), Antitrust Guidelines for International Enforcement and Cooperation, U.S. Department of Justice and Federal Trade Commission, January 30, 2017, p.2.

2 Lee, John Sanghyun, *Strategies to Achieve a Binding International Agreement of Regulating Cartels*, Springer, 2016, p.96.

3 Ibid.

4 Taylor, Martyn, *International Competition Law*, Cambridge University Press, 2006, p.74; Chu, Yu-Peng, Wu, Rong I, ed., *Business, Markets and Governments in the Asia Pacific*, Routledge, 1998, p.133.
5 Schaede, Ulrike, *Cooperative Capitalism*, Oxford University Press, 2000, p.219; de Bary, Wm. Theodore, Keene, Donald, Tanabe, George, Varley, Paul, *Sources of Japanese Tradition*, Vol. 1, Columbia University Press, 2001, p.xx.
6 77 Eng Rep 1260, 11 Co Rep 84; Gellhorn, Ernest, Kovacic, William E., *Antitrust Law and Economics*, West Group, 1994, p.10. In this case, it seems that Queen Elizabeth I had granted Darcy, her alleged lover, the exclusive right to import playing cards into England. When a certain Allein challenged this monopoly and started making and selling playing cards, Darcy claimed an infringement of his monopoly. When the charge was brought before the Court of Queen's Bench, the court unanimously dismissed the suit and held the monopoly to be void with the arguments that "letters patent" from the Crown infringed upon the privileges and rights of the Crown's subjects to freely engage in trade. The court furthermore noted that monopoly harmed competitors and consumers as well by forcing on them products with higher prices and lower quality.
7 Taylor, op.cit., pp.74–75.
8 Duhaime, Lloyd, Canadian Legal History, 1889, Canada Wheels Out World's First Competition Statute, Duhaime.org, April 6, 2014, Online. Available http://www.duhaime.org/LawMuseum/CanadianLegalHistory/LawArticle-1420/1889-Canada-Wheels-Out-Worlds-First-Competition-Statute.aspx (accessed May 1, 2019).
9 Christophers, Brett, *The Great Leveler*, Harvard University Press, 2016, p.149; Gellhorn, Kovacic, op.cit., pp.15–20.
10 Constitutional Rights Foundation, Progressives and the Era of Trust Busting, Vol. 23, No. 1, CRF, 2007, Online. Available https://www.crf-usa.org/terms-of-use.html (accessed June 16, 2019).
11 Ibid.
12 Ibid.
13 Ibid.
14 15 U.S.C. Ch.1 Sec. 1–7.
15 Gellhorn, Kovacic, op.cit., p.1; Christophers, op.cit., p.149.
16 Gellhorn, Kovacic, op.cit., p.1.
17 15 U.S.C. Ch.1 Sec. 1.
18 15 U.S.C. Ch.1 Sec. 2.
19 Martin, Stephen, *The Goal of Antitrust and Competition Policy*, Purdue University, July 2007, p.10.
20 193 U.S.197.
21 Ibid.
22 USDJ, FTC, op.cit., p.5.
23 Gellhorn, Kovacic, op.cit., p.363.
24 156 U.S. 1.
25 Gellhorn, Kovacic, op.cit., p.360.
26 221 U.S. 1.
27 Gellhorn, Kovacic, op.cit., p.26.
28 Ibid., p.363.
29 U.S. Code, 15 U.S.C. Ch.1 Sec. 12–27. Legislation for the Act was introduced by House of Representatives congressman Henry Clayton Jr. of Alabama.
30 USDJ, FTC, op.cit., p.6.
31 15 U.S.C. Ch.1 Sec. 13(a).
32 15 U.S.C. Ch.1 Sec. 14.
33 Ibid.
34 Wu, Tim, Be Afraid of Economic "Bigness". Be Very Afraid, *New York Times*, November 14, 2018. Wu suggests that the view that industrial monopolies were used

by the Nazis as instruments of aggression influenced Congress in enacting the Anti-merger Act to curb dangerous concentrations of political and economic power.

35 15 U.S.C. Ch.1 Sec. 18.
36 15 U.S.C. Ch.2, Subch. I Sec. 41–58.
37 15 U.S.C. Ch.2, Subch. I Sec. 45(a)(1).
38 USDJ, FTC, op.cit., pp.5–6.
39 15 U.S.C. Ch.2, Subch. I Sec. 53(b)(2).
40 Gellhorn, Kovacic, op.cit., p.29.
41 251 U.S. 417.
42 Maseritz, Guy B., "No Inventions, No Innovations": Reassessing the Government's Antitrust Case Against United States Steel Corporation, 7 J. Bus. & Tech. L. 247, 2012. Online. Available https://digitalcommons.law.umaryland.edu/jbtl/vol7/iss2/1 (accessed June 17, 2019).
43 Gellhorn, Kovacic, op.cit., pp.123–124.
44 Maseritz, op.cit.
45 Ibid., p.361.
46 15 U.S.C. Ch.1 Sec. 13.
47 Graham, Edward M., Richardson, J. David., ed., *Global Competition Policy*, Institute of International Economics, p.236.
48 15 U.S.C. Ch.1 Sec. 13.
49 Ibid.
50 USDJ, FTC, op.cit., p.25.
51 15 U.S.C. Ch.1 Sec. 18(a).
52 Ibid. USDJ, FTC, op.cit., pp.7–8.
53 Odagiri, Hiroyuki, Remarks as Prepared for the Chatham House Conference, Aligning Antitrust Enforcement with Broader Policy Goals, June 18, 2015, p.3. Online. Available http://www.jftc.go.jp/en/policy_enforcement/speeches/2015.files/Chatham House.pdf (accessed July 13, 2019); Haley, John Owen, *Authority Without Power*, Oxford University Press, 1991, p.146. Pre-WWII Japan did have laws regulating some aspects of competition such as a 1916 decree prohibiting price fixing.
54 Haley, op.cit., pp.141–147; Mason, R.H.P., Caiger, J.G., *A History of Japan*, Tuttle Publishing, 1997, p.336. The four combines between them controlled between 50% to 95% of copper, steel, coal, oil, electricity, ammonium sulfate, rayon, sugar refining, and spinning enterprises in Japan. Banking, insurance, shipping, and trading enterprises associated with the four combines handled the distribution of the combines' products.
55 Japan Fair Trade Commission, The Antimonopoly Act, Article 1. Online. Available https://www.jftc.go.jp/en/legislation_gls/amended_ama09/index.html (accessed July 13, 2019).
56 Schaede, op.cit., p.75.
57 See Article 7–2 of the Antimonopoly Act.
58 Gerber, David J., *Global Competition*, Oxford University Press, 2012, p.169.
59 European Commission, Internal Market, Industry, Entrepreneurship, and SMEs, Online. Available https://ec.europa.eu/growth/single-market_en (accessed July 13, 2019). According to the European Commission, the Single Market, encompassing the 28 EU member states at the time, refers to the EU as one territory without any internal borders or other regulatory obstacles to the free movement of goods and services.
60 European Commission, Competition, Online. Available http://ec.europa.eu/competition/antitrust/overview_en.html (accessed July 13, 2019).
61 European Council, Council of the European Union, New measures to fight against illegal competition practices in the internal market, Online. Available https://www.consilium.europa.eu/en/press/press-releases/2018/06/20/new-measures-to-fight-against-illegal-competition-practises-in-the-internal-market/ (accessed July 13, 2019). The EC also implements decisions of the European Parliament and the Council of the EU.

62 Gerber, op.cit., p.159.
63 Rudo, Joachim, The 1999 Amendments to the German Act Against Restraints of Competition, Online. Available http://www.antitrust.de/ (accessed July 13, 2019).
64 European Commission, Procedures in Anticompetitive Agreements (Article 101 TFEU cases), Online. Available http://ec.europa.eu/competition/antitrust/procedures_101_en.html (accessed July 28, 2019).
65 Ibid.
66 Ibid.
67 White, Lawrence J., The Role of Competition Policy in the Promotion of Economic Growth, CPRC Discussion Paper Series, May 2008, p.3; Brooks, Douglas H., Competition Policy and Development, Asian Development Bank, October 2005, p.2.
68 Gilpin, Robert, *Global Political Economy*, Princeton University Press, 2001, p.51.
69 Ibid.
70 Manne, Geoffrey A., Weinberger, Seth, International Signals: The political dimension of international competition law, *The Antitrust Bulletin*, Vol. 57, No. 3/Fall, 2012, p.503.
71 Fidler, David P., *Competition Law and International Relations*, Maurer School of Law, Indiana University, 1992, p.57.
72 Taylor, op.cit., p.150.
73 Sokol, D. Daniel, Monopolists Without Borders: The Institutional Challenge of International Antitrust in a Global Gilded Age, University of Wisconsin Law School, Legal Studies Research Paper Series, Paper No. 1034, February 2007, p.44.
74 Phan, Thanh, Realism and International Cooperation in Competition Law, *Houston Journal of International Law*, Vol. 40, No. 1/Fall, 2017, p.326.
75 Hufbauer, Gary, Kim, Jisun, International Competition Policy and the WTO, Peterson Institute for International Economics, April 11, 2008. Online. Available https://piie.com/commentary/speeches-papers/international-competition-policy-and-wto (accessed July 13, 2019).
76 Gerber, op.cit., p.52.
77 World Trade Organization, The General Agreement on Tariffs and Trade (GATT 1947), Online. Available https://www.wto.org/english/docs_e/legal_e/gatt47_01_e.htm#articleIII (accessed July 13, 2019).
78 Ibid. The principle of non-discrimination is stated under the clause National Treatment on Internal Taxation and Regulation.
79 Ibid. Article XI is entitled General Elimination of Quantitative Restrictions.
80 Hufbauer, Kim, op.cit.
81 Ibid.
82 Fidler, op.cit., p.57.
83 Taylor, op.cit., p.44.
84 Bradford, Anu, International Antitrust Negotiations and the False Hope of the WTO, *Harvard International Law Journal*, Vol. 48, No. 2/Summer, 2007, p.384.
85 Kearns, Jason E., International Competition Policy and the GATS: A Proposal to Address Market Access Limitations in the Distribution Services Sector, *University of Pennsylvania Journal of International Law*, Vol. 22, No.2, 2014, Art. 2, p.285.
86 Manne, Weinberger, op.cit., p.505.
87 Waltz, Kenneth N., *Theory of International Politics*, McGraw-Hill Inc., 1979, p.134.
88 Gilpin, op.cit., p.18.
89 Walt, Stephen M., America's IR Schools are Broken, Foreign Policy, February 20, 2018. Online. Available http://foreignpolicy.com/2018/02/20/americans-ir-schools-are-broken-international-relations-foreign-policy/ (accessed July 13, 2019).

3 Overview of International Relations theories

Introduction

Since at least the time when the economist John Maynard Keynes noted that an inhabitant of London in the early 20th century "could order by telephone, sipping his morning tea in bed, the various products of the whole Earth, in such quantity as he might see fit, and reasonably expect their early delivery upon his doorstep," and could at the same moment and by the same means invest in the natural resources and new enterprises in any part of the world,[1] business activity had become global in scale. The internationalization of business in turn has meant that the conduct of enterprises, including acts that may entail anticompetitive behavior as well as the competition policies undertaken by governments may impact the national interests of not just the state where an enterprise may be domiciled but also of other states as well. As this book argues that the national interests of a state are determined by the views on the condition of international relations held by its leaders and people, and this in turn will shape a state's competition policy and its application of competition law, in this chapter I will look at several major theories of International Relations (IR) that will provide a framework in understanding what the national interests of state leaders may be depending on their outlook on the condition of IR.

At its very basic level there is an invariable component of the concept of national interest for every state which is to ensure its protection and security. IR theorists have highlighted in their studies the subtle, yet distinct differences of what states consider to be what I will call here their extended national interests that are built upon the base of the prime national interest, that of survival. Those differences are determined by the historical, political, and cultural traditions of a nation which ultimately shape its foreign policy. Accordingly, and as articulated by the IR scholar Hans Morgenthau, the concept of the national interest contains two elements, one that is required as fundamentally necessary, "unaffected by the circumstances of time and place" and linked to the survival of the state such as the maintenance of territorial integrity, and the other that is "variable and determined by circumstances" and is different from state to state and time to time.[2] The question arises, however, as to what those extended national interests, or those interests that go beyond that of ensuring the survival of the state, are. In attempting to answer this question, as it is beyond the scope of this work to analyze the foreign policies and national interests of all of the major states currently in existence, I will instead present in what follows brief overviews of what constitutes the national interest of states according to the IR theories of Realism, Liberalism, and Power Transition, with the assumption that states have common threads of international behavior that can be largely explained within the framework of either one or several of these IR theories.

The three IR theories presented here offer different perspectives as to what constitute a state's national interests. Despite the diversity of views, the overall underlying assumption of IR is that in a sovereign state there is a political community that can speak with a common voice which is effectively capable of containing or suspending individual interests by undertaking measures that will bind all members of the community. The Swiss philosopher Jean-Jacques Rousseau described such a common voice as the "general will." As he envisioned it, each state or the "body politic," can be considered as an organized, living body, resembling that of a man. The head, for example, is represented by the sovereign power and the brain by the laws and customs of the state, while the public income is the blood which distributes nutrients throughout the body. Furthermore, the "body politic…is…a moral being possessed of a will" or the "general will," which alone "can direct the state according to the object for which it was instituted, i.e., the common good."[3] This general will, according to Rousseau, will always tend towards "the preservation and welfare of the whole and of every part, and is the source of laws…for all the members of the state."[4] And in line with the idea of present-day IR theorists that survival is the basic national interest of all states, Rousseau writes that "as long as several men in assembly regard themselves as a single body, they have only a single will which is concerned with their common preservation and general wellbeing."[5] In such a case, there is no conflict of interests and "the common good is everywhere clearly apparent."[6] Rousseau in making this statement does not, however, elaborate as to what exactly is this "common good." Assuming that the common good is in effect the national interest of a state going beyond that of simple survival and holding that the state has a common or general will which is representative of all of its people and not just its leaders, I will attempt to further clarify in what follows what this "clearly apparent" common good, or national interests, is within the context of the IR theories of Realism, Liberalism, and Power Transition.

Realism

Introduction

When the study of IR first emerged as an academic discipline in the United Kingdom (UK) and United States (US) after World War I,[7] Realism was from the start one of the core doctrines that was taught to IR students. Most of the early scholarship and concepts to emerge from IR studies were based on Realist models, and over the decades Realism became the most influential school of thought in IR in both Europe and the US. In the 20th century Realism as a theory gained prominence through the writings of theologians, theorists, scholars, and historians such as Reinhold Niebuhr, E.H. Carr, George F. Kennan, and Hans Morgenthau. The dynamism of the theory is apparent in the further contributions to its development and evolution by scholars such as Kenneth Waltz and John Mearsheimer, who proposed different approaches in Realist thought that are widely known as Neo- or Defensive Realism and Offensive Realism respectively. Accordingly, Realism is today an epistemic body of thought where we have several theories that coexist within a single Realist framework.

A detailed examination of all the various approaches of Realism is beyond the scope of this work. What will be presented instead in the following, for the primary purpose of use in a theoretical analysis as to how and why states may use their competition policies for promoting their national interests, is an overview of Realism that encompasses some of the major assumptions of Realists derived over the centuries from the Western classical texts of Realism, such as those written primarily by the ancient 5th-century BCE Thracian historian Thucydides, the 16th-century Florentine historian Niccolò Machiavelli, and the 17th-century English philosopher Thomas Hobbes.

Assumptions of Realism

In the Realist paradigm, the sovereign state is the key player in IR.[8] And since the state is the aggregate of individuals, Realists see human nature as an underlying factor that impacts and drives the conduct and behavior of states in the realm of politics, business, and diplomacy. One such view that is espoused in the Realist literary tradition is that given by Machiavelli in his no-nonsense Renaissance guide to statecraft, *The Prince*. Men, according to Machiavelli, are selfish creatures who are driven towards fulfilling their own self-interests.[9] Accordingly, to deal with such egregious traits in his advice to rulers of states Machiavelli stated that the rulers themselves must not keep their word or act virtuously if it puts them at a disadvantage or they are no longer able to keep it.[10] He warned that a ruler who may want to act virtuously among many who are not virtuous will always come to grief and therefore if he wants to live he must learn how not to be virtuous and to make use of this according to his needs.[11] For Machiavelli, a ruler needs the power of the lion to terrify the wolves among men and the cleverness of the fox to avoid traps if he wants to preserve his state and ensure his own survival.[12]

A century after Machiavelli expounded his advice to princes on how to behave, the English philosopher Thomas Hobbes in his treatise *Leviathan* observed "the condition of man" as being in a "condition of war of every man against every man."[13] This Hobbesian view of man was later finetuned in the 20th century by IR scholar Kenneth Waltz who wrote in his *Theory of International Politics* that among nations "the state of nature is a state of war…with each state deciding for itself whether or not to use force."[14] As such, a state "conducts its affairs in the brooding shadow of violence" and the international political realm is correspondingly anarchic, that is, decentralized and horizontal with no overriding authority.[15]

In the 20th century IR scholars such as Morgenthau and Mearsheimer argued that the condition of IR is essentially determined by man lusting after power and seeking self-aggrandizement and dominance over other others in their pursuit of national security and other goals, a Realist view often referred to as Offensive Realism.[16] As elaborated by Morgenthau, all politics is a struggle for power (a view stipulated earlier by Hobbes who wrote that mankind has a "perpetual desire of power after power, that ceaseth only in death")[17] and that whatever the ultimate goal of peoples or states, whether it be that of obtaining freedom, security, or prosperity, in the arena of international affairs the end is achieved by striving for power.[18]

This recognition of the primacy of power in the context of international relations is nothing new; indeed it was Thucydides who in his *The History of the Peloponnesian War*, an account of the wars fought between the Peloponnesian League led by the ancient Greek city state of Sparta and the Delian League led by Athens, highlighted the driver for power in a fictionalized dialogue between the representatives of Athens and the people of another state, Melos, when he had the Athenian plenipotentiaries, who were demanding the submission of Melos to Athens remark in a matter of fact tone to the Melians, "it is a general and necessary law of nature to rule wherever one can…and we know that you or anybody else with the same power as ours would be acting in precisely the same way."[19]

It should be added, however, that for Realists power is not the only driver of humans. The German philosopher Georg W.F. Hegel interpreted a human drive for dominating others as being based on a primal aspiration of humans to be recognized by others as having worth and dignity. This quest for recognition was a fundamental factor that distinguished humans from other animals.[20] Morgenthau also considered the factor of recognition a significant manifestation of the struggle for power, and that the desire for it is a potent dynamic force that determines social relations, the prime purpose being to impress, and to seek the confirmation of others of one's own importance and of the power that one has in possession.[21] And along with the drive for power, recognition, and self-aggrandizement, the factor of fear looms large for Realists. As was demonstrated by Thucydides in his account of the clash between Sparta and Athens, for Realists it is the feelings of fear and insecurity that will induce states to build up their own defense capabilities for the purposes of maximizing their own security, in effect creating another dimension in the competition for power as they are all interested in survival above anything else.[22]

The Realist view of national interests

Given their worldview and their views about human nature, for Realists competition and conflict is endemic in the international relations of a state. Without any overarching world government or authority, states will basically have to fend for themselves to ensure their security and other national interests although they may have the alternative of seeking an alliance or alliances to achieve a balance of power against a third party that is considered as threatening. On this regard, however, for states with a Realist bent in their foreign policy no alliance is perpetual and they may change their alliance partner according to the change in circumstances, a point noted by the British prime minister and statesman Palmerston (1784–1865) who said of Britain that it has no permanent allies or enemies, only permanent interests. And for Realists it is only the growth of the crucial factor of power that is needed to ensure the state's permanent interest which is that of survival. The more power that a state has, the more its survival is ensured. Hence, a state with a Realist outlook will undertake what it considers to be the necessary measures to fortify this power including economic, political, and military power. Behind the belief that a state needs to increase its power lies the assumption that this expansion of power is undertaken with the intent of increasing its relative power vis-à-vis another state. That is to say, the weaker the power of other states will be, the higher the probability that your state will be able to survive.

Accordingly, Realism sees the struggle for power as essentially a zero-sum game. Most Realists consider achieving a balance of power among states as the best means to keep the zero-sum struggle from completely getting out of hand and to ensure a temporary peace.[23] For Realists, any policy that ultimately results in the fortification of a state's security by increasing its economic, political, and/or military powers at the expense of other states will be in the national interest of the state. A state may, for example, encourage or tacitly approve its industries forming export cartels which would execute measures such as predatory pricing, quantitative supply restrictions, and dumping for dominating a market or industry of another state. A state may also set up high tariffs or import restrictions with the intent of protecting its infant or declining industries at the expense of the industries and consumers of other states.

The execution of what are arguably all hypothetical examples of competition policies inspired by Realism would be based on an underlying assumption that these policies are unanimously supported by the amalgamation of the will (or Rousseau's "general will" as described earlier) of all or most individuals of a state, and that they are executed in the best interests of this "general will." There is, however, the gap between theory and reality that needs to be taken into consideration in understanding and comprehending the limits of theory. In the case of a "general will," it will need to be considered as to whether there is such a thing, when there are often examples of policies executed that are supported by the will of certain vested interests that do not necessarily constitute or represent a majority of citizens of a state. For example, Japan's high tariffs on foreign rice and other agricultural products are set ostensibly to ensure food security, a major component of Japan's stated basic national interest that is arguably related to the Realist theme of survival of the state. The burden of this policy is borne primarily by Japanese consumers in the form of higher food prices and an inordinately high share (for an industrialized nation) of disposable income devoted to food consumption.[24] Meanwhile, farmers, who constitute approximately 2% of the working population, have had, until very recently, their livelihood largely protected from global competition through government sanctioned cartelization (led and organized by the nationally operated Japanese agricultural cooperative Nokyo) leading to subsidized production output and reduction agreements, income support, and high import tariffs. Constant reminders made by the government and media directed towards the public over several decades that purport to show Japan's low ratio of food self-sufficiency as measured in calories and the simultaneous call from virtually all of the major political parties for protecting Japanese farmers from the ravages of global competition have in effect conditioned the majority of the non-farming population up to very recently into accepting high food prices without question. That is, the majority of white- and blue-collar Japanese workers who are in industries that are not protected from global competition by high tariffs or subsidies have up to now gladly sacrificed their livelihoods and standard of living by paying higher prices for imported food products and have been further willing to subsidize out of their paid taxes the income of farmers and have them protected from more efficient foreign farmers, all for the sake of ensuring Japan's national food security. The widespread support for this policy is further maintained by an electoral voting system that currently places a disproportionate weight on the votes of constituents from rural areas compared to those from major urban cities.[25] As such, this example raises the question, aside from what is the "general will," as to who ultimately decides what is in the best interest of the state, and whether it is always the case that state policies, regardless of whether they are Realism-inspired or not, are truly executed in the best interests of the state. On this point, the IR scholar James Rosenau noted that what is best for a nation "is not...knowable as a single truth," that is, in reality, the goals and interests of a state are constituted by values and subjective preferences, so that there are potentially as many different interpretations of the national interest as there are citizens of a state.[26] This is an argument that runs counter to the claim of Realists of the existence of a unified view of the national interests held by all citizens of a state and is also a central component of Liberalism which we will next review in more detail.

Liberalism

Introduction

For many IR theorists the principal alternative to Realism is Liberalism.[27] As a theory it can be argued to partly have its origins in the writings of the German philosopher Immanuel Kant who set forth three "definitive articles" in his *Perpetual Peace* (1795) as a means of ensuring a universal peace: 1) the establishment of "republican constitutions" or governments that are accountable to its people and that are based on three principles; freedom for all members of society, dependence on a common body of legislation, and legal equality for all citizens, 2) a "federation of free states" or the creation of international institutions dedicated to maintaining peace, and 3) the realization of "universal hospitality" or the ensuring of the right of the non-state citizen or foreigner in another state to be treated with friendliness in the state that he or she had arrived in.[28] These three conditions have in turn over several centuries become the roots of different strands of

Liberalism leading to a situation akin to that of Realist theory where we currently have not one unified theory but different variations. Hence, it has been the case that there have been continuing efforts to reduce the variations of Liberalism so as to lead to the development of a set of common assumptions that can be stated as succinctly as their Realist counterparts.[29] As it is beyond the scope of this work to look at all of the subgroups of Liberalism, what I will focus on here instead will be what is arguably the most widely known variation of Liberalism, "liberal internationalism," which, while firmly having its roots in Kantian thought, was fortified with the writings of Adam Smith and later on in the 20th century was further substantively articulated by US President Woodrow Wilson and fine-tuned in the writings of IR scholars such as Andrew Moravcsik and Anne Marie Slaughter; the following is a summary that was woven together using the writings of these various advocates of Liberalism.

Assumptions of Liberalism

Unlike Realists who view the state as the primary actor in international relations, Liberals see individuals and groups working in the realms of both domestic and transnational societies as the main players in international relations. Like Realists, Liberals view international society to be in a condition of anarchy.[30] But as states have embedded within them a domestic society that in most cases is based on laws and has various societal groups, and at the same time as states coexist with other states, Liberals argue that incentives are accordingly created for cross-border economic, social, and cultural interactions. A state of anarchy does exist within international relations, but it is tempered by the possibility that creating interdependence among states will in turn restrain state behavior. If there is no such interdependence, a state will not conduct international relations and in effect will isolate itself into an autarkic existence of which Tokugawa Japan (1603–1867) may arguably be one example. Hence, for Liberals, it is not the balance of power that will determine state behavior and maintain peace as Realists claim, but the relationships of various domestic social actors and governments representing their interests and the alignment of such interests through changing individual or group preferences. For Liberals, states are not monolithic organisms, but rather are rational actors that represent various societal groups whose views and social pressures determine state preferences. And it is the interdependence among state preferences that will influence state policy.

Liberals, as with Realists, do not think highly of human nature.[31] As Kant stated, in a condition of lawless freedom, humans would "rather engage in incessant strife than submit to a legal constraint which they might impose upon themselves, for they prefer the freedom of folly to the freedom of reason."[32] The Scottish economist Adam Smith saw humans as creatures of self-love who are likely to help other humans only when it can be shown that "it is for their own advantage to do for him what he requires of them." It is in vain to expect help from an individual "from their benevolence only."[33] Despite this negative view of human nature, Liberals do not see the primary conflict among states as coming from the aggregation of individual power struggles within a state as Realists claim, but rather from the conflict of interests and goals which create incentives for political dispute.[34] Liberals assume that these interests vary among states due to the preferences of individuals and groups within a society, the distribution of different preferences within a society, and the degree to which a particular government represents individuals and groups in its society and within the larger international community.[35] For Liberals the existence of divergent fundamental beliefs, the scarcity of material goods, and inequalities in domestic political power among states and social actors also makes it inevitable that there will be competition among states.[36] Unlike Realists, however, Liberals do not see this competition as being zero-sum in nature.[37]

National interests of Liberalism

Because of the prevalence of various social groups and individuals within each state and the varying degrees of domestic and inter-state interdependence, as Moravcsik stated, most modern states are not made in the mode of Sparta; states compromise on security or even on their sovereignty in order to achieve other ends, such as to save money. Nor is it necessarily the case that modern states all seek "wealth." Instead, a state would often seek various trade-offs between economic, social, and political goals for the purpose of balancing the interests of various social groups and individuals. Liberals also do not assume as Realists do that each state pursues the sole specific goal of amassing power for the sake of increasing its security. That is, state preferences or national interests cannot be reduced to a simple metric such as "security" or "wealth."[38] And, contrary to the central argument of Realists, most states have not and do not seek to struggle for power in the sense of dominating another state; instead they would, if circumstances allow it, "spend money on butter rather than on guns."[39] Accordingly, it becomes clear from this view that the concept of power for Liberals is distinctively different from those held by Realists. For Liberals, power is a factor that arises from an interdependence among preferences that IR scholars Robert Keohane and Joseph Nye had labeled "asymmetrical interdependence."[40] That is, all other things being equal, the more interdependent a state is, the more intense its preference for a given outcome, the more power other states potentially have over it; while conversely the less that a state wants something, the less that state cares about the outcomes, the less intense its preferences, and the less power other states have over it.[41]

Liberalism has championed limited government and scientific rationality coupled with a belief that individuals should be free from arbitrary and excessive state power and the power of organized religions.[42] In the domestic realm of national politics, Liberals have often advocated political freedom, separation of church and state, constitutional rights, equality before the law, and liberty for the individual. In the arena of international relations, Liberals have called for the spread of democratic values and the spread of market capitalism based on the belief that it is the best economic vehicle in promoting the general welfare of peoples and in efficiently allocating limited natural resources.[43] The emphasis on promoting democracy arguably has its origins in the writings of Kant who stated that having a republican form of government that effectively reflects the will of the people at large and not the personal whims of a single ruler would ensure a higher prospect of perpetual peace as people in general "would have great hesitation in embarking on so dangerous an enterprise" as war.[44] More recently, this view of Kant's was restated somewhat differently by the American journalist Thomas Friedman who hypothesized that states that were wealthy and economically and politically open enough to welcome the American hamburger restaurant McDonald's would not go to war with each other as they would have so much to lose economically (including their American hamburgers) if they did.[45] Hence, the creation of a federation of democratic states as advocated by Kant would be in the interest of all peace-loving as well as McDonald's-loving states.

In the 20th century Woodrow Wilson evoked the Kantian idea of a federation of democratic states in his Fourteen Points, the statement of principles outlined in a speech given by him to the US Congress in 1918 in which, aside from calling for free trade, open agreements, self-determination, and democracy, he also proposed the formation of a general association of nations for the purposes of affording mutual guarantees of political independence and territorial integrity. It was the Fourteen Points and its underlying premise of making the world safe for democracy that became the basis for the concept of international liberalism. In such an international society where the pursuit of distinct preferences or interests of states, whatever they may be, is constrained by the interdependence of states and the general aversion of free citizens of a state to resort to war to resolve conflicts, the implementation of policies by Liberals is undertaken with a fundamentally different tone when compared to their execution by Realists.

In the realm of competition policy, as we have seen, Realists may argue that states seek to enact protectionist policies such as high tariffs or import restrictions for industries that are deemed to be essential for national security.[46] Liberals, however, may contend that states act upon implementing protectionist policies in reaction to the preferences of domestic producers who are globally uncompetitive as well as to the preferences of consumers who are sympathetic to the social and economic plight of the uncompetitive domestic producers which they are faced with as a result of global competition. Hence, Liberals would most likely be favorable to the proposal that Franklin D. Roosevelt had made in 1944 when he called for the global monitoring of illegal cartel activity, as well as towards his vision of a US (stated in his 1944 State of the Union Message to Congress) where "every businessman, large and small" would be guaranteed the freedom "from unfair competition and domination from monopolies at home or abroad."[47] This Liberal perspective is clearly different from Realist explanations of the execution by states of trade protectionist competition policies which tends to stress the role of power in structuring trade relations or the need to defend self-sufficiency for purposes of national security within the context of zero-sum geopolitical competition, that is, without any regard to the consequent economic externalities.

A state with a Realist bent would also find it difficult to accept a global competition policy or law that is impartial to all and does not confer any special benefits or advantages that would allow it to increase its power over other states. For

Liberals, however, a global competition policy or law may become a reality if there is an alignment between the positions and views of various domestic interest and societal groups. This would entail having all influential societal and interest groups in each state agreeing with each other (domestically and internationally) that a global competition policy is in their mutual interests and is therefore worth having.

Power Transition

Introduction

Power Transition (PT) theory has its origins in the writings of the University of Michigan IR scholar A.F.K. Organski. While the theory has evolved over several decades since its first publication in 1958 with additional academic contributions from other prominent IR scholars, in contrast to the widespread teaching of Realism and its ubiquitous mentioning in IR textbooks, PT theory has received considerably less attention from scholars and students. IR specialists have speculated that this relative neglect may have been due to the fact that the notions behind this theory are so clearly against and in contrast to the precepts of Realist, and for that matter Liberal, perceptions of international affairs.[48] I will argue, however, that the choice of PT theory as another framework for analyzing the formation and execution of competition policy is relevant to the focus of this book as the theory is able to provide an explanation of the possible motives behind the execution of a state's competition policy in an international context. Another reason for choosing this theory is for the contrasting assumptions that it holds compared to those of Realist and Liberal theories of IR. This affords us the possibility of creating a considerably different but equally compelling scenario as to how a state may use its competition laws and policies for furthering its national interests. It also allows us to consider the likelihood of the realization of a global competition policy from a PT perspective.

Assumptions

While PT theory shares the view with Realism that the primary actor in international relations is the state, its three major theoretical assumptions in their totality essentially reject the basic Realist and Liberal view of the condition of international politics. First, while both Realism and Liberalism view international affairs to be in a state of anarchy, PT sees that instead there exists an international order that is hierarchically organized much in the manner of a political system within a state. Rules of behavior for states exist in this order and states accept their position and wield their influence in accordance with the relative differences of their power and wealth. Second, although PT shares with Realism a view of the centrality of the role of power and sees it as a critical variable that shapes how the international order functions, in contrast to Realism, which sees international competition among states as a struggle for power to maximize their respective self-interests and their national security, the view of PT is that, while states are indeed in a state of constant competition, the objective of states is to maximize their net gains within the hierarchical order they belong to.[49] And third, while Realism sees certain aspects of human nature such as a preoccupation with self-survival leading to the pursuit of self-aggrandizement and security as one of the motivating drivers behind decisions for war and peace, PT argues that it is primarily the aggregate dissatisfaction or satisfaction of states with the rules of the international hierarchical order and their relative power that is the essential precondition for determining war or peace in the international system.[50]

A major underlying theoretical foundation behind the assumptions of PT theory is the existence of a hierarchy among humans. Social hierarchies have been in existence since the beginning of recorded history, prompting some social scientists to suggest that they are a manifestation of the law of nature that helped communities to function more efficiently and consequently survive.[51] According to Organski, all states within an international hierarchical order recognize the existence of a hierarchy and the relative distribution of power among states within it, a view that is in contrast to Realists who argue that states sees the condition of international relations as being an anarchical zero-sum game and to Liberals who see states restrained in their behavior in an anarchical system by the factor of interstate interdependence. In PT theory, the distribution of power is uneven and is concentrated in the hands of a few powers. A Dominant Power sits at the top of this system and controls the largest proportion of resources within the system through rules that guide political, economic, diplomatic, and military interactions among the powers. That state today is the US.[52] The Dominant Power, however, is not a hegemon as it cannot singlehandedly control the actions of other powerful nations. Its position as the Dominant Power is maintained by achieving preponderance in power over potential rivals and by managing the rules of the international system so that they benefit not only itself in terms of obtaining wealth, security, and recognition, but also its allies who are thus also satisfied with having their national aspirations met. Below the Dominant Power are the Great Powers. These states are very powerful. They cannot, however, match the power of the Dominant Power on a one-on-one basis at a given point in time although they have the potential to do so in the future. Currently, the Great Powers, are China, Germany or the European Union (EU), India, Japan, and Russia. Below this group are the Middle Powers, substantive states of the size of Brazil, France, or Italy, with a considerable amount of resources but insufficient power to challenge the Dominant Power for control of the international order. Further down are the Small Powers which constitute the largest number of states with few resources compared to the Middle and Great Powers. They constitute no threat to the Dominant Power's leadership of the international hierarchical order. As such, with one Dominant Power at the top and an increase in the number of powers the further we go down the power hierarchy, the international order can perhaps be best visualized as being in the shape of a pyramid.

Another foundation of PT theory is power. While modern IR scholars such as James Dougherty and Robert Pfaltzgraff Jr. define power as the ability of one actor (whether it be a state or an individual) to compel another actor to do or not to do something which is not necessarily in accordance with the will of the latter,[53] power, as defined by Organski, is "the ability to influence the behavior of others in accordance with one's own needs,"[54] and in a state is defined by a combination of three elements: the population of those who can work and fight, the level of political development, and the level of economic development. Of the three, Organski considers population as the most important determinant of power, as the number of people in a state, especially of those who are able to work and to serve in its armed forces, sets a clear limit on the size of a state's military establishment and its ability to coerce or resist other states. Population also limits the size of the labor force and the domestic economic which in turn impacts the ability of a state to coerce or influence others by economic means. Finally, a large and growing population is a source of talented individuals who can contribute to the further economic growth of the state. As for the political development of a population, this is essentially about the effectiveness of the political system of a state in being able to extract and mobilize the state's human and material resources in order to project its power, that is, to influence the behavior of other states. And almost equally important as the level of political development is the level of economic development, or more specifically the level of industrialization of a state and the economic productivity of its people. The level of economic development contributes to the ability a state has to churn out consumer and capital goods for trade and aid, as well as weapons for its military or for export which in turn will have an impact on its ability to influence the behavior of other states.

For PT theory, all of the above three determinants of power are interrelated and tend to change together. Accordingly, PT considers the size of a state's gross national product (GNP)[55] to be a credible index of measuring national power as it depends on both the number of people in a state and the per capita level of economic productivity. Organski admits that GNP does not give enough consideration to the level of a state's political development, but he nevertheless views it as the best index of power available. Hence, power in PT theory is the per capita economic productivity of a state multiplied by its population.[56]

As we have noted previously many Realists claim that peace is best maintained when states support a power distribution arrangement or balance of power that limits their respective power ambitions. PT theory, in contrast, sees the level of satisfaction of each state with the rules of the international hierarchical order they are a part of as a major factor for driving the decisions for peace or war. The international hierarchical order is headed by the most powerful state in the world, that is, the Dominant Power. As this state has created the order to begin with, and accordingly has used its power to obtain whatever major benefits there may be, such as establishing rules of the order that will perpetuate its privileges and dominance, the Dominant Power is naturally satisfied with the international hierarchical order or status quo that it has created. Accordingly, the Dominant Power is also most likely to be relatively more satisfied with the order and its rules than the lesser powers in the hierarchy. Because of this level of relative satisfaction, and specifically in the absence of any state challenging its dominance, the Dominant Power becomes in effect the defender of the status quo. The Dominant Power, however, is not a hegemon and it cannot control the actions of other powerful states on its own. Accordingly, it follows that to maintain the international order the Dominant Power needs and has power allies, or Great Powers, that are also satisfied with and willingly accept the status quo international order. Below the Great Powers are the lesser powers that are too weak to do anything but accept the international order, whether they are satisfied or not with it. While there are states that are satisfied with the international order, the few dissatisfied states that may be at either the top or bottom of the hierarchy are dissatisfied because they see and believe that the international order does not confer equal benefits to all and is not in their long-term interests. They view the international order as being unfair, corrupt, biased, skewed, and dominated by hostile powers. For them the status quo is unacceptable.[57]

In such a condition of international relations, peace in the order is maintained by the Dominant Power with the willing support and cooperation of its Great and Middle Power allies that are satisfied with the distribution of benefits and the rules of the order. The Dominant Power has a large power advantage over every other single state or a combination of most countries making it futile for others to resist. For this reason, during periods of power preponderance exercised by the Dominant Power and the prevalence of satisfaction with the order among the Great and Middle Powers, the international order is peaceful and stable. And PT sees that it is this existence of a preponderance of power rather than the operation of a balance of power among states that creates a condition of peace. A case may arise, however, when not all powers are satisfied with the way benefits are distributed or with the leadership of the Dominant Power. When such a dissatisfied state approaches parity with the power level of the Dominant Power by growing its power (i.e., gross national product) more rapidly than the Dominant Power and becomes, in essence, a potential challenger, instability increases and the conditions for conflict are born. PT theory quantitatively defines such challenger states as those with 80% or more of the power (as measured by GNP) held by the Dominant Power. The appearance of a potential challenger will make the Dominant Power fear that its position is being challenged and will accordingly undertake preparations to resist the challenger.

According to Organski, ordinarily such challenges by rising powers will lead to war which he believes has been substantiated by the major wars of recent history that have involved the biggest power in the world, i.e., the US and its allies, against a fast industrializing challenger and its allies, i.e., Nazi Germany and Imperial Japan. While Organski concludes from empirical studies of past history that the rise of a challenger state guarantees a major war,[58] he does see the possibility of a peaceful transition of power from the Dominant Power to the challenger and cites the passing of dominance of the international order from the UK to the US after the First World War as an example.[59] To ensure such a peaceful transition, past history suggests that certain conditions may be needed, such as the challenger being willing to accept the status quo international order and being satisfied with its rules, or that, if the challenger is not willing, the Dominant Power is willing to accommodate the changes in the status quo demanded by the challenger, including the rewriting of the rules of the order leading to a redistribution of power that in effect leads to a change in position between the challenger and the Dominant Power. All other states that are dissatisfied with the order will either have to follow the rules of the order as they are too weak to do anything about it, or they will seek to change the rules or even attempt to overthrow the order if their power approaches that of the Dominant Power.

The PT theory view of what constitutes a state's national interests

It can be inferred from the assumptions and arguments of PT that the prime national interest for a state is, as it is with Realism, its survival and the pursuit of power in order to protect its sovereignty. Where PT diverges from Realism, however, is when it comes to the view held by Realists that the struggle for power is essentially a zero-sum game played in a condition of anarchy. As we have seen, PT views the condition of mankind as being organized into a hierarchical order (or orders) and that states interact with each other within this order. Only when the situation occurs that this hierarchy is threatened by the rise of a challenger state that is intent on changing the rules of the order does the possibility of peace breaking down occur. Accordingly, for states, their national interests extending beyond that of ensuring their survival will depend on what category of state they belong to. For the Dominant Power, its national interest is to see that the order which it dominates, or the status quo, continues indefinitely and is stable. This entails that all other states follow the rules of the order which in most cases are established by the Dominant Power. To this end, the Dominant Power will execute national policies that will ensure its ability to maintain a preponderance of power to the extent that all other Powers will continue to recognize it as the leader of the order. For the Great and Middle Powers, it is in their national interests to ensure that the rules of the order are to their satisfaction, and to maximize their power within the order as much as possible. For a state that is either in the position of approaching the power level of the Dominant Power or is too weak to change the order, it is in their national interest to work towards changing those aspects of the order that they are dissatisfied with or see as unfair and reshape the order (possibly by force in the case of the rising power and by collective means in the case of the weak power) so that it better accommodates their national aspirations.

As such, in a PT view of the world, it will only be the Dominant Power that will primarily be able to establish the rules or global policies of international trade or competition for the order. It cannot, however, unilaterally impose them on the order as it will, despite its preponderance of power, need the cooperation of the Great and Middle Powers in accepting its rules and enforcing them throughout the order. If, accordingly, the Dominant Power decides that there should be an order-wide competition policy that is dedicated to protecting competition within the order and that other Great and Middle Powers can agree to such a policy, PT theory suggests that the implementation of such a competition policy will be possible. Conversely, so long as the Dominant Power is against such a policy, there is little likelihood for it to come into existence. This is arguably substantiated by the fact that ever since the US had opposed the creation of a global competition law since the demise of the Havana Charter in 1950, the US-led economic order of industrialized democratic states including the EU and Japan that has been in place since 1945 and been built on the foundation of such organizations as the IMF and WTO has not had a global competition policy or law to this day. The question then arises, what will move the Dominant Power into implementing, in this example, the rules for a global competition policy within the order? In the context of PT theory, the answer is simply when the Dominant Power feels that the implementation of a global competition policy will further strengthen its power and its capability to remain as the Dominant Power of the international order that it sits on top of.

Conclusion

For the political elite of a state that adheres to the views of Realism, the condition of anarchy in the zero-sum environment of international relations dictates that the prime national interest of a state will be to seek as much power as possible. Accordingly, such leaders will have little hesitation in initiating competition policies that have a detrimental impact on the power of other states. They may argue this is their reason, for example, in seeking to enact protectionist policies such as high tariffs or import restrictions for industries that are deemed to be essential for national security.[60] Liberals, on the other hand, may contend that states implement protectionist policies in reaction to the preferences of domestic producers who are globally uncompetitive as well as to the preferences of consumers who are sympathetic to the social and economic plight that uncompetitive domestic producers face as a result of global competition. This perspective is clearly different from Realists who tend to stress the role of power in structuring trade relations or the need to defend self-sufficiency for purposes of national security within the context of zero-sum geopolitical competition, that is, without any regard to the consequent economic externalities.

A state with a Realist bent would also find it difficult to accept a global competition policy or law that is impartial to all and does not confer any special benefits or advantages that would allow it to increase its power over other states. For Liberals, however, a global competition policy or law may become a reality if there is alignment of the positions and views of various domestic interest and societal groups. For Liberals, to have all democratic states accept a global competition policy or law would entail getting all influential societal and interest groups in each state to agree with each other (domestically and internationally) that a global competition policy is in their mutual interests and therefore worth having. As for PT theory followers who view international society as a hierarchical international order dominated by one Dominant Power, a global competition policy or law may have an opportunity of coming into existence if the Dominant Power so desires it and the other Great Powers find it in their interests to align themselves with the Dominant Power and support such a policy.

In the previous chapter I have stated the hypothesis that the views of a state's political leaders and its people on the condition of international relations will determine their perception of their national interests and accordingly influence the extent to which the state may or may not use its competition laws as a means for fulfilling those interests. This state behavior in turn may lead to either helping or hindering the prospects of the creation of a global competition law or policy. Having completed this review of the IR theories of Realism, Liberalism, and Power Transition, I should perhaps in conclusion add to my hypothesis the argument that, so long as most states including the major industrialized economies of the US, EU, and Japan adhere to a Realist view of international relations (as being in a state of anarchy and as being a zero-sum struggle for power by nations) which leads to states to pursue policies favoring their national interests over the interests of global consumer welfare, there will be limited likelihood of a global consensus developing on a global competition policy that focuses on promoting open and transparent markets and equal commercial opportunity for all enterprises regardless of their national origin.

Notes

1 Keynes, John Maynard, The Economic Consequences of the Peace, *The Globalist*, November 17, 2001, Online. Available https://www.theglobalist.com/global-man-circa-1913/ (accessed May 4, 2019).
2 Burchill, Scott, *The National Interest in International Relations Theory*, Palgrave Macmillan, 2005, p.37.
3 Rosseau, Jean Jacques, *On Political Economy*, Encyclopedia Britannica Inc., 1982, p.396.
4 Ibid.
5 Ibid., p.425.
6 Ibid.
7 Aberystwyth University in Wales and the School of Foreign Service of Georgetown University in Washington D.C. both began offering courses on IR in 1919.
8 Slaughter, Anne Marie, Liberal International Relations Theory and International Economic Law, *American University International Law Review*, Vol. 10, No. 2, 1995, p.722.
9 Machiavelli, Niccolò, *The Prince*, Encyclopaedia Britannica Inc., p.25.
10 Ibid., p.22.
11 Ibid.
12 Ibid., p.25.
13 Hobbes, Thomas, *Leviathan*, Encyclopaedia Britannica Inc., 1982, p.85.
14 Waltz, Kenneth, N., *Theory of International Politics*, McGraw Hill, 1979, p.102.
15 Ibid.
16 Daddow, Oliver, *International Relations Theory*, Sage Publications Ltd., 2013, p.121. In contrast to Offensive Realism it is Defensive Realism which argues that the anarchical nature of the international system restrains and moderates the behavior of states in their pursuit of attaining national security.
17 Hobbes, op.cit., p.76.
18 Morgenthau, Hans J., *Politics Among Nations*, McGraw Hill, Inc., 1985, p.31.
19 Brown, Chris, Nardin, Terry, Rengger, Nicholas, ed., *International Relations in Political Thought*, Cambridge University Press, 2010, p.57.
20 Fukuyama, Francis, *The End of History and the Last Man*, Free Press, 2006, p.xvi.
21 Morgenthau, op.cit., p.87.

22 IR theorists generally define this phenomenon as the Thucydides Trap.
23 Unoki, Ko, *International Relations and the Origins of the Pacific War*, Palgrave Macmillan, 2016, pp.13–15.
24 Nikkei Shimbun, Engeru keisu 29 nenburi kosuijun (Engel Coefficient at a 29 Year High), February 17, 2018, Online. Available https://www.nikkei.com/article/DGXLASFS17H4O_X10C17A2EE8000/ (accessed July 13, 2019); Honkawa Data Tribune, Shuyoukoku Engeru keisu no suii (Trends of the Engel Coefficient of Major Countries) October 30, 2018, Online. Available http://www2.ttcn.ne.jp/honkawa/0211.html (accessed July 5, 2019). According to data released by the Japanese Ministry of General Affairs, its Engel coefficient, which is used to measure the ratio of food consumption value compared to disposable income, was at 25.8% in 2016 while that of the US (according to Organisation for Economic Co-operation and Development data) was at about 15% in 2015.
25 *Japan Times*, Eliminate Disparity in the Value of Votes, December 24, 2018. The maximum disparity in the value of votes between electoral districts was 2.43 to 1 in 2012. Since then the Japanese Supreme Court put a cap on the growing disparity by ruling in October 2017 that a disparity of 1.98 to 1 is constitutional, making in effect the weight of a vote in a less populated area almost twice that of one in a more populated area.
26 Burchill, op.cit., p.50.
27 Slaughter, op.cit., p.727.
28 Kant, Immanuel, *Perpetual Peace: A Philosophical Sketch*, pp.436–437, in Brown, Nardin, Rengger, op.cit.
29 Slaughter, op.cit., p.727.
30 Moravcsik, Andrew, *Liberal Theories of International Relations: A Primer*, Princeton University, 2010, p.2.
31 Kant, op.cit., p.439.
32 Ibid.
33 Smith, Adam, *An Inquiry into the Causes of the Wealth of Nations*, Book II, Chapter 2, Encyclopedia Britannica Inc., 1982, p.7.
34 Moravcsik, op.cit., p.4.
35 Slaughter, op.cit., p.728.
36 Moravcsik, op.cit., p.4.
37 Ibid.
38 Ibid.
39 Ibid.
40 Ibid., p.5.
41 Ibid., p.4.
42 Burchill, op.cit., p.104.
43 Ibid.
44 Kant, op.cit., p.437.
45 Friedman, Thomas, *The Lexus and the Olive Tree*, Thorndike Press, 1999, p.384.
46 Burchill, op.cit., p.108; Smith, op.cit., p.197. Realists are not the only ones that may call for trade protectionism in the name of national security. Even so-called liberals such as Adam Smith have at one point viewed it as possible that trade restrictions be introduced out of considerations of national security. He writes that free trade cannot exist where "national animosity" threatens the very survival of a state, "defence, however, is of much more importance than opulence."
47 Roosevelt, Franklin D., State of the Union Message to Congress, January 11, 1944, Online. Available http://www.fdrlibrary.marist.edu/archives/pdfs/state_union.pdf (accessed July 5, 2019).
48 Fujiwara, Kiichi, Japan in Decline? Power Transition in Asia and its Implications, Online. Available http://www.jfcairo.org/FF.htm (accessed July 5, 2019).

49 Kugler, Jacek, Organski, A.F.K., *The Power Transition: A Retrospective and Prospective Evaluation, Handbook of War Studies*, Routledge, 1989, pp.172–173.
50 Tammen, Ronald L., Kugler, Jacek, Lemke, Douglas, Stam III, Allan C., Alsharabati, Carole, Abdollahian, Mark Andrew, Efrid, Brian, Organski, A.F.K., *Power Transitions*, CQ Press, 2000, p.8.
51 BBC, Why all Men are Not Created Equal, July 16, 2012, Online. Available http://www.bbc.com/future/story/201220713-why-all-men-are-not-created-equal (accessed July 13, 2019).
52 Midlarsky, Mansul, ed., *Handbook of War Studies*, Routledge, 1989, p.173; Tammen, Kugler, Lemke, Stam III, Alsharabati, Abdollahian, Efrid, Organski, op.cit., pp.6-7.
53 Dougherty, James E., Pfaltzgraff Jr., Robert L., *Contending Theories of International Relations*, Addison Wesley Longman Inc., 2001, p.72.
54 Organski, A.F.K., *World Politics*, Alfred A. Knopf Inc., 1968, p.426.
55 Gross national product being the aggregate of consumer expenditure, government expenditure, capital investment (the sum equaling gross domestic product, or GDP), plus income from abroad (i.e., exports) less the amount of money flowing abroad from the state (i.e., imports).
56 Kugler, Organski, op.cit., p.190.
57 Tammen, Kugler, Lemke, Stam III, Alsharabati, Abdollahian, Efrid, Organski, op.cit., p.9.
58 Organski, op.cit., p.361.
59 Ibid., p.356.
60 Burchill, op.cit., p.108.

4 Cartels

Illegal and/or in the national interest?

Introduction: the definition and nature of cartels

As with many of the jargon and concepts used in modern-day business studies that are in one way or another associated with war or battle, the word "cartel" also seems to have an origin related to war. According to G.W. Stocking and M.W. Watkins, cartel comes from the Latin *charta* meaning a paper or letter and was used to describe a military agreement between belligerent nations to settle matters such as the exchange of prisoners of war.[1] Currently the term "cartel" is generally used to describe a certain form of collaborative association, an example being that of a business cartel composed of various enterprises cooperating with each other on business-related objectives such as maintaining market prices by agreeing to restrict production output. Sir Alfred Mond, the organizer and head of the British chemical trust Imperial Chemical Industries (ICI), defined a cartel as being "a combination of producers for the purpose of regulating...production, and... prices" that does not give up the separate identity of the different enterprises, and does not usually last more than a limited time.[2] The European Parliament and Council defined the term cartel as being an "agreement or a concerted practice" between more than two competitors that has as its objective the coordination of their respective competitive behavior in the market such as fixing or coordinating purchase or selling prices or other conditions, the sharing of intellectual property rights, the allocation of production or sales quotas, and the division of markets and customers through agreements such as bid rigging, restricting imports or exports, or coordinated anticompetitive actions against other competitors.[3] Such aforementioned acts of cartels including price fixing and market allocation that "have as their object or effect the prevention, restriction, or distortion of competition" within the European Union (EU) are prohibited under Article 101 paragraph 1 of the Treaty on the Functioning of the European Union (TFEU).[4]

In the Japanese Antimonopoly Act (AMA) the term "cartel" is not specifically mentioned. However, Article 2(6) does describe what a cartel is and does; that is, it is an arrangement where enterprises work "in concert with other enterprises," to engage in acts that lead to the "unreasonable restraint of trade," or such activities conducted by any enterprise that "fix, maintain, or increase prices, or limit production, technology, products, facilities...thereby causing, contrary to the public interest, a substantial restraint of competition in any particular field of trade."[5] And in Article 3, enterprises are prohibited from undertaking such "unreasonable restraints of trade."[6]

In the United States' (US) Sherman Act there is also no mention of the word "cartel" within its text. Instead, Section (§) 1 of the Act broadly states the prohibition on "every contract, combination in the form of trust or otherwise, or conspiracy, in restraint of trade or commerce among the several States or with foreign nations."[7] The US Supreme Court had interpreted the Sherman Act as rendering per se illegal[8] cartel acts to include collusive agreements among horizontally positioned competitors to fix prices, restrict production output, rig bids or allocated markets.[9] In the 1940 case, United States v. Socony-Vacuum Oil Co. (Socony),[10] that concerned a group of major oil refining companies agreeing to buy surplus gasoline from independent refiners (who were unable to store surplus gasoline and were dumping gasoline onto the market with give-away prices) in order to prevent an acceleration in the decline of gasoline prices and the depression of the oil industry in general, the court adopted a rigid condemnation of all price-fixing arrangements as being illegal per se. Upon handing down its decision, the court gave its view that the oil cartel's true purpose was to restrain competition and raise market prices. The court stated that, although the buying program of surplus gasoline did stabilize the market, it did this by doing nothing more than to rectify "competitive evils."[11] Although the court acknowledged that it was beyond its power to determine "whether or not particular price-fixing schemes are wise or unwise, healthy or destructive," it confirmed that "under the Sherman Act a combination for the purpose and with the effect of raising, depressing, fixing, pegging, or stabilizing the price of a commodity in interstate or foreign commerce is illegal per se."[12] The legal scholars Ernest Gellhorn and William E. Kovacic consider the ruling given in Socony the "foundation" for analyzing horizontal price-fixing cartels within the context of the Sherman Act.[13]

To understand the goal of a cartel comprising of several enterprises we must perhaps remind ourselves that the activities of a for-profit private enterprise are generally devoted to ultimately make as much profit as possible, as the Supreme Court arguably seemed to suggest in its views given in its Socony ruling. As the economist Joseph Stiglitz stated, corporations strive for profit.[14] And in the long history of commercial activity going back to ancient times this fundamental aspect of a business has basically not changed. Towards this goal of making as much profit as possible, enterprises will compete to produce better goods and services at the lowest possible cost and sell them at the highest possible price to consumers. Another sure way of maximizing profits is to restrict competition, whether it be by buying out competitors or squashing them.[15] And accordingly, for a cartel consisting of likeminded enterprises working in league to maximize their profits, a generic strategy is to attain a near or total monopoly position by driving out competitors, using abusive anticompetitive measures such as predatory pricing (e.g., "dumping" of products onto a market at super low prices), or by absorbing competitors outside of a cartel and raising prices or restricting the supply for its products and services to the extent that it would lead to monopoly profits for the cartel. Keeping in mind the Realist concept of human nature as we reviewed in the previous chapter and its central tenet of self-interest and survival as the prime motivator of human beings, such a strategy from enterprises participating in a cartel seeking profit maximization is perhaps not difficult to imagine. As Adam Smith observed, people of the same trade seldom ever meet together "for merriment and diversion" but when they do, "the conversation ends in a conspiracy against the public, or in some contrivance to raise prices."[16]

By having such objectives as dominating a market and extracting monopoly profits, business for cartels is essentially a zero-sum affair. And aside from eliminating the competition, cartels will exploit consumers by giving them no alternative but to pay high prices for their products. There is in effect little difference in the objectives and behavior of such cartels compared to those of the conquering imperialists of world history; in the case of the former, cartels dominate a market by eliminating potential new rivals, and in the latter imperialists subjugate a nation or territory by eliminating any opposing political or military threat.[17] In the parlance of IR theory, a cartel intent upon monopolizing a market by eliminating its competitors is a manifestation coming from a Realist's view of the world. Cartels behave as they do, that is, pursue collective monopoly power, because doing so will ensure their survival and, as the ancient Athenians told the hapless people of Melos before they were to be conquered, because they could. For cartels, a condition of unrestricted, free for all "competition" is an anathema. In a situation where cartels are allowed to pursue a monopoly position, the Swedish economist Gustav Cassel predicted that through their anticompetitive activities, cartels and other monopolistic forces will obstruct "the world from moving to better occupations," with the result that industry will find "it difficult to maintain itself," and labor will face unemployment.[18]

Globalization and cartels

The concept of a cartel as elaborated in the above laws have been in existence since the rise of commercial activity in ancient times.[19] There are examples of cartels from medieval Europe while in Japan the kabu-nakama or trade associations of the Tokugawa period (1603–1867) were also arguably cartels that restricted membership and regulated business among its members.[20] Some business historians state the first modern cartels to have materialized after the 1870s, partly as a reaction to a global economic turndown that was occurring at the time.[21] In Japan, cartels appeared in 1880 with the formation of the Japan Paper Manufacturers Federation, and the Japanese Cotton Spinning Federation in 1882. In both cases the Meiji government encouraged their formation to prevent excessive competition.[22] In Germany, from the moment the German Empire consisting of a motley of German states was established under the leadership of Prussia and the Prussian statesman Otto von Bismarck in 1871, the number of cartels grew at a rapid pace as financial capitalists used direct financial pressure as well as their system of interlocking boards of directors to integrate enterprises and reduce competition, prompting some economic historians to call Germany the "fatherland" of the cartel movement.[23] A major example of a German cartel from this period is the Rhenisch-Westphalian Coal Syndicate consisting of over 67 enterprises which was formed in 1893 with the purpose of managing over a thousand different prices for varying types of coal.[24] While there are no official numbers on cartels in Germany before 1905, historian Carroll Quigley notes that in 1896 there were already 250 cartels of which 80 were in the iron and steel industry alone, and by 1905 according to an official Reichstag survey there were 385 cartels of which 92 were in coal and metals.[25] The German Reichstag by this time had actively supported the formation of cartels, the most famous example as highlighted by Quigley being the enactment of a law in 1910 that forced potash manufacturers to become members of the potash cartel.[26]

Along with the rise of national cartels, another phenomenon was developing which Stiglitz defines as "globalization," that is, the closer economic integration of the states of the world through the increased flow of goods, services, capital, and labor.[27] Although some economists consider globalization as a phenomenon to have emerged in the 1970s,[28] from the 1870s and until the beginning of World War I (WWI) in 1914, the advancement of science and the refining of mass production techniques coming from the industrial revolution, the hegemony of the British Empire or the reign of Pax Britannica (leading to the spread of British legal institutions, the English language, and British political and social values), improvements in long-distance communication, and progress in management and manufacturing techniques in industries such as chemicals, steel, and oil, had all fused together to allow wealthy urbanites at the beginning of the 20th century a life style that would be familiar to affluent people in industrialized countries today. And concurrent with the march of technological progress and the expansion of international trade at that time was the spread of the liberal belief all over Europe and other parts of the world, propagated by the English parliamentarian Norman Angell in his widely read book *The Great Illusion*, that a European war would not likely occur anymore as "the economic cost of war was so great that no one could possibly hope to gain by starting a war, the consequences of which would be so disastrous."[29] According to Angell, nationalism was no longer a concern as a capitalist has no country and knows that "arms and conquests and jugglery with frontiers serve no ends of his, and may very well defeat them."[30] As with the view stated by the American political scientist Francis Fukuyama in his article The End of History? published in 1989[31] (that is, with the triumph of Western liberal democracy over the empire of the Soviet Union, the historic ideological struggles of humans may have come to an end), so too Angell's view that a European war would be nearly unthinkable would turn out to have been sorely premature with the advent of WWI in 1914. Be that as it may, the growth of globalization from the 1870s had accelerated the rise of another business phenomenon: the international cartel.

The international cartel

International law scholar Martyn Taylor defines an international cartel as being a horizontal agreement between a number of enterprises from different countries operating in international markets under typical collusive arrangements that allocate markets, reduce or increase total production, and increase or decrease market prices.[32] International cartels first appeared in the 1880s and 1890s in the steel rails, aluminum, zinc, electric lamp, explosives, synthetic alkali, and shipping sectors.[33] What follows below is a brief look at some prominent examples of international cartels that later appeared from the 1890s up to the 1920s.

In 1896 the Aluminum Company of America (Alcoa), an American aluminum producer based in Pittsburgh, reached a marketing agreement with Aluminium Industrie AG, a Swiss-German company, not to export into each other's markets.[34] In 1899 the American miner and business magnate Francis Marion Smith established an organization called Borax Consolidated with headquarters in London, England, that comprised of an alliance of mining and mineral enterprises in Germany, France, Austria, the United Kingdom (UK), and the US. The mining and mineral supply enterprise under Smith became a leader in the global supply of refined borates and earned him the title of the "Borax King."[35] In 1904 a group of French and Belgium enterprises combined to form an international cartel for the distribution of plate glass.[36] Three years later bottle manufacturers in central Europe and Scandinavia combined to form a glass bottle cartel.[37] By 1914 according to one survey there were 114 international cartels in existence.[38] Although WWI had severely disrupted international business transactions, international cartel activity resumed almost immediately after the ending of hostilities and even when there was some bitterness remaining between the governments of former enemies. In 1922 a 20-year arrangement was concluded by the US-based manufacturer of electric equipment, General Electric (GE), with A.E.G. of Germany that provided for the exchange of patents between the two companies and the division of the world market with GE obtaining the markets of the US, Central America, and partly Canada, and A.E.G. getting hold of the markets of Eastern and Central Europe.[39] In 1924 the German potash cartel and French potash suppliers concluded an agreement to share quotas for the US market. This arrangement later led to a full-blown international cartel agreement in 1926 with the chief objective of eliminating competitors in the US market.[40] In September 1926 the major steel producers of Europe combined to form the international steel entente where an agreement was made to control steel output and penalties set for overproduction and premiums for underproduction.[41] In 1929 the cartel agreement concluded between the American E.I. duPont de Nemours Co. and the British monopoly ICI resulted in the world being divided up for all their chemical products. This cartel agreement was later expanded to include an agreement between ICI and the German cartel I.G. Farbenindustrie (Farben), thus resulting in the division of the world market among the chemical conglomerates of Germany, the UK, and the US.[42]

The German cartel I.G. Farben, which had initially been formed in 1904 by the combination of three enterprises, had, by 1926, come to control about two-thirds of Germany's chemical output, spreading out into every branch of industry, including drugs, plastics, explosives, light metals, and holding a total monopoly on dyes.[43] In 1927 I.G. Farben concluded a European dyestuff cartel with a French organization (Kuhlmann Group) which together with a Swiss cartel became the European Dyestuff Cartel in 1929. ICI, which had a near monopoly in dyestuff in

British territories, later joined this cartel in 1931. ICI, as we have seen, had concluded a cartel arrangement with duPont in 1929. Partly through this indirect connection with duPont, I.G. Farben then concluded many individual cartel agreements with the latter and other American corporations.[44]

As it is beyond the scope of this work to delve into the respective reasons as to why these international cartels were created, I will instead take the liberty of mentioning some generic reasons for international cartelization as suggested by Schumpeter in his International Cartels and Their Relation to World Trade.[45] First on his list was the need of European enterprises in general to recoup their foreign market positions that had been lost as a result of WWI. Second, cartelization was undertaken to deal with excess production capacity. Third, cartelization came about from the desire of war-weary and demoralized businesses to eliminate cut-throat competition and also wasteful practices in production. Fourth, enterprises looked to using cartels as a means of restoring old pre-war business ties and getting access to raw materials that had been made inaccessible during the war. And finally, fifth, international cartels were formed for the purpose of achieving market price stabilization.[46] Aside from these reasons, Schumpeter saw the movement towards the formation of international cartels as "the natural and inevitable outcome of the movement towards economic concentration and national combination in general."[47] Although the formation of international cartels arguably spurred the internationalization of business and globalization and for some represented a vital factor in promoting more orderly marketing conditions, economic integration, and accordingly more orderly international relations,[48] for others the rise of international cartels added a different dimension to the struggle and conflict among capitalist nations for new colonies and markets. As with Schumpeter, the Russian revolutionary Vladimir Lenin saw the creation of international cartels as a natural phenomenon in capitalism. In his *Imperialism: The Highest Stage of Capitalism*, written in 1916, Lenin viewed the activities of cartels to be those of dividing up among "themselves...the whole internal market of a country", and imposing "their control...upon the industry of that country... As the export of capital increased, and as the foreign and colonial relations and the 'spheres of influence' of the big monopolist combines expanded, things 'naturally' gravitated towards...the formation of international cartels."[49] For Lenin the creation of international cartels represented "a new stage of world concentration of capital and production" in which the "international cartels dominate the *whole* world market, dividing it 'amicably' among themselves – until war brings about a re-division."[50] That is, along with Gatling guns, tanks, ships, and planes, the international cartel had also become another weapon or partner of the capitalist nations in their struggle for power and hegemony, leading to the further conquest of markets and the expansion of colonies by means other than waging war. As the German Minister for Economic Affairs from 1926 to 1929, Julius Curtius, noted, "these great modern economic organisms transcend the bounds of purely private business and have gradually become public institutions with national responsibilities."[51]

The crisis of capitalism and the increase in cartel activity

Although the end of WWI in 1918 had raised expectations among consumers in the major belligerent countries that wartime restrictions and austerity measures imposed on economic activities that led to limitations on the production of consumer goods and the rationing of consumption would be lifted, the end of the war had also led to the beginning of a crisis of overproduction created by the expansion and mobilization of many industries such as chemicals and steel for the war effort. Countries such as Japan that had faced a boom in demand for its products from Europe, Asia, and the Pacific during the war now saw a collapse in their trade and economy in the depression of 1920 to 1921 as the European economies began to resume their export of consumer goods to Asia and as Europe and the US began to raise trade tariffs against imported goods. In 1922 the so-called "Washington System" of naval disarmament and collective security came into effect, with France, Italy, Japan, the UK, and the US agreeing to downsize their respective naval forces in the western Pacific region. Disarmament would have entailed a peace dividend for these countries in terms of tax money released for non-military public expenditure but most states retrenched on spending as overall tax revenues declined. Disarmament also added extra pressure on labor markets as navy and military personnel were being decommissioned and forced to compete for civilian jobs in depressed markets leading to a rise in unemployment and a further fall in consumer demand. A deflationary mood had come to pervade the economies of the world, leading to countries setting up trade protectionist measures in the form of high tariff and import restrictions. In 1921 the UK introduced the Safeguarding of Industries Act which placed a duty on those imported goods that were considered as being sold below the cost of production. The US enacted the Fordney–McCumber Tariff Act in 1922 which raised the tariff rates on imported goods to an overall average of 14% and on some imported items to as high as 38.5%.[52]

To counter the rise of protectionist measures as well as to deal with industry overcapacity, the governments of several countries resorted to encouraging the creation of cartels. In the UK, various domestic industry associations had formed export cartels even before the end of WWI in preparation for expanding into foreign markets once hostilities ceased.[53] In 1920 the governments of the UK and the Netherlands reached an agreement to defend the price of tin through the creation of the Bandoeng Pool, a de facto cartel which bought up surplus tin until the price of tin increased. As noted by historian Peter Roddy, in making such an agreement no consideration was given to the welfare of consumers.[54] Between 1926 and 1929 cartels were formed in Spain for the promotion of products such as coal, lead mines, paper, and wine.

In Germany, cartels had become a ubiquitous feature of German economic life by the mid-1920s. According to the Federation of German Industrialists, there were already 1,500 cartels in Germany in 1923.[55] As a means of extending state control over prices and production the German government forced non-cartelized companies into joining existing state sponsored cartels.[56] During the time of the financial collapse of 1931 there were 2,500 cartels.[57] Immediately after Adolf Hitler and the Nazis ascended to power in 1933 a law was enacted in July of that year that gave the government the right to create certain cartels and prohibit the formation of new enterprises. Other new legislation enacted by the Nazis allowed cartels to engage in anticompetitive activities that had formerly been prohibited such as boycotts against non-cartel members.[58] By the time the Nazis were fully entrenched in power in the mid-1930s all major areas of German industry had become subject to some form of private cartel agreement.[59]

The US legally permitted the formation of export cartels after 1918 under the Webb–Pomerene Act[60] with the condition that such cartel activity would have no impact on the domestic US economy. Even though the US had arguably the strictest and most unambiguous legislation prohibiting abusive behavior associated with cartels as stated in §1 of the Sherman Act, the post-WWI economic downturn and the subsequent Great Depression led to a significant cartelization of key sectors of the US economy during the the 1920s and 1930s with an estimated 47.4% of all agricultural products measured by value and 86.9% of all minerals produced subject to control by cartels by 1939.[61]

As for Japan, immediately after WWI the Japanese government enacted two export promotion laws which sanctioned the creation of cartels for producing bleaching powder, wool, cement, coal, copper, and canned crab meat.[62] In the post-WWI period, however, Japan, as pointed out by legal scholar John Haley, was more of a victim than a player in the race to form cartels as Japanese consumers were forced to buy from the most successful international cartels and import almost all of their foodstuffs, chemical fertilizer, minerals, oil, and other raw materials. The majority of Japanese producers who provided the bulk of Japanese exports, mostly textile manufacturers, were unorganized and engaged at the time in fierce competition among themselves. Attempts by the Japanese government to encourage the formation of cartels to restrain competition had been largely unsuccessful and those cartels that did come into existence on a voluntary basis were small-scale exporters but even these export cartels did not last long. It would not be until the gradual militarization of Japanese politics that the business combines, or zaibatsu, would gain their dominant position in the Japanese economy in the mid-1930s.[63]

While cartel activity increased in the 1920s it was the erecting of tariff barriers by countries such as the US and UK that led to calls by various states for international cooperation in dealing with the depressed world economy. Although the League of Nations, the precursor to the United Nations, was formed in 1919 and provided a forum for member states to discuss and cooperate with each other on a wide range of topics of international concern, it would not be until 1927 that the World Economic Conference (WEC) was held with the specific purpose of facilitating discussion and cooperation among the major economies of the world in coming up with measures to restore economic growth to Europe. State officials from 29 countries as well as representatives of businesses, workers, and consumers attended the WEC. The idea for the conference was originally proposed by the French minister Louis Loucheur who believed that the conflicting national interests of states were a major obstacle to economic recovery in Europe and that only through the close cooperation between governments and private businesses could the situation of low economic growth be rectified.[64] Aside from hammering out a resolution calling for measures such as independent action by several states in removing or lowering tariff barriers and concerted action in expanding trade through commercial treaties,[65] the WEC was notable for taking up the topic of competition in its agenda and in particular on the issue of regulating international cartel activity.

Changing views of cartels

In 1998 the Organisation for Economic Co-operation and Development (OECD) announced and urged OECD member states in its Cartel Recommendation to prohibit cartels by enacting domestic competition legislation banning collusive price fixing, tendering, output restrictions and market division, and furthermore recommended that the member states cooperate with each other to eliminate cartel activity. This recommendation was arguably made based on the assumption that cartels and activities associated with cartels were not in the interests of capitalism, competition, or global consumer welfare. At the beginning of the 20th century and up to the 1920s, however, opinion on cartels was far from uniform.[66] Loucheur believed that cartels could help in reducing overproduction and improving stability in worker employment. That is, cartels offered a means to rationalize an industry by improving efficiency and eliminating excess capacity.[67] This belief was shared and put into practice by many governments in Europe that encouraged the formation of cartels as mentioned previously. The German economist Julius Hirsch saw the formation of cartels and trusts as a possible means to increase productivity and lower the total costs of industry and trade by allowing the elimination of waste and redundancy.[68] Given the growing proliferation of cartels in Germany at the time in the 1920s, such a positive view on the role of cartels from a German economist is perhaps not unexpected. Alberto Pirelli, an Italian member of the Supreme Economic Council of Versailles, believed that cartels could contribute to industrial rationalization and stability in the labor market.[69] In short, the common view in the pre-World War II (WWII) decade of the 1920s was that cartels provided both benefits and harm and that one could differentiate between what was "good" and "bad" cartel behavior.[70] This mixed view on cartels was aired at the WEC in 1927. In its summary opinion, the WEC noted that cartels may "secure a more methodical organization of production and a reduction in cost, and act as a check on uneconomic competition and reduce the evils resulting from fluctuation in industrial activity." On the other hand, the WEC also noted that "if they encourage monopolistic tendencies and the application of unsound business methods," cartels may "check technical progress in production and involve dangers to the legitimate interests of important sections of society and of particular countries."[71]

Despite this balanced presentation of views made on the merits and threats of cartels, as the conference proceeded, the idea that the international community should establish a regime to deter cartels from bad behavior gradually spread among the participating states. In support of this trend, concern especially began to be raised by speakers who urged measures to prevent cartels from inordinately raising prices to consumers, as well as from labor union leaders such as Léon Jouhaux of the French CGT labor union who argued that cartels that were not willing to share their monopoly profits with their workers should be made to do so.[72] At the end of the conference, a final recommendation was issued by the WEC which called upon the League of Nations to collect information on international cartels, monitor their conduct and investigate the impact of their activities, and publicize incidents of harmful conduct undertaken by the cartels.[73] The WEC did not establish an international judicial regime regulating cartel activity citing that it was "impossible" given the divergent views and measures considered necessary by various member states and "on account of the objections of principle which a number of states would feel on national and constitutional grounds to any such system." Furthermore, the WEC took the view that "the laws and tribunals of each individual country can take action with regard to international agreements so far as they involve operations in its own territory."[74] The inability of the WEC to set up an international legal regime was to some a sign of a lack of progress.[75] Be that as it may, however, the significance of this action taken at the WEC was that it was done at a time when the global economy had lacked an international authority to deal with issues of competition that crossed national borders and that for the first time in modern history states had agreed to discuss collaborating on regulating private competition, a realm that traditionally had been under the scope of private domestic laws.

Yet while it may have seemed that an international consensus towards regulating cartel activity would eventually develop, the Great Depression of 1929 had given way to a further increase in international cartel activity supported by national governments and international treaties for products such as tin, aluminum, nitrogen, dyestuff, and enamel goods. According to one estimate, during the 1930s international cartels controlled 40% to 50% of world trade with monopoly pricing for their products.[76]

The national interest and cartels

As mentioned previously, WWII had convinced people such as the US president Franklin D. Roosevelt that cartels were partly to blame for the coming of the war and that cartel activity needed to be monitored and regulated by the international community. What was considered a tool by governments for managing the economy in the 1920s and 1930s was now looked upon as an enemy of democracy and an instrument of power of totalitarian dictators such as Hitler and the Japanese militarists. This is not to say, however, that the cartelization of economic life was a phenomenon limited particularly to Germany and Japan. Indeed, as we have seen, American and British enterprises were also actively pursuing the formation of cartels at one point or another. Quigley argues, however, that the major difference between Germany and the UK was that in contrast to the former where the existence of cartels was well publicized and acknowledged, British cartels were notable not for "their rarity or weakness so much as their unobtrusiveness" according to a report issued by the British Committee on Trusts in 1929.[77] Indeed, in an attempt to study the British vegetable oil monopoly controlled by Unilever founded by William H. Lever which was as substantial as the monopoly that I.G. Farben had on chemicals, the American business magazine *Fortune* lamented that "[n]o other industry…is quite so exasperatingly secretive as the soap and shortening industries."[78] But perhaps a major factor that made Roosevelt and others including Lenin consider that cartels were inimical to the interest of maintaining peace was the inclination demonstrated by German cartels and monopolistic organizations before and during WWII to be used and exploited by the state for furthering nationalistic purposes. That is, as pointed out by Quigley, while in countries such as the US and UK monopoly capitalists were businessmen seeking maximization of profits first and patriots later, in Germany they were nationalists first and businessmen later.[79] Consequently, the political goals of cartels and the state there frequently coincided, augmenting the view that cartels are an instrument of the state for furthering its national interests. Be that as it may, the perceived benefits arising from cartels such as encouraging production efficiency and stabilizing prices were now swept away in favor of the view of Adam Smith that cartels resulted in "conspiracies against the public." With the US the undisputed leader of the post-war international economic order created after WWII in 1945, this negative view of cartels became the dominant narrative among the industrialized states of Europe and Japan.

Accordingly, the US had sought to establish an international legal regime that would regulate the activities of international cartels through attempts such as the establishing of the International Trade Organization (ITO) and the drawing up of the Havana Charter. Both endeavors however, as mentioned previously, ended in failure. And to this day global enforcement against cartels is fragmented with each jurisdiction looking basically only after its own citizens. Although at its Ministerial Conference in Singapore in 1996 the World Trade Organization (WTO)[80] set up the Working Group on the Interaction between Trade and Competition Policy (WGTCP) to consider issues relating to the interrelationship between trade and competition and to deliberate on whether or not to include competition policy within the framework of the WTO, no common consensus was formed. The WTO is currently without a mandate to deal with cartel issues.[81]

A development in international relations that has perhaps complicated the efforts towards the formation of a global consensus on banning cartels is the use of cartels by developing countries as part of their decolonization and national development process in gaining leverage over wealthy industrialized nations. The Group of 77 (G-77) at the United Nations, a coalition of developing nations that had originally banded together to promote their collective economic interests (now expanded to 134 member countries and with the participation of China), had advocated the creation of stronger commodity cartels for products such as bananas, coffee, coffee, cocoa, rubber, tin, and sugar since the 1960s, so as to allow these developing countries to improve their terms of trade[82] vis a vis the industrialized nations. Perhaps the most prominent example of developing countries using a cartel to exert leverage over developed nations is that of the Organization of Petroleum Exporting Countries (OPEC), a cartel that was founded on September 14, 1960, by the five founding nations of Iran, Iraq, Kuwait, Saudi Arabia, and Venezuela (which now consists of 14 member states),[83] at a time when the global oil market was controlled by seven private multinational companies known as the "Seven Sisters" which held 85% of the world's oil production.[84] OPEC's stated mission was to seek "to coordinate and unify the petroleum policies of its Member Countries and ensure the stabilization of oil markets" so that not only would there be a secure and regular supply of petroleum to consumers, but most importantly for the oil producers "a fair return on capital for those investing in the petroleum industry."[85] That is, OPEC's implicit goal was to reclaim their oil resources from their former colonizers, in particular the oil company proxies of the Netherlands, the UK, and the US. To this end OPEC flexed its muscles for the first time in 1973 when it embargoed oil shipments to the US and its allies that supported Israel in the Arab–Israeli War, leading to the quadrupling of the price of a barrel of oil. OPEC was then able to maintain some control over the price of oil until the mid-1980s.[86]

That the consumers of a state in most cases have only their own government to rely upon in protecting them from anticompetitive acts stemming from cartel activities is a reflection of not only the current reality of international politics, but arguably also of the anarchic condition of international society and the absolute aspect of national sovereignty we have seen touted by Realists in particular.[87] While consumers will have to live with this situation until the time when the international community may develop a consensus and agree upon having a global competition law that encompasses measures against illegal cartel activity, what is perhaps an egregious aspect for consumers is that, while many governments, such as the EU, Japan, and the US, have on the one hand laws to ban abusive collusive anticompetitive activities, virtually all[88] have on the other hand legally allowed the formation of cartels that have engaged in anticompetitive activities arguably at the expense of the interests of domestic and/or foreign consumers. And at times governments have even cooperated with each other to maintain cartels at the expense of their own respective domestic consumers. An example is the formation of a global aluminum cartel initially urged by Paul O'Neil, the head of Alcoa, the world's largest aluminum producer, as a means to stabilize the market and protect the US from "destructive" competition by Russia, which at the time was making its transition to a market economy.[89] The "destructive" competition which O'Neil was alluding to was a rapid surge in Russian aluminum exports from 300,000 tons in 1990 to 1.6 million tons in 1993.[90] Despite some opposition from the Department of Justice (DoJ), the negotiated agreement was signed on March 1, 1994 by Australia, Canada, the EU, Norway, Russia, and the US Clinton administration, creating an international aluminum cartel that resulted in reduced worldwide aluminum production capacity, higher prices and profits for Alcoa, and higher prices for consumers regardless of where they resided.[91]

The mammoth Japan Agricultural Cooperative (Nokyo), or JA, is another prominent example of a de facto authorized cartel, comprised of a large family of several agricultural cooperatives that had over several decades engaged in anticompetitive activities such as regulating rice production, distribution, and pricing, and supplying farmers with financing for purchasing agricultural equipment, fertilizer, seeds, and fuels at uncompetitive prices.[92] The JA cartel, through its strong links to Japanese politicians and the bureaucracy, had forced the Japanese consumer to pay higher than world market prices for staple products such as rice[93] and for imported food products such as beef.[94] While hurting the purses of consumers, the cartel activities of JA and their lobbying pressure on politicians, resulting in generous government farm subsidies and high import tariffs, have also until recently arguably impacted the motivation of Japanese farmers to become more productive and internationally cost competitive. Unlike the dubious legal status of the international aluminum cartel, however, the activities of the JA and other so-called cooperatives are permitted under Article 22 of the AMA that allows a voluntary partnership that is meant to provide mutual support to small-scale enterprises.[95]

Aside from the JA, between 1953 and 1961 the Japanese parliament legislated over 20 statutes permitting the formation of cartels in almost every major industry in the Japanese economy. Laws such as the Medium and Small Industry Stabilization Law, the Marine Products Export Industry Act, the Ammonium Sulphate Industry Rationalization Act, and the Ammonium Export Adjustment Temporary Measures Act authorized the formation of recession and rationalization cartels as well as cartels for the purpose of promoting or stabilizing certain specific industries, to protect small to medium-sized enterprises, and to achieve rapid increases in production capacity and international competitiveness.[96] Such separate legislation has allowed the exemption of cartels from the provisions of Article 2(6) and 3 of the AMA.[97]

The tolerance by governments of cartels and cartel activities that has led to damaging the economic welfare of consumers as well as protecting economic inefficiency is perhaps a reflection of their ability to actively respond only to powerful and vocal interest groups, resulting in their forgetting about the prime purpose of enforcing their competition laws: to protect consumer welfare and competition by ensuring open, transparent markets, equal business opportunities for all enterprises regardless of national origin, and the allocation of market resources in accordance with consumer demand. As such, while the formation of cartels by developing nations as a means of gaining leverage over developed nations as in the case of the formation of OPEC can be considered as being within the context of promoting the national interests of expanding national power and enhancing national security, the national interest as perceived by some other governments such as those of Japan and the US have at times arguably come to mean ensuring that the profitability of private enterprises or special interest groups takes precedence over the economic welfare of their consumers, rather than having anything to do with what are arguably the traditional concerns of national interest according to Realist IR theory, that is, enforcing national security or expanding national power vis-à-vis other states, in effect making a farce not only of competition laws that were meant to protect innovation-driving competition and to promote the liberal concern of consumer welfare, but also of casting doubt on whether a state is able to always comprehend what its national interests truly are.

Export cartels

Another example of a cartel supported by virtually all governments that have competition laws banning collusive anticompetitive activities is the export cartel. Export cartels consist of cooperative arrangements among enterprises that have the explicit purpose of promoting their exports to foreign markets. While export cartels usually consist of enterprises from the same nation, an export cartel can also be an international cartel comprising of enterprises from various countries who collude on pricing or production output for exports to markets other than those of the cartel member states. An example is that of OPEC mentioned earlier. Export cartels allow domestic enterprises to pool their resources and spread risks, thus enabling the attainment of economies of scale and other efficiencies not possible if the enterprises worked on their own. The advocates of export cartels have also considered them to be helpful to small and medium-sized enterprises in dealing with the market power of foreign purchases, particularly in the case when such purchasers have formed import cartels.[98]

In an export cartel, certain enterprises with products for exports collaborate in areas such as fixing pricing, output, and distribution, thus allowing them to increase their market power. Export cartels essentially enable enterprises in exporting states to gain inordinately high levels of profits at the expense of consumers in the importing state by engaging in anticompetitive behavior that is prohibited in various competition laws such as §1 of the US Sherman Act. An example of an arguably government-authorized export cartel is the arrangement by Japanese automakers in restricting their exports to the US under the 1981 Japanese automobile Voluntary Restraint Agreement (VRA) negotiated between Japan and the US. The cartel was formed at the time when the US car industry was being hard pressed by a surge of imported Japanese cars. The VRA resulted in the temporary recovery of the US automobile industry, higher prices for Japanese cars for US consumers owing to restricted supply, and price increases for US cars as US automakers decided to improve profitability rather than regain lost market share.[99] Such a detrimental outcome for the interests of American consumers from the formation of the Japanese automobile export cartel would suggest that, as pointed out by legal scholar Daniel Gifford, VRAs concluded between governments including the 1981 Japan–US automobile VRA would be a per se violation of §1 of the Sherman Act, were it not for the fact that a government-sponsored VRA is immune to antitrust attack when the adherence to the agreement by foreign producers is mandated by their government (in such circumstances the foreign producer being entitled to a defense known as the "foreign sovereign compulsion" defense).[100]

As mentioned earlier, in the 1940 Socony case the US Supreme Court ruled that the Sherman Act applied also to "foreign commerce." Yet, in 1918 the Webb–Pomerene Act (WPA) was enacted with the purpose of exempting US enterprises from the Sherman Act. The formation of export cartels under this Act was allowed with the prerequisite that the cartel does not restrain domestic trade or impact the exports of a domestic competitor. The enterprises in the export cartel were also not allowed to enter into any agreement that depressed or increased prices of commodities sold within the US. That is to say, in accordance with Chapter 50 of the WPA, enterprises within an export cartel were given permission to engage in anticompetitive behavior so long as there was no impact on domestic competition and on the welfare of consumers within the US.[101]

In 1982 the US further enacted two laws that were to compliment the WPA, the Export Trading Act (ETA)[102] and the Foreign Trade Antitrust Improvements Act (FTAIA).[103] The ETA was passed with the purpose of increasing "United States exports of products and services" by "modifying the application" of antitrust laws "to certain export trade." The law established an office within the Department of Commerce dedicated to promoting the formation of export trade associations and export trading companies and provided a specific mechanism involving the application for Export Trade Certificates which allowed American enterprises to enter into collaborative relationships, with the condition that they met certain specific standards such as limiting conduct to export trade and avoiding any "substantial lessening of competition or restraint of trade" in the US or "a substantial restraint of the export trade of any competitor of the applicant."[104]

While the ETA thus provided a means for American export ventures to protect themselves from the application of antitrust regulations, the FTAIA had an arguably more substantial positive impact on exporters as it further narrowed the application of the Sherman Act with respect to export transactions.[105] The FTAIA amended §7 of the Clayton Act covering corporate mergers and acquisitions to exempt US joint ventures that were limited in scope to doing business with foreign nations from provisions prohibiting them "from acquiring the stock or assets of another corporation to lessen competition or create a monopoly."[106] The FTAIA also amended §5(a) of the Federal Trade Commission Act[107] so that the Act would not prohibit "unfair methods of competition involving commerce with foreign nations…unless such methods have a direct, substantial, and reasonably foreseeable effect" on domestic business or on the export commerce of a domestic business.[108]

The FTAIA was enacted in response to the perception among American businessmen that "American antitrust laws are a barrier to joint export activities that promote efficiencies in the export of American goods and services" and in order to "encourage the business community to engage in efficiency producing joint conduct in the export of American goods and services."[109] While a concern was raised in the deliberations preceeding the Act's enactment that the legislation could be misinterpreted as American approval for American enterprises to engage in international cartel activity such as was prevalent before WWII and that there might be a risk that such cartels would give rise to "a secret agreement to include the United States in the market allocation to round things out," the Senate Committee on the Judiciary that reviewed the bill did not believe, after "weighing this and similar arguments carefully," that "the legislation will result in a rejuvenation of international cartels." Regardless of this point of concern, however, the Committee went on to allude that, however, even if international cartels with American companies within it were formed, so long as their activities did not have a "spillover" effect and there would not be "a direct, substantial, and reasonably foreseeable effect" on commerce within the US, the existence of such international cartels and their cartel activities would be permitted.[110] Several years after the FTAIA was enacted, at the 2004 WTO Working Group on the Interaction between Trade and Competition Policy, the US publicly stated its opposition to the prohibition of export cartels, citing their ability to enhance efficiencies, bringing innovation, and lowering prices.[111]

In Japan, while cartels were prohibited under Article 2(6) or 8 of the AMA where it is stated that a trade association must not engage in any act which substantially restrains competition in any particular field of trade, the Export-Import Transaction Act (EITA, Yushutsu-nyu torihiki ho) of 1952 exempted the formation of export cartels from the provisions of the AMA in Article 5. The EITA allowed (upon notifying the Minister of Economy, Trade, and Industry) exporters to enter into an agreement with regard to pricing, quantity, quality, design, and other matters in export transactions for specific type of goods to be exported to a specific destination.[112] The export cartel was, however, obliged to observe six requirements, one of them being that the export cartel agreement would not violate any treaties concluded with foreign governments. If all requirements stated in the EITA were fulfilled, the restraint of competition caused by the formation of an export cartel would be allowed and prohibited only if it was considered "unreasonable," which under Article 2(6) of the AMA was defined as being "contrary to the public interest."[113]

The EITA was legislated upon the suggestion of the American occupation authorities (SCAP) who in response to growing concerns of the dumping of Japanese exports of canned crab and tuna in the US market in the late 1940s had suggested to the Japanese government the enactment of an act similar to that of the Webb–Pomerene Act so that Japanese exporters would be able to practice "orderly marketing," or self-regulation in terms of prices and market quotas on export markets.[114] Over the course of several years the EITA was amended four times to allow more joint activities which led to the burgeoning of Japanese export cartels. By 1960, 172 export cartels in 65 industries were in existence which accounted for almost half of all export product categories.[115] As most of the companies, however, that initially took advantage of the EITA were small and medium-sized enterprises, the rationale behind the EITA shifted from that of ensuring "orderly marketing" and protecting, to some extent, foreign producers to that of allowing and encouraging the growth and protection of Japanese infant industries. Eventually enterprises of the large-scale industries of paper, vinyl chloride, chemical fertilizers (ammonium sulfate), cement, steel products, and synthetic fibers also formed export cartels under the provisions of the EITA to promote not only the exports of their products but also to rationalize their respective industries to overcome economic recession.[116] By the time they had achieved a level of international competitiveness, many of these cartels had disbanded. While there were 209 export cartels in 1969, this number had dropped to 56 by the 1980s.[117]

While it could be argued that the EITA had worked to further the national interests of Japan in terms of strengthening the international competitiveness of the Japanese economy (and through this its national security) at the expense of the market shares of foreign producers, a major loser was the Japanese consumer who, according to one estimate, ended up paying market prices for Japanese produced goods that were 20% to 30% more expensive than those same products that were "dumped" onto foreign markets by the Japanese export cartels.[118]

In the EU, cartels including export cartels are prohibited under Article 101 of the Treaty on the Functioning of the European Union (TFEU). In paragraph 1 it is stated that all agreements that may affect trade between the member states which have as their objective or may bring about the "prevention, restriction or distortion of competition within the internal market" are prohibited. The Article in addition specifically states the prohibition of acts such as fixing purchase or selling prices, limiting or controlling production, markets, technical development, or investment, and sharing markets or sources of supply.[119]

While exports made from one EU member country to another by an export cartel are banned in accordance with Article 101, it was made clear in a case involving a UK export cartel exporting crude oil to a non-EU member country (Israel), Bulk Oil v. Sun, 1986, E.C.R., that export cartel activity undertaken by EU member states towards a non-EU country would not be prohibited given that the cartel activity was "not intended to provide a particular advantage" for either the production of oil in the UK or for the domestic UK market. The EU also reasoned that the UK export cartel would not "restrict or distort competition" within the EU.[120]

In addition to the above exemption on the prohibition of export cartels, cartels in general may be exempted from Section 1 of Article 101 in accordance with the provisions of Section 3 of the same Article which states that a cartel may be allowed if its formation may contribute to "improving the production or distribution of goods or to promoting technical or economic progress," allows consumers "a fair share of the resulting benefit," and does not bring about the possibility that "competition in respect of a substantial part of the products in question" is eliminated.[121] An example where an exemption concerning a cartel was applied was in the 1984–1985 Synthetic Fibers case. Using the provision of Article 101 Section 3, the European Commission gave its approval to ten of the largest European manufacturers of synthetic fibers for a crisis cartel (i.e., a rationalization cartel formed in an industry with chronic overcapacity) that led to an 18% reduction of capacity over several years, with the expectation that it would bring about a more efficient industry with no impact on competition and in a socially accepted way by retaining workers and redeployment of redundant workers.[122]

Conclusion

Through the application of laws such as those of the EU, Japan, and the US, governments have legally allowed the formation of cartels in certain instances or encouraged such collusive activities as price fixing and market distribution that would be considered illegal under their domestic competition laws. That is, as in the case of cartels formed for the purpose of promoting exports, governments have from time to time allowed illegal conduct so long that it would have no major adverse effect on their own domestic market or consumers, with total disregard of the impact on consumers in other states or any detriment to total global welfare.[123] Taylor calls such a stance one of "under-regulation," that is, an exporting nation would permit anticompetitive conduct or "underregulate" anticompetition activity that is consistent with its perceived national interest and would ultimately lead to a reduction in the welfare of the entire global community.[124] This focus of states on promoting their national interests rather than on the welfare of the global community creates what is called in economic theory an "economic externality."[125] As to what those national interests are (assuming that a government is not at the mercy of powerful special interest groups that are able to dictate to the former what the national interest should be), first and foremost they are: strengthening national security. Export cartels arguably support national security by positively contributing to the national economy by increasing exports that would advance the economic growth of the exporting country leading to the creation of new jobs, more investment, and economic growth. That is, export cartels are in the national interest because they positively contribute to the national economy which in turn strengthens national security. And they do this by essentially extracting surplus profits from foreign consumers and transferring them into the coffers of the export cartels and their home country tax revenues. It should be noted, however, that there is a danger that the anticompetitive effects coming from the activities of an export cartel in foreign markets may spillover into its domestic market. An increase in the production quantity of an export product by the cartel, for example, may impact the production levels of a similar product for the domestic market, leading to possible detrimental changes in domestic market prices. In short, for the governments that promote the formation of export cartels, protecting competition or the welfare of the global consumer is of secondary or of no importance.[126] States in such instances are behaving as Realists with only one thing in mind: increasing their respective power through increasing exports. Increasing the welfare of consumers in importing states would not increase the power of an exporting state. Liberal concepts of promoting global welfare, promoting cooperation among various societal groups across various states, as well as achieving a harmonious state of international relations through removing issues of contention are basically thrown to the winds. Internationalist concepts of the equality of nations also become a farce when states deliberately promote export cartels. In the context of Realist IR theory the use of cartels by states for the purposes of promoting exports, or for some other purpose perceived to relate to increasing national power such as accelerating industrial rationalization, can be explained as a manifestation of one aspect of a state's struggle for power with the goal of strengthening its national security or of achieving dominance over other powers. This has been most apparent in the case of cartels being used by the Nazi government to further strengthen its economy and war machine and arguably also with OPEC as the developing states attempted to gain power and leverage vis-à-vis the industrialized states, using the supply of oil as a political weapon. On the other hand, the existence of cartels such as the international aluminum cartel mentioned earlier which was instigated at the strong urging of a private enterprise can be explained within the context of liberal theories of IR which hold that state preferences cannot be reduced to a simple metric such as struggling for power to achieve security or wealth but rather come about as a response to the interests of various social groups and individuals, which in the case of the aluminum cartel was the end result of a state response coming from the pressure of a company that arguably wielded a considerable amount of political and economic influence within the US.

Be that as it may, while developed regions such as the EU, Japan, and the US may counter state-sanctioned export cartels and protect their consumers by extraterritorially applying their respective competition laws or by forming import cartels,[127] the people that lose the most to export cartels are arguably those in developing countries who on their own lack the political and economic clout to take measures against such export cartels.[128] Or, to use the parlance of Power Transition, the major losers are the consumers in the states that are at the bottom of the hierarchical international order. Such states have little or no clout in changing the rules of the order. Indeed, in 2002 the government of Thailand, for example, claimed that export cartels were potentially damaging to developing countries as they worsened their terms of trade and called for the abolition of export cartels in industrialized nations, considering it "unacceptable" for developed nations to make "use of export cartels as a strategic trade policy to extract 'rents' from foreign countries."[129] Accordingly, the Thai government argued that developing countries be allowed to form import cartels so as to enable them to gain countervailing power against buyers or sellers from developed countries. This proposal was supported not only by Indonesia and China, but also received support by UNCTAD which suggested that developed countries should abolish export cartel exemptions on a non-reciprocal basis.[130] Such calls for reform, however, have so far failed to compel the advanced industrial states to rescind legislation allowing the formation of export cartels.

Such disagreement on export cartels and the divide it creates between the developed and underdeveloped nations, as well as evoking tensions in diplomatic relations, are perhaps other reasons besides of ensuring the protection of competition that an impartial international authority should be established to monitor and regulate international cartel activity with the goal of ensuring a just distribution of economic welfare and the protection of consumers wherever they may reside. For this to happen, however, first and foremost the international community will need to be in agreement what the concept of global welfare means. To this end states, and particularly the developed regions of the EU, Japan, and the US may have to first discard their Realist notion of international relations as being a struggle for power and a zero-sum game, as well as do away with their arguably contradictory stance on competition policy of claiming to be in favor of protecting competition and the consumer, while harming both through their support of cartels that protect certain industries or enterprises and the endorsement of export cartels.

It can be argued that the more states bind themselves with nationalistic calls of "our country first!" and intertwines this with a primitive mercantilist belief that having a trade surplus means that the state is "winning," the greater possibility there is to see states attempt to get around domestic competition laws and encourage the formation of export cartels or for states to increase import tariffs that arguably skew competition and hit the purses of consumers, leading ultimately to more diplomatic and economic conflict among nations. We can perhaps also expect to see attempts by governments (especially those that are vulnerable to specific domestic interest groups) affiliated to the WTO including China, the EU, Japan, and the US to circumvent the current ban on the use of VRAs that has been in place since the Uruguay Round Agreement of 1994 (with exceptions granted to one sector in each importing state) and to conclude VRAs that will curtail imports and enable domestic producers and foreign exporters to divide up monopoly profits at the expense of domestic consumers. If, on the other hand, states take the view of Power Transitionists and considers themselves as existing within an international hierarchical order that has at its apex a Dominant Power that determines, along with its Great Power allies, the rules, norms, and values for the order, all that it may take for an international authority with the power to monitor and regulate cartel activity to come into existence would be for the Dominant Power and its Great Power allies to actually want such an overarching legal authority, and for the rest of the lesser powers of the international community to accept it. In one respect, this perhaps entails the further globalization of the international community, but in a form that is more akin to what imperialism has been; an incorporation of states and peoples into a political and economic framework of rules and customs that is established and dominated by the imperial powers. And, as a start, the US, which is arguably for now the dominant power of the international economic order, will need to want such a cartel-regulating authority – an unlikely prospect for the foreseeable future, given the increasingly strident antiglobalization and economic nationalist message emanating from the Trump administration along with the backlash against globalization that seems to be growing within certain states such as the UK.[131]

Notes

1 Lee, J.S., *Strategies to Achieve a Binding International Agreement on Regulating Cartels*, Springer Nature Singapore, 2016, p.10.
2 Allen, James S., *The Cartel System*, International Publishers, 1946, p.9.
3 EUR-Lex, Directive 2014/104/EU of the European Parliament and of the Council of November 26, 2014 on certain rules governing actions for damages under national law for infringements of the competition law provisions of the Member States and of the European Union Text with EEA relevance, December 5, 2014, Online. Available https://eur-lex.europa.eu/legal-content/EN/TXT/?uri=CELEX%3A32014L0104 (accessed May 26, 2019).

4 EUR-Lex, Consolidated version of the Treaty on the Functioning of the European Union – Part Three: Union Policies and Internal Actions – Title VII: Common Rules on Competition, Taxation and Approximation of Laws - Chapter 1: Rules on competition – Section 1: Rules applying to undertakings – Article 101 (ex-Article 81 TEC), Online, Available https://eur-lex.europa.eu/legal-content/EN/ALL/?uri=CELEX%3A12008E101 (accessed May 26, 2019).

5 International Competition Network, Anti-Cartel Enforcement Template, Japan, November 15, 2015, p.4, Online. Available https://www.jftc.go.jp/en/policy_enforcement/cartels_bidriggings/anti_cartel_files/set_ICN_Cartel_Template_Japan2015.pdf (accessed May 26, 2019); Matsushita, Mitsuo, The Antimonopoly Act of Japan, Global Competition Policy, Institute of International Economics, December 1997, p.172. In theory, a cartel activity would not be prohibited if it were not contrary to the "public interest." As to what exactly is the "public interest" is not clear and has not been elaborated upon in the courts. In a Japanese Supreme Court decision given in the Oil Cartel (Price Fixing) Case in 1984 (Decision of the Supreme Court, February 24, 1984, Keishu, 38(4), 1287 et seq. (1984)), however, the Court ruled that "public interest" in Article 2(6) of the AMA means free competition in principle. However, there are, according to the Court, exceptional instances where an agreement that restrains competition is necessary to meet a valid objective. Accordingly, courts should weigh the benefits of maintaining competition and the benefits of maintaining such an agreement; when the benefits of the latter outweighs those of the former, then such an agreement is not contrary to the public interest and therefore such a cartel would not be illegal.

6 Japan Fair Trade Commission, The Antimonopoly Act, Chapter II, Article 3, Online. Available https://www.jftc.go.jp/en/legislation_gls/amended_ama09/amended_ama15_02.html (accessed May 26, 2019).

7 15 U.S. Code §1, Legal Information Institute, Cornell Law School, Online. Available https://www.law.cornell.edu/uscode/text/15/1 (accessed May 26, 2019).

8 That is, an act that is inherently illegal.

9 International Competition Network, Anti-Cartel Enforcement Template, United States Department of Justice Antitrust Division, November 17, 2016, Online. Available https://www.justice.gov/atr/page/file/957596/download (accessed August 2, 2019).

10 310 U.S. 150.

11 Gellhorn, Ernest, Kovacic, William E., *Antitrust Law and Economics*, West Group, 1994, p.183.

12 Ibid.

13 Ibid., p.182.

14 Stiglitz, Joseph E., *Making Globalization Work*, Norton, 2006, p.199.

15 Ibid., p.200.

16 Smith, Adam, *The Wealth of Nations*, Encyclopedia Britannica, 1982, p.55.

17 Fear, Jeffrey, Cartels and Competition: Neither Markets nor Hierarchies, 2006, working paper, p.7. Online. Available http://www.hbs.edu/faculty/publication%20files/07-011.pdf (accessed August 2, 2019). As noted by Fear, however, not all cartels were established to eliminate competitors; rather some cartels were formed with the aim of preserving competitors by positioning themselves to control similar product markets in a horizontal fashion, thereby avoiding ruinous competition.

18 Gerber, David J., *Global Competition*, Oxford University Press, p.29.

19 Lee, op.cit., p.9.

20 Starkey, David J., Harlaftis, Gelinda, ed., *Global Markets: The Internationalization of the Sea Transport Industries Since 1850*, St. John's, 1998, p.58; Schaede, Ulrike, *Cooperative Capitalism*, Oxford University Press, 2000, p.226.

21 Fear, op.cit., p.10.

22 Ibid., p.11.

23 Haley, John Owen, *Authority Without Power*, Oxford University Press, 1991, p.146; Quigley, Carroll, *Tragedy and Hope*, Macmillan Company, 1974, p.510.
24 Fear, op.cit., p.4.
25 Quigley, op.cit., p.510.
26 Ibid.
27 Stiglitz, op.cit., p.4.
28 Saul, John Ralston, *The Collapse of Globalism*, Atlantic Books, 2018, p.3.
29 Joll, James, *The Origins of the First World War*, Longman, 1992, p.202.
30 Angell, Norman, *The Great Illusion*, Cosmo Inc., 2007, p.309.
31 Fukuyama, Francis, *The End of History?*, The National Interest, Summer 1989, Online. Available https://www.embl.de/aboutus/science_society/discussion/discussion_2006/ref1-22june06.pdf (accessed August 15, 2019).
32 Taylor, Martyn, *International Competition Law*, Cambridge University Press, 2006, p.213.
33 Fear, op.cit., p.12.
34 Ibid., p.13.
35 Klein, Julius, International Cartels, Foreign Affairs, April, 1928, Online. Available https://www.foreignaffairs.com/articles/1928-04-01/international cartels (accessed August 2, 2019).
36 Ibid.
37 Ibid.
38 Allen, op.cit., p.21.
39 Ibid., p.17.
40 Klein, op.cit.
41 Ibid.
42 Teichova, Alice, *An Economic Background to Munich*, Cambridge University Press, 1974, p.313.
43 Quigley, op.cit., p.512.
44 Ibid.
45 Schumpeter, Joseph, International Cartels and their Relation to World Trade, *Proceedings of the Academy of Political Science in the City of New York*, Vol. 12, No. 4, America as a Creditor Nation (Jan., 1928).
46 Schumpeter, op.cit., pp.110–113.
47 Ibid., p.112.
48 Klein, op.cit.
49 Allen, op.cit., p.5.
50 Ibid.
51 Klein, op.cit.
52 Martos, Luis Palma, Hidalgo, Jose-Luis Garcia, Solan, Christian Chase, The Controversy Over International Cartels in the League of Nations (1925–1927), Eshet Conference Paper, p.5. Online. Available http://www.eshet.net/conference/paper_view.php?id=1361&p=39 (accessed August 2, 2019).
53 Allen, op.cit., p.8.
54 Roddy, Peter, *The International Tin Trade*, Woodhead Publishing, 1995, p.18.
55 Quigley, op.cit., p.510.
56 Fear, op.cit., p.12.
57 Quigley, op.cit., p.510.
58 Ibid., p.453.
59 Haley, op.cit., p.146.
60 15 U.S. Code §66.
61 Haley, op.cit., p.146.
62 Ibid., p.11.
63 Haley, op.cit., p.146; Quigley, op.cit., p.564. By the 1930s eight zaibatsu controlled 75% of the Japanese nation's wealth. They frequently cooperated with each other, a

prime example being the cooperation between Mitsui and Mitsubishi in eliminating a smaller competitor, the Suzuki Shoten of Kobe, which precipitated a financial panic leading to a closure of most banks in Japan in 1927.

64 Gerber, op.cit., p.25.

65 *The Spectator*, The World Economic Conference, July 30, 1927. Online. Available http://archive.spectator.co.uk/article/30th-july-1927/4/the-world-economic-conference (accessed August 2, 2019).

66 Taylor, op.cit., p.134. The recommendation was titled "Recommendation of the OECD Council Concerning Effective Action Against Hard Core Cartels," and was released on March 30, 1998. The OECD was originally established to facilitate the post-WWII distribution of economic aid in Europe. It subsequently gained the role of promoting discussion and coordination of economic and social policies among the advanced industrialized nations of Europe, Japan, and the US. Today it consists of 35 nations.

67 Gerber, op.cit., p.28.

68 Martos, Hidalgo, Solan, op.cit., p.9.

69 Ibid., p.10.

70 Gerber, op.cit., p.29.

71 CQ Researcher, The International Cartel Movement, Editorial Research Reports, Vol. II, Washington D.C., CQ Press, 1928, Online. Available http://library.cqpress.com/cqresearcher/document.php?id=cqresrre1928060400 (accessed May 26, 2019).

72 Gerber, op.cit., p.30.

73 CQ Researcher, op.cit.

74 Ibid.

75 Gerber, op.cit., p.31.

76 Lee, op.cit., p.51.

77 Quigley, op.cit., p.513.

78 Ibid.

79 Ibid. Quigley points out that cartels such as I.G. Farben and others were constantly working to help Germany in its struggle for power by espionage, gaining economic advantages for Germany, and by attempting to cripple the ability of other countries to mobilize their resources for waging war.

80 The intergovernmental trade regulating organization founded in 1995 that replaced the General Agreement on Tariff and Trade (GATT) and which deals with regulating trade in goods, services, and intellectual property. It is the largest economic organization in the world with over 160 member states.

81 Martyniszyn, Marek, Export Cartels: Is it Legal to Target Your Neighbor? *Journal of International Economic Law*, Vol. 15, No. 1, 2012, p.11. Online. Available https://ssrn.com/abstract=2012838 (accessed August 2, 2019).

82 The terms of trade being the ratio of export prices to import prices or the amount of imported goods per each unit of its exports a state can purchase.

83 Other member states include: Qatar (1961), Indonesia (1962), Libya (1962), the United Arab Emirates (1967), Algeria (1969), Nigeria (1971), Ecuador (1973), Gabon (1975), Angola (2007), and Equatorial Guinea (2017). Indonesia suspended its membership in 2016.

84 *Focus Economics*, The History of OPEC: Has it been a success? Online. Available https://www.focus-economics.com/blog/opec-history-has-opec-been-a-success (accessed July 13, 2019).

85 Ibid. The Seven Sisters being: British Petroleum, Gulf Oil, Royal Dutch Shell, Standard Oil of Southern California, New York, and New Jersey, and Texaco.

86 Fear, op.cit., p.17.

87 UNCTAD, Model Law on Competition (2010), Chapter I, Online. Available http://unctad.org/en/Docs/tdrbpconf7L1_en.pdf (accessed July 13, 2019). There has, however, been some development of soft-law instruments including the Model

Law on Competition developed by UNCTAD in which it states that its objective is "[t]o control or eliminate restrictive agreements or arrangements among enterprises, or mergers and acquisitions or abuse of dominant positions of market power, which limit access to markets or otherwise unduly restrain competition, adversely affecting domestic or international trade or economic development."

88 Martyniszyn, op.cit., p.10. Some countries that prohibit export cartels include Luxembourg, Russia, Thailand, and Uruguay.

89 Stiglitz, op.cit., p.201.

90 Gifford, Daniel J., Antitrust and Trade Issues: Similarities, Differences, and Relationships, *University of Minnesota Law School DePaul Law Review*, Vol. 44, 1995, p.1080.

91 Stiglitz, op.cit., p.201.

92 Cutts, Robert L., Capitalism in Japan: Cartels and Keiretsu, *Harvard Business Review*, July–August 1992; Shukan Diamond, Mokaru Nogyo (Money making agriculture) 2018, Diamond-sha, February 24, 2018, p.30. Major structural reforms, however, have been undertaken leading to a reduction in the role of Nokyo starting from March 2019 when it will lose its oversight and auditing powers over farmers. Government subsidies for reducing rice cultivation acreage that started in 1970 were eliminated in 2018.

93 Numbeo, Price Rankings by Country of Rice, Online. Available https://www.numbeo.com/cost-of-living/country_price_rankings?itemId=115 (accessed June 22, 2019); Japanese Ministry of Agriculture Forestry and Fisheries, Norinsuisangyo no yushutsuryoku kyoka senryaku (Fortification strategy for Japanese agriculture, forestry, and fisheries industries), May 19, 2017, Online. Available http://www.maff.go.jp/j/council/seisaku/syokuryo/160729/pdf/13_ref_data3_6.pdf (accessed July 13, 2019).

94 Shukan Diamond, op.cit., p.30. The Japanese import tariff for foreign rice is 778% while the import tariff for beef imported from the US is 38.5% and 26.6% for beef from states that are members of the Comprehensive and Progressive Agreement for Trans-Pacific Partnership (CPTPP).

95 Japan Fair Trade Commission, Antimonopoly Act, Chapter VI, Article 22, Online. Available https://www.jftc.go.jp/en/legislation_gls/amended_ama09/amended_ama15_06.html (accessed July 13, 2019).

96 Haley, op.cit., p.152.

97 Takahashi, Iwakazu, Anti-Monopoly Exemptions in Japan, The Specific Workshop between the Drafting Committee on Competition Law of Vietnam and the Japan Fair Trade Commission, August 8, 2003, p.7. Online. Available https://www.jftc.go.jp/eacpf/05/hanoiTaka.pdf. Other such laws exempting cartels from Article 2(6) and 3 of the AMA include Article 18 of the Road Transport Law which allows agreements relating to the joint operation by bus operators of routes that are less viable due to falling demand, and the Insurance Business Law (overseen by the Financial Services Agency) which in Article 101(1), No.1.2, exempts insurance cartels from the provisions of the AMA.

98 Taylor, op.cit., p.231.

99 Gifford, op.cit., p.1077.

100 Ibid., p.1088. In Mannington Mills, Inc. v. Congoleum Corp., 595 F.2d 1287, 1293 (3d Cir. 1979), it was noted that the "defense is not principally concerned with the validity or legality of the foreign government's order," but rather whether it compelled the defendant business to violate American antitrust law.

101 Federal Trade Commission, Webb Pomerene Act, Online. Available http://uscode.house.gov/view.xhtml?req=granuleid%3AUSC-prelim-title15-chapter2-subchapter2&edition=prelim (accessed July 13, 2019).

102 15 U.S.C. §4001.

103 15 U.S.C. §6a.

104 International Trade Administration, Export Trading Company Act of 1982, Title III, Export Trade Certificate of Review, Online. Available https://www.trade.gov/mas/ian/etca/tg_ian_002137.asp (accessed May 26, 2019).

105 The FTAIA inserted in Section 6(a) of the Sherman Act, Conduct Involving Trade with or Commerce with Foreign Nations. Sherman Act, Available. Online http://www.linfo.org/sherman_txt.html (accessed May 13, 2019).

106 15 U.S.C. §18. In this Section it is stated that no person engaged in commercial activity is allowed to "acquire…the whole or any part of the stock or other share capital…or any part of the assets of another person" also engaged in commerce if the effect of the acquisition "may be to lessen competition or to create a monopoly…"

107 15 U.S.C. §45.

108 Congress.Gov, H.R.5235 Foreign Trade Antitrust Improvements Act of1982, Online. Available https://www.congress.gov/bill/97th-congress/house-bill/5235 (accessed May 26, 2019).

109 House of Representatives, Report No. 97–686, Foreign Trade Antitrust Improvements Act of 1982-Report together with Additional Views, August 2, 1982, p.2, Online. Available http://www.appliedantitrust.com/26_extraterritoriality/statutes/hr_rep_97_686__8_2_1982.pdf (accessed May 26, 2019).

110 Ibid., p.13.

111 Martyniszyn, op.cit., p.8.

112 Ministry of Justice, Japanese Law Translation, Export and Import Transaction Act, Online. Available http://www.japaneselawtranslation.go.jp/law/detail_main?re=&vm=&id=2854 (accessed May 26, 2019).

113 Aside from export cartels, other cartels that have been authorized by the Japanese government and deemed as within the boundaries of law include depression (fukyo) cartels, rationalization (gorika) cartels, medium and small enterprise cartels, shipping conferences, and insurance industry cartels.

114 Schaede, op.cit., p.85.

115 Ibid.

116 Ibid.

117 Ibid., p.86.

118 Ibid.

119 EUR-Lex, Treaty on the Functioning of the European Union, Article 101, Online. Available http://eur-lex.europa.eu/legal-content/EN-LT/TXT/?uri=CELEX:12008E101&fromTab=ALL&from=EN (accessed May 26, 2019).

120 EUR-Lex, Judgment of the Court of 18 February 1986, Bulk Oil (Zug) AG v Sun International Limited and Sun Oil Trading Company, Online. Available http://eur-lex.europa.eu/legal-content/EN/TXT/?uri=CELEX%3A61984CC0174 (accessed May 26, 2019).

121 EUR-Lex, Consolidated version of the Treaty on the Functioning of the European Union – Part Three: Union Policies and Internal Actions – Title VII: Common Rules on Competition, Taxation and Approximation of Laws – Chapter 1: Rules on competition – Section 1: Rules applying to undertakings – Article 101 (ex-Article 81 TEC), May 9, 2008, Online. Available https://eur-lex.europa.eu/LexUriServ/LexUriServ.do?uri=CELEX:12008E101:EN:HTML (accessed May 26, 2019).

122 Hay, Donald, United Kingdom, *Global Competition Policy*, Institute of International Economics, 1997, p.223; Kokkoris, Ioannis, Should Crisis Cartels Exist Amidst Crises?, *The Antitrust Bulletin*, Vol. 55, No. 4/Winter, 2010, p.739.

123 Martyniszyn, op.cit., p.37; Gellhorn, Kovacic, op.cit., pp.140–141; Sher, Scott A., Ji, Yuan, The Involvement of the Chinese Government in the US Vitamin C Antitrust Legislation, LexisNexis, *China Antitrust Law Journal*, Vol.1, Issue 1/Summer, 2017, p.10; Davis Polk, U.S. Supreme Court to Decide Whether to Defer to Chinese Government's Interpretation of PRC Laws in Vitamin C Antitrust Case, January 18, 2018, Online. Available https://www.davispolk.com/publications/us-supreme-court-decide-

whether-defer-chinese-government's-interpretation-prc-laws (accessed June 22, 2019). In Matsushita Electric Industrial Co. v. Zenith Radio Corp. (Matsushita), 475 U.S. 574 (1986), US TV manufacturers alleged that 21 Japanese TV manufacturers created a cartel and applied predatory pricing in the US for the purpose of driving the former out of business. In an amicus brief to the US Supreme Court, the Japanese government stated in its support of the Japanese TV manufacturers that it had directed the TV manufacturers to organize themselves as a cartel and that it had implemented the regulatory regime. According to the amicus brief, "it is the position of the Japanese Government the formal representations of foreign governments concerning their sovereign acts are to be given conclusive effect, and that when the exercise of a state's sovereignty involves only control of the activity of its own nationals within its territory, with respect to its own export trade, foreign governments and foreign courts should not question or punish such activity." In response, the US government supported the same position, advising the Court that a foreign government's assertions concerning the existence and meaning of its own domestic laws should be accepted at "face value" and deemed "conclusive." The government (Department of Justice and State Department) further stated that failing to give "dispositive weight" to the statements of foreign governments would trigger "deep concern" among "significant trading partners of the United States." The Supreme Court did not, however, rule on the issue of foreign sovereign compulsion, finding instead that the conduct at issue allegedly committed by the TV manufacturers did not cause injury to the plaintiffs.

124 Taylor, op.cit., p.45.

125 Ibid., p.44.

126 Gifford, op.cit., p.1088. Likewise, the adherence and observance of the principles of antitrust legislation by states comes into question when a state may form an export cartel as the result of a state-to-state agreement such as in the case of a VRA. The importing state in such a case will, as the US has done, grant immunity to the exporting state's export cartel even though it would be a per se violation of domestic competition laws on the grounds of state coercion.

127 Taylor, op.cit., pp.233–234; Martyniszyn, op.cit., p.17; The United States Department of Justice, Summary of Outbound Restraint Cases, Online. Available https://www.justice.gov/atr/annex-5 (accessed June 22, 2019). In Daishowa International v. North Coast Export Co., 1982–2 Trade Reg Rep (CCH) 64,774, at 71785 (ND Cal, 1982), this case involved a group of US wood pulp exporters who formed a US-based export cartel as permitted under US domestic competition laws. In retaliation, a group of Japanese wood pulp importers formed an import cartel in Japan to boycott US wood pulp. Simultaneously the Japanese wood pulp importers challenged the validity of the US export cartel under US antitrust laws, alleging price fixing and a refusal to supply. The US pulp exporters in response countersued the Japanese importers through the extraterritorial application of US antitrust law to the import cartel in Japan. A US federal district court in San Francisco ruled that a US export cartel was exempted from US antitrust laws but the Japanese import cartel was not. Accordingly, it awarded damages to the US pulp exporters and granted an injunction against the boycott. The case was not appealed and no other higher court was given the opportunity of further ruling on the issue of extraterritoriality. The judgement was nevertheless seen by the Japanese as being unfair and a diplomatic row broke out over the case. In another case, the American Soda Ash Export Cartel (ANSAC) which was established under the WPA in 1984 was found by the European Commission in 1990 to have violated EU competition laws on price fixing. In response, ANSAC organized another export cartel for the sake of solely exporting to the EU and focusing only on collaborating on logistics-related activities.

128 Martyniszyn, op.cit., pp.18–19; Taylor, op.cit., pp.215–216. A case in point is that which involved ANSAC against which claims were made by the Alkali Manufacturers Association of India (AMAI), an association which represented producers of soda ash

in India for various infringements of Indian competition law in 1996. AMAI accused ANSAC of predatory pricing (selling below cost) and of circumventing Indian competition law by trying to sell its products indirectly through a Singaporean entity. In response to the complaint, the Indian antitrust authority, the Monopoly and Restrictive Trade Practice (MRTP) Commission issued an injunction against ANSAC in accordance with Section 12A of the Indian competition law, the Monopoly and Restrictive Trade Act Practice of 1969 (the MRTP Act) under which a temporary injunction was allowed during an inquiry before the Commission for proving any unfair trade practice. After further appeals for repeal of the injunction and rejections applied by ANSAC and the Commission respectively, the case was brought before the Supreme Court in Haridas Exports v. All India Float Glass Manufacturers' Association, 6SCC600 (India Supreme Court, 2002), at which the Court ruled that the MRTP Act had no extraterritorial jurisdiction, that court jurisdiction existed only after the importation of the goods, while in this case the goods were only intended to be imported. In effect, the lack of an explicit textual statement within the MRTP Act providing for extraterritoriality prevented the Indian government from taking any further measures in countering the activities of the American export cartel. There is, however, the occasional rare case in which a developed nation is unable to legally counter the allegedly illegal anticompetitive activities of an international export cartel formed by nations from the developing world. In International Association of Machinists (IAM) v. OPEC (477 F Supp 553(CD Cal 1979), aff'd, 649 F 2d 1354 (9th Cir 1981), cert denied, 454 US 1163 (1982)), a US union sued OPEC under the "effects doctrine" of US antitrust law alleging that the price fixing of oil had a detrimental impact on US markets. A federal District Court and the US Court of Appeal declined to apply US antitrust laws against OPEC. The former held that OPEC, with its governmental character comprising of state-backed oil companies, was protected by the sovereign immunity doctrine which provides that each sovereign nation is beyond the jurisdiction of national courts. The Court of Appeal reached the same conclusion, relying on the "act of state" doctrine which stipulates that a US court will not rule on a politically sensitive dispute as it would require the court to judge the legality of the sovereign act of a foreign state. In another case involving OPEC, Prewitt Enterprises Inc. v. Organization of Petroleum Exporting Countries (U.S. Court of Appeals (11th Cir)), Appeal from the US District Court for the Northern District of Alabama, December 18, 2003, a class action suit was filed by Prewitt Enterprises, a small petroleum products seller, against OPEC in Alabama. In response to Prewitt's claim of OPEC violating US antitrust laws on the basis of their extraterritorial application, the US District Court ruled that OPEC was in violation and issued an injunction against OPEC to refrain from further production cuts in oil. OPEC succeeded in having the ruling dismissed on the basis of a technicality (lack of jurisdiction). The dismissal was further upheld on appeal.

129 Martyniszyn, op.cit., p.9.

130 Ibid.

131 Davis Polk, op.cit.; *Wall Street Journal*, Justices Unanimously Rule Lower Court was too Deferential to Chinese Government, June 14, 2018. In a case that had gone all the way to the US Supreme Court for deliberation, Animal Science Products, Inc. v Hebei Welcome Pharmaceutical Co. Ltd. (Hebei), the defendants, Hebei and its holding company North China Pharmaceutical Group Corporation (North China), had claimed that their collusive conduct and actions of price fixing and supply limitation of vitamin C on the international market was compelled by Chinese law. The Chinese Ministry of Commerce through an amicus brief supported the defendants by confirming their assertion, adding that the cartel was created to improve the competitiveness of Chinese vitamin C manufacturers in the global market and to promote the Chinese vitamin C export industry. The District Court declined to give conclusive deference to the Ministry's submission and instead found the defendants liable for

violating US antitrust laws. They were told to pay US$147 million in damages. The Ministry of Commerce in response expressed "deep dissatisfaction" about the ruling and complained that the court showed "disrespect" for China. An appeal was made to the Second Circuit Court of Appeals which concluded that international comity required the lower court to abstain from asserting its jurisdiction over the case. This time the Ministry praised the Second Circuit Court decision. After the plaintiff petitioned for certiorari, the Supreme Court invited the US Solicitor General who represents the US Government's official position, or the view of the newly elected President Donald Trump's administration, to submit an amicus brief on the deference question. In November 2017, the Solicitor General issued a statement disagreeing with the Second Circuit Court's position, arguing that the characterization given by foreign governments towards their own laws should be given "substantial" but not "conclusive" deference as federal courts have a responsibility to consider other relevant materials when interpreting foreign law. On June 14, 2018 the Supreme Court finally issued a unanimous ruling against the Chinese manufacturers in which they stated that while US courts should show "respectful consideration" of a foreign government's views, they are not, however, "bound to accord conclusive effect to the foreign government's statements."

5 The extraterritorial application of competition laws

Introduction

The previous chapter had looked at the interrelatedness of the activities of business cartels with international relations (IR) and how the existence of cartels may be explained using the framework of IR theory. In this chapter, I will look at another topic that also arguably connects the two fields of competition law and international relations: the extraterritorial application of domestic competition laws. In presenting my arguments the focus of this chapter will be on the development of the exercise of judicial extraterritoriality under the so-called "effects doctrine," which will be explained in the next section. Although international law jurists have generally and historically taken the view that a state has jurisdiction over all persons and property within its territory, the effects doctrine which is at the foundation of the extraterritorial application of national competition laws by national law courts and competition enforcement authorities has, ever since a decision rendered by the United States (US) Supreme Court in 1945, become accepted not only by the US, but also by the European Union (EU), and Japan. The inclusion of the effects doctrine in the Comprehensive and Progressive Agreement for Trans-Pacific Partnership (CPTPP)[1] which includes as member states Chile, Malaysia, Mexico, and Vietnam suggests that the concept of the extraterritorial application of national competition laws is also becoming accepted by a growing number of other states, including those of the emerging market economies. Despite this trend, however, as I will show, the extraterritorial application of competition laws is not without conflict. Differences over interpretation and enforcement have arisen as a result of different concepts of competition and the existence of concerns over the protection of national interests which will be shown through various cases.

Extraterritoriality

The effects doctrine

With the end of the Thirty Years War and the signing of the Treaty of Westphalia in 1648, what is known today in international public law as the "territorial principle," that the right of a state to proscribe and enforce laws is limited to that state's territory (*cuius regio, eius religio*), was first mentioned in the West and has been a major foundation for the conduct of international relations and the concept of national sovereignty. States in principle and as a matter of international public law are not to interfere in the internal affairs of another sovereign state. As stated in the Charter of the United Nations (UN) Article 2.4, "[a]ll Members shall refrain in their international relations from the threat or use of force against the territorial integrity or political independence of any state, or in any other manner inconsistent with the Purposes of the United Nations." Even before the UN Charter was enacted, however, jurists have generally and historically taken the view that a state has jurisdiction over all persons and property within its territory.[2] Legal opinions pronounced in US court cases such as Schooner Exchange v. McFaddon (1812) have supported this position. As elucidated by Judge C.J. Marshall the state has "exclusive and absolute" jurisdiction over all persons and property within its territory and that it is not susceptible to any limitation that is "not imposed by itself."[3] In American Banana Co. v. United Fruit Co. (1909),[4] Judge Oliver Wendell Holmes Jr. stated that "the general and almost universal rule" in determining whether an act is lawful or not must be determined by the laws of the country where the act was perpetrated. If another jurisdiction should lay hold of the perpetrator and treat him in accordance to its own notions of justice rather than those of the place where the acts were committed, not only would this "be unjust, but would be an interference with the authority of another sovereign, contrary to the comity of nations." Accordingly, concluded Holmes, all "legislation is prime facie territorial."[5] Yet within a few years after the American Banana Co. case, legalists had begun to challenge this traditional jurisdictional principle of a state having authority in regulating conduct only within its territory. In Strassheim v. Daily (1911),[6] the US Supreme Court delivered the opinion that "[a]cts done outside a jurisdiction, but intended to produce and producing detrimental effects within it, justify a state in punishing cause of the harm as if he had been present at the effect."[7] In a landmark international court case brought before the Permanent Court of International Justice (PCIJ),[8] the S.S. Lotus (France v. Turkey, P.C.I.J., Ser. A, No. 10 [1927], 2 Hudson World Court), in the ruling it handed down the court essentially expanded the territorial principle.[9] This case involved that of the collision between the French mail steamer the Lotus with a Turkish steamer, the Boz-Kourt, resulting in the deaths of eight Turkish nationals. Towards the issue as to whether Turkey had the right to arrest the officer of the watch on board the Lotus, a French citizen, the court ruled that Turkey had not acted in conflict with the principles of international law, that a state may exercise prescriptive jurisdiction over conduct that took place outside of its territory on the grounds that it caused harm within its borders. This ruling came to be known as the objective territoriality principle. After World War II (WWII) a Harvard University hosted research project, the Harvard Research in International Law, undertook a study that led to the objective territoriality principle being presented as an extension of the basic territorial principle. The extension, however, was presented in very narrow terms using the example where, if a certain individual A stands in country A on one side of a river and shoots individual B in country B on the other side of the same river that flows between both countries, country B should have jurisdiction to punish A for the crime since the crime of shooting individual B was "committed" in the territory of B. That is, the consequence of the crime was specifically located in the territory of B.[10]

While the territorial principle has generally been observed by the international community (except on occasions where a similar incident to that of the Lotus case had arisen, or when power politics or war come into play, or when such actions for military intervention had been approved by the UN Security Council under Articles 41 to 43 in the UN Charter), international trade and globalization has, however, blurred the distinction of what is considered foreign or domestic, leading at times to a situation where conduct taking place in one country has had a detrimental impact on markets elsewhere. For example, the formation of the aluminum export cartel mentioned in the previous chapter has led to an increase in the price of aluminum sold in various countries. Accordingly, in the realm of competition policy the need to strengthen the enforcement efficacy of competition laws for protecting domestic consumers becoming impacted by anticompetitive abuses committed outside of a state's territory has led to the expansion of the jurisdictional coverage of competition laws to include also acts committed outside of a country's borders, in effect unshackling domestic competition laws from the territorial principle. In United States v. Aluminum Co. of America (Alcoa),[11] the US Court of Appeals for the Second Circuit held that any state may impose liabilities, even upon individuals not within its allegiance for conduct outside its borders that had consequences within its territory. As the court put it, "it is settled law...that any state may impose liabilities, even upon persons not within its allegiance, for conduct outside its borders that has consequences within its border which the state reprehends; and these liabilities which other states will ordinarily recognize...."[12] The court went on to further state that agreements made by the foreign companies, although concluded outside of the US, were unlawful if they were intended to affect imports and did affect them.[13] As an example, the court mentioned that, "the limitation of the supply of goods in Europe...or in South America, may have repercussions in the United States if there is trade between the two."[14] In conclusion, the court ruled that it found the Sherman Act applicable to foreign conduct because such conduct was "intended to affect imports" into the US and did actually affect them.[15]

The idea as laid down in the Alcoa case allowing a state to regulate conduct that occurs outside of its territory where that conduct brings about particular effects within its borders came to be known as the effects doctrine, and as WWII ended the US increasingly adopted it as a basis for regulating conduct outside its territorial borders.[16] The effects doctrine, has not, however, been without its detractors with some having criticized its application as an example of American unilateralism and an excess of jurisdiction under public international law. In the British Yearbook of International Law, International Court of Justice judge R.Y. Jennings pointed out that the doctrine "apparently comprehends the exercise of jurisdiction over agreements made abroad, by foreigners with foreigners, provided only that the agreement was intended to have repercussions upon American imports or exports," while legal scholar F.A. Mann, in reference to the Alcoa case argued that the ruling "has nothing in common with the effect which by virtue of established principles of international jurisdiction confers the right of regulation."[17] On July 28, 1978, the United Kingdom (UK) government stated that "Her Majesty's Government considers that in the present state of international law there is no basis for the extension of one country's antitrust jurisdiction to activities outside of the country of the foreign national."[18] This view was further fortified with legislation; in 1980, the Protection of Trading Interest Law was enacted which provided measures to thwart the extraterritorial application of US antitrust laws.[19]

As for Japan, the country has up to recent years rejected the effects doctrine. In the Comments of the Government of Japan on the draft of the 1995 US Antitrust Enforcement Guidelines for International Operations, the Japanese government stated the view that the extraterritorial application of US domestic laws (including US antitrust laws) based on the effects doctrine is not allowed under general international law.[20] Indeed in United States v. Nippon Paper Industries Co.[21] where a Japanese paper company was prosecuted under the Sherman Act for involvement in cartel price fixing of fax paper, the Japanese government reacted by submitting an amicus brief where it stated that the extraterritorial application of the Act was unlawful under international law. Despite this objection, the US court of appeals reversed a district court decision,[22] thereby making this case the first time that §1 of the Sherman Act had been applied to a criminal case on an extraterritorial basis.[23]

Yet despite past objections to the extraterritorial application of US antitrust laws, there has been a general global trend towards acceptance of the effects doctrine. Beginning in the 1960s, the European Commission (EC) – the executive body of the EU responsible for proposing and enforcing EU laws – declared that the relevant provisions concerning the European Economic Community's (i.e., the predecessor to the EU) competition laws were applicable to all arrangements affecting competition within the member states of the Community.[24] In 1972 the International Law Association (an international nonprofit organization founded in Brussels, Belgium, in 1873 for the study of international law) approved for the first time the effects doctrine as a principle of international law at the 55th Conference in New York. In 1977 L'Institut du Droit International (an organization also founded in 1873 and devoted to the study of international law) stated that the effects doctrine could be applied extraterritorially if an illegal action had "intentional, or at least foreseeable, substantial, direct, and immediate effects within a territory."[25] In the Wood Pulp case (A. Ahlstrom Oy v. Commission, Cases 114/85, 1988) brought before the European Court of Justice (ECJ) that involved a Finnish cartel consisting of two wood pulp producers situated outside of the Community, the ECJ found that the two producers had infringed upon Article 81 (ex-Article 85) of the Treaty of Rome by adopting and agreeing to practices leading to higher than normal prices (in a competitive environment) in the Community for wood pulp. In giving its decision, the ECJ ruled that while the Community's jurisdiction to apply its competition rules within the Community was covered under the universally recognized territorial principle of international law, with regard to the rules of competition law the "decisive factor" in its application was "where the agreement, decision or concerted practice [of the cartel members] is implemented … . It is immaterial whether or not the producers had recourse to subsidiaries…or branches within the Community in order to make their contacts with purchasers within the Community."[26] In effect, the ECJ had for the first time endorsed the effects doctrine.[27] And since the Wood Pulp case the ECJ has repeatedly applied the effects doctrine in its decisions.[28]

An arguably significant recent development in the acceptance of the effects doctrine within international law was its inclusion as a concept in a major international economic trade treaty. In December 2018, the CPTPP Agreement, signed by the countries of Australia, Brunei, Canada, Chile, Japan, Malaysia, Mexico, New Zealand, Peru, Singapore, and Vietnam came into effect. In addition to providing for the elimination of trade tariffs, the Agreement covered a range of non-tariff-related matters with a broad set of rules for trade and investment. With its ratification by all the member states the CPTPP Agreement creates a single economic area whose members account for 13% of the world's gross domestic product[29] and would help to facilitate the movement of goods, money, services, information, and people.[30] A point of significance of the Agreement is its mention of competition policy. In Chapter 16 Article 16.1 paragraph 2 it is stated that each "Party shall endeavor to apply its national competition laws to all commercial activities in its territory" which is in effect saying that the parties to the Agreement are to have comprehensive competition policies in place and enforced within their territories. Interestingly, however, in a footnote to paragraph 2 it is stated that "for greater certainty, nothing in paragraph 2 shall be construed to preclude a Party from applying its competition laws to commercial activities outside its borders that have anticompetitive effects within its jurisdiction,"[31] i.e., the effects doctrine and the extraterritorial application of competition law are to be observed by the member nations of the CPTPP Agreement.

An expansion in the application of the effects doctrine? The CRT case

The fact that Japan had agreed to have the effects doctrine reflected in the CPTPP agreement arguably goes to show how much that nation has changed its outlook concerning the extraterritorial application of competition law since its government issued its opposition in the Comments of the Government of Japan on the draft of the 1995 US Antitrust Enforcement Guidelines for International Operations mentioned earlier. Some argue, however, that Japan may recently have perhaps gone too far in applying the principles of the effects doctrine. A case in point is the Japan Fair Trade Commission (JFTC) 2015 Cathode Ray Tubes (CRT) ruling, based on the Antimonopoly Act (AMA), for a surcharge to four cathode-ray tube (CRT) manufacturers located in southeast Asia. A CRT is the key component which is used in the production of televisions. The companies MT Picture Display of Indonesia, MT Picture Display of Malaysia, MT Picture Display of Thailand, all of which belonged to the Japanese electronics conglomerate the Panasonic Corporation, and Samsung SDI of Malaysia, which belonged to the Samsung Group, were ordered to pay total surcharges (calculated by the JFTC based on the sales amount of all CRTs sold outside of Japan) amounting to approximately JP¥3.2 billion (US$26 million). The May 22, 2015 ruling is the culmination of a case going back to October 2009 and February 2010 when the JFTC fined six foreign firms (including foreign subsidiaries of Japanese firms) and issued cease and desist orders to two companies for involvement in a cartel made up of 11 CRT manufacturers in total (i.e., MT Picture Display, Samsung SDI, LG Philips Displays, Chunghwa Picture Tubes, Chunghwa Picture Tubes Malaysia, Thailand CRT, P.T. LP Displays Indonesia, plus the above four companies of the 2015 ruling) that was fixing prices of CRTs and engaging in the "unreasonable restraint of trade" as prohibited under the AMA. According to the JFTC, the eleven CRT manufacturers held meetings from around May 2003 during which they agreed to stabilize and maintain the price of CRTs to be sold to local subsidiaries of TV manufacturers such as Sharp and JVC who manufactured TVs in southeast Asia to be sold in various markets outside of Japan. The cartelists did not sell any of their CRTs in Japan nor was it ever made clear by the JFTC to what extent the final finished TV product was sold in Japan.[32] The JFTC at this time had issued cease and desist orders to MT Pictures Display and to Samsung SDI. The JFTC also ordered six companies who had manufactured and supplied CRTs to pay a surcharge amounting to JP¥4.3 billion (US$36 million) in total.[33] Two companies filed an appeal with the JFTC against the cease and desist order and four companies filed appeals against the surcharge which eventually resulted in the 2015 JFTC decision against the four companies mentioned above. Marek Martyniszyn of Queen's University of Belfast views this case as an example which not only demonstrates how far Japan had gone to accept reliance upon the effects doctrine but that also goes beyond, asserting that this is possibly the "furthest-reaching" claim for extraterritorial application of competition law the international community has seen to date.[34] Indeed, the anomaly with this case is that in contrast to the concept of the effects doctrine as laid down in the Alcoa case mentioned earlier, i.e., "any state may impose liabilities, even upon persons not within its allegiance, for conduct outside its borders that has consequences within its border which the state reprehends,"[35] the JFTC justified their ruling by claiming that, although the price fixing was undertaken outside of Japan, competition was restrained because the cartelists could control the prices for CRTs in the relevant market, i.e., mainly in Japan in this case.[36] The only customers, however, in this case were the Japanese-headquartered TV manufacturers (in this case Sharp, JVC, and three other manufacturers) whose TV manufacturing subsidiaries in southeast Asia were being supplied with foreign-made CRTs. Furthermore, it was never made apparent by the JFTC that the final TV product was sold in Japan or that there was any disadvantageous effect on the Japanese TV manufacturers in Japan (which would have been difficult to show since no TVs were manufactured in Japan). Accordingly, the JFTC calculated the penalty surcharges based on the sales amount of CRTs sold outside of Japan, which may be the only case so far where a surcharge or a fine for an anticompetitive act has been imposed as such.[37] This JFTC decision on the charge of restraining competition in relevant markets (not necessarily in Japan as the JFTC seems to assert) impacted the

Japanese and foreign CRT manufacturers who did not manufacture or sell their product in Japanese territory; this suggests that a door may have opened leading to the possibility that the JFTC may in the future render a ruling against a foreign company even if its conduct cannot be proven to have any detrimental impact on Japanese consumers or competition in Japan.[38]

Conclusion

As the CRT case as well as previous other cases mentioned above have demonstrated, although it may well be that the practice of the extraterritorial application of competition laws has been accepted by at least the major industrialized economies and to some extent by some emerging economies such as those that have agreed to the CPTPP Agreement, what is an arguably unresolved issue is the lack of uniformity in its application. The CRT example may be indeed, as Martyniszyn asserts, a new and controversial precedent that extends the traditional application of extraterritoriality and the effects doctrine and presents further possible challenges to the concept of national sovereignty as well as to other nations' understanding of the scope of application of the effects doctrine, thus possibly giving rise to international tensions.[39] Indeed, the outcome of the CRT case suggests that the CPTPP member states may need to work on harmonizing the extraterritorial application of their competition laws if they want to avoid conflict when observing the footnote to Article 16.1 paragraph 2 of the treaty. In this regard, it is perhaps worth mentioning that in an attempt to provide uniformity and end any confusion in the application of the effects doctrine, in 1982 the US Congress passed the Foreign Trade Antitrust Improvements Act (FTAIA). As we have seen in the previous chapter, the FTAIA was enacted to provide immunity from US antitrust laws for cartels that were formed for the express purpose of promoting US exports. Conversely, the FTAIA also essentially limits the scope of the extraterritorial application of the Sherman Act to conduct that involves trade or commerce with foreign states that "has a direct, substantial, and reasonable foreseeable effect" on domestic (US) commerce, such as raising prices that US consumers must pay for products in the US or restricting or eliminating US exports to a particular foreign market.[40] Hence, while the definition of a "direct, substantial, and reasonably foreseeable effect" has differed in different court rulings,[41] it may be argued that if the CRT case was judged in accordance with the principles of the FTAIA, a considerably different ruling might have been issued by the JFTC as they probably would have been unlikely to be able to show what direct impact there was on Japanese consumers who did not buy the foreign-made TVs to begin with. The JFTC would also have found it difficult to show the impact on Japanese exporters as none of the TVs that used the CRTs in question were manufactured in or exported from Japan.

Ideally, competition laws should be applied, whether domestically or extraterritorially, with consistency and fairness. In this regard, as recommended by the Organisation for Economic Co-operation and Development (OECD), for avoiding international conflicts over the extraterritorial application of competition laws, the concept of comity, or the voluntary policy that a country undertakes in giving full consideration to another nation's important interests when enforcing its own competition law, has a significant importance.[42] Comity can be classified into two aspects, one being that of active or positive comity where a country may ask another nation to enforce the latter's laws or take appropriate measures against anticompetitive behavior taking place in that nation that is affecting the important interests of the requesting country. The second aspect is that of negative or passive comity where a country agrees to take into account the important interests of other nations when applying its own competition laws. The reality is, however, that the governments enforcing competition laws are (at least in the EU, Japan, and the US) accountable to their respective peoples and accordingly, despite comity, the influence of domestic social and interest groups as well as the execution of national policies related to the economy, industry, foreign trade, and market access cannot be ruled out and may take precedence over observing international comity and may affect rulings on competition law cases and on the application of competition law. That is, the objectives of promoting national interests focused on strengthening national security or national power come into play, especially with those nations that view the arena of international relations through the lens of Realism.

Ideally, getting consensus by the international community on agreeing to a global competition policy would be a solution for achieving fairness and consistency in the extraterritorial enforcement of competition laws. To the extent that the globalization of the world economy is giving rise to a global consumer-oriented society that is increasingly becoming homogenous in outlook and tastes, there may be room for optimism that we may see the birth of such a policy that is based on a common view of the purposes of competition. Towards this end, former chief Democratic Counsel of the House Judiciary Committee Julian Epstein had proposed that the per se rules of US antitrust laws may be a template for developing an international consensus on competition policy.[43] Although some nations may object to such a proposal on the grounds that this smacks of an American attempt to force its values on others, it is true that the competition laws of the EU, Japan, and the US generally hold the same view as to what activities are considered anticompetitive such as horizontal price fixing leading to a detrimental impact on consumers in the form of higher prices. Yet, as we have seen, whereas in the US the Supreme Court ruling given out in United States v. Socony-Vacuum Oil Co.[44] had essentially established that a combination, i.e., cartel, "formed for the purpose and with the effect of raising, depressing, fixing, pegging, or stabilizing the price of a commodity in interstate of foreign commerce is illegal per se," in Japan, a cartel, while in principle unlawful as it represented an "unreasonable restraint of trade" under Article 2(6) of the AMA, nevertheless could be considered legal if its actions were not "contrary to the public interest."[45] In a ruling issued in 1984 by the Japanese Supreme Court in the Oil Cartel case the court ruled that there may be exceptional situations in which an agreement that substantially reduces competition is necessary to meet certain valid objectives, and so long as the benefits from allowing a cartel agreement outweigh the objective of maintaining competition, such a cartel agreement would not be against the public interest and therefore not be illegal.[46] In the EU's Treaty on the Functioning of the European Union (TFEU), while in Article 101(1) it is stated that agreements that lead to concerted practices, i.e., cartels, which prevent, restrict, or distort competition are prohibited, nevertheless in Article 101(3) it is also stated that in circumstances where such concerted practices may also contribute to production or distribution (while benefiting consumers) and not impose restrictions to or eliminate competition such cartels may be exempted from prohibition.[47] Given the differences in national positions that exist on a point of competition law so fundamental such as whether or not price fixing cartels are illegal per se, or given that the US Supreme Court for that matter had overturned an almost century old ban on vertical price restraints in Leegin Creative Leather Products Inc. v. PSKS[48] in 2007 by ruling that vertical price restraints were not necessarily per se illegal, Epstein's proposal to use the per se rules of US antitrust laws as a template for a global competition policy may be difficult if not impossible to realize, in a situation where not only divergent views among countries on what is per se illegal exists but also where even in the US the concept of what is considered per se illegal changes over time.

Differences also exist between the EU, Japan, and the US over the severity of penalties meted out to offenders against competition laws. While in the US and Japan there are criminal penalties for cartels and monopolization, in the EU there are no criminal penalties although some member states such as the UK have criminal penalties for cartels. Private parties in the EU member states, Japan, and the US can raise a civil suit against an enterprise but the US stands out in terms of the amount of damages that a victim can claim against an enterprise.[49] Major differences exist between Japan and the EU/US over the process of investigation for anticompetitive behavior involving the availability of attorney-client privilege and certain due process issues such as the right to legal counsel at interviews.

Furthermore, we must also contend with the assertions of Realist IR theorists that states struggle among themselves for power to achieve certain national interests aside from strengthening national security such as making their country "great again" as Donald Trump has reminded the world. Indeed, to this end some states have suggested that their national competition laws could be used to protect their national or certain vested interests such as export industries. A case in point regards the interlocking vertical relationships (keiretsu) in Japan consisting of a group of companies centered around a bank. Although the keiretsu has been viewed by Japanese economic planning authorities and businesses as a structure to promote exports and stable economic relationships, during the bilateral Structural Impediments Initiative (SII) talks that took place from 1989 to 1990 the US viewed it as an impediment to competition and to US exports to Japan.[50] As if spurred on by the SII, in 1992 the US Department of Justice (DoJ) announced that it would begin to enforce US antitrust laws against "conduct occurring overseas that restrains" US exports regardless of whether there is or not any direct harm to US consumers.[51]

So long as states continue to put their national interests first, the most one can probably hope for in the meantime is the building of better cooperation and understanding of best practices among the competition authorities of each nation by working (as previously and currently undertaken) through avenues such as the International Competition Network (ICN),[52] the harmonization in the extraterritorial application of competition laws through comity, the conclusion of international economic partnership agreements such as the CPTPP, and the development of a global consensus that recognizes that when applying domestic competition laws the aim is not to be for the purpose of promoting narrow national interests while allowing governments to ostensibly claim that they are protecting competition, but to protect competition so as to promote innovation, productivity growth, and the increase in the standard of living of consumers regardless of where they may reside.

Notes

1 The successor to the Trans-Pacific Partnership Agreement (TPP) which was formed by the 11 member states after the US had withdrawn from the TPP. The CPTPP came into force in December 2018.
2 Bishop, William W., *International Law*, Little, Brown and Company, 1971, p.535.
3 Ibid., 11 U.S. 116.
4 213 U.S. 347.
5 Bishop, op.cit., pp.567–568.
6 221 U.S. 280.
7 Bishop, op.cit., p.559.
8 International Court of Justice, *Permanent Court of International Justice*, Online. Available https://www.icj-cij.org/en/pcij (accessed September 8, 2019). The PCIJ was established in 1922 under the Covenant of the League of Nations. It was dissolved in 1946 with the establishment of its successor, the International Court of Justice. The PCIJ was the first international tribunal in the world with general jurisdiction over matters that were brought to its attention primarily by states. Aside from giving rulings on international law cases the PCIJ also contributed to the development of international law.
9 Bishop, op.cit., p.559; Gerber, David J., *Global Competition*, Oxford University Press, 2012, p.61.
10 Ibid. (Gerber).
11 148 F.2d 416 (2nd Cir. 1945).
12 Ibid.
13 Kojima, Takaaki, *International Conflicts over the Extraterritorial Application of Competition Law in a Borderless Economy*, Weatherhead Center for International Affairs, 2002, p.3.
14 Bishop, op.cit., p.568.
15 Gerber, op.cit., p.64.
16 Ibid., p.60.
17 Kojima, op.cit., pp.3–4.
18 Ibid., p.4.
19 Ibid.
20 Ibid., p.6.
21 FindLaw, U.S. Court of Appeals, First Circuit, 96–2001, decided March 17, 1997, Online. Available https://caselaw.findlaw.com/us-1st-circuit/1316485.html (accessed June 22, 2019).
22 Justia, 944 F. Supp.55 D. Mass. 1996, Online. Available https://law.justia.com/cases/federal/district-courts/FSupp/944/55/1486090/ (accessed June 22, 2019).

23 FindLaw, op.cit.
24 Martyniszyn, Marek, Japanese Approaches to Extraterritoriality in Competition Law, *International and Comparative Law Quarterly*, 66(3), Cambridge Core, 2017, p.3. Online. Available https://papers.ssrn.com/sol3/papers.cfm?abstract_id=3116898 (accessed August 2, 2019).
25 Ministry of Economy, Trade and Industry (METI), Excessive Extraterritorial Application of Competition Laws, p.478. Online. Available http://www.meti.go.jp/english/report/downloadfiles/2008WTO/2-14-2ExcessiveExtraterritorial.pdf (accessed July 8, 2017).
26 EUR-Lex, Judgement of the Court of 27, September 1988, Online. Available http://eur-lex.europa.eu/legal-content/EN/TXT/?uri=CELEX%3A61985CJ0089 (accessed June 13, 2017).
27 Martyniszyn, op.cit., p.3.
28 Calster, Geert van, International Law and Sovereignty in the Age of Globalization, *Encyclopedia of Life Support Systems*, Online. Available http://www.eolss.net/sample-chapters/c14/e1-36-01-04.pdf (accessed June 13, 2017).
29 Reuters, Asia Pacific Nations Sign Sweeping Trade Deal Without U.S., March 8, 2018, Online. Available https://www.reuters.com/article/us-trade-tpp/asia-pacific-nations-sign-sweeping-trade-deal-without-u-s-idUSKCN1GK0JM (accessed July 13, 2019).
30 Shiraishi, Takashi, The Geostrategic Significance of the TPP Agreement for the Asia Pacific, Nippon.com, January 28, 2016, Online. Available http://www.nippon.com/en/column/g00338/ (accessed June 13, 2017).
31 WTO Center, Full Text of CPTPP, Chapter 16 Competition Policy, Online. Available http://www.wtocenter.vn/upload/files/fta/174-ftas-concluded/175-cptpp-tpp11/177-full-text/16.-Competition-Policy-Chapter.pdf (accessed May 26, 2019).
32 Martyniszyn, op.cit., p.13.
33 ABE & Partners, JFTC applies Antimonopoly Act beyond borders for first time, Managingip.com, November 2015, Online. Available http://www.managingip.com/Article/3501783/Japan-JFTC-applies-Antimonopoly-Act-beyond-borders-for-first-time.html (accessed June 14, 2017).
34 The companies were MT Picture Display Malaysia, MT Picture Display Indonesia, MT Picture Display Thailand, Samsung SDI Malaysia, LG Philips Display Korea, P.T. LP Displays Indonesia; Martyniszyn, op.cit., p.13.
35 Bishop, op.cit., p.61.
36 ABE & Partners, op.cit.
37 Ibid.
38 Nikkei, Japan can go after foreign cartels, Supreme Court rules, December 13, 2017. In December 2017, after the ruling on the fine was appealed to the JFTC by Samsung SDI and then to a high court, both of which upheld the fine, the Japanese Supreme Court also upheld the decision of the JFTC of imposing a fine against Samsung SDI. The ruling marked the first occasion of the Court approving the enforcement of Japanese competition law against cartel activity outside of Japan and more controversially against such anticompetitive acts that arguably did not have any impact on consumers in Japan.
39 Martyniszyn., op.cit, p.15.
40 Beckler, Richard W., Kirtland, Mathew H., Extraterritorial Application of U.S. Antitrust Law: What is a “Direct, Substantial, and Reasonable Foreseeable Effect” Under the Foreign Trade Antitrust Improvements Act?, *Texas International Law Journal*, Vol. 38, No. 11, pp.13–14. Online. Available http://www.tilj.org/content/journal/38/num1/Beckler-Kirtland11.pdf (accessed June 25, 2017).
41 Ibid., p.15.
42 Kojima, op.cit., p.25; Concurrences, Glossary of Competition Terms, Online. Available http://www.concurrences.com/en/droit-de-la-concurrence/glossary-of-competition-terms/Comity (accessed June 25, 2017).

43 Epstein, Julian, The Other Side of Harmony: Can Trade and Competition Laws Together in the International Marketplace?, *American University International Law Review*, January, 2002, p.365.
44 310 U.S. 150.
45 Japan Fair Trade Commission, Legislations and Guidelines, Online. Available http://www.jftc.go.jp/en/legislation_gls/amended_ama09/amended_ama15_01.html (accessed June 26, 2017).
46 Matsushita, Mitsuo, The Antimonopoly Law of Japan, in Graham, Edward M., Richardson, J. David, ed., *Global Competition Policy*, Institute for International Economics, 1997, p.172.
47 Vesey, Caleb, Per se Rules in U.S. and EU Antitrust/Competition Law, New York Law School, Online. Available http://www.eucomplaw.com/comparing-eu-and-us-competition-law/per-se-rules/ (accessed June 26, 2017).
48 Ibid. In Leegin Creative Leather Products, Inc. v. PSKS, Inc. (2007), 551 US 877, the Supreme Court ruled that vertical price restraints in the form of resale price maintenance in this particular case were not necessarily illegal per se, thereby overturning the almost century old per se ban on vertical price fixing established in the Supreme Court case Dr. Miles Medical Co. v. John D. Park & Sons Co., 220 US 373 of 1911.
49 In the US, the victim can get three times the loss they received as a result of damage incurred as a result of an enterprise violating antitrust laws plus attorney's fees. In contrast, in the EU, private suits are left to the jurisdiction of each state.
50 Gerber, op.cit., p.215.
51 Gellhorn, Ernest, Kovacic, William E., *Antitrust Law and Economics*, West Group, 1994, pp.478–479.
52 The ICN was launched in 2001 and provides a venue for competition agencies to deal with competition policy and enforcement issues.

6 Mergers and acquisitions and national interests

Introduction

Mergers and acquisitions (M&A) refer to financial transactions which result in the consolidation of companies or assets. Some of the transactions, which involve at least two companies, include cases where one company totally or partially acquires the assets of another, or where one company combines its assets with that of another to form a new enterprise.

Since their first appearance in modern history, business enterprises have engaged in the act of merging with or acquiring other enterprises or their assets. Indeed, what was arguably the world's first joint stock company, the Dutch East India Company established in 1602, came into existence when six Dutch trading companies merged with the primary objectives of avoiding the deleterious effects of excessive domestic competition and achieving the economies of scale that would allow them to effectively compete with colonial traders from Spain and Portugal and the English East India Company which had been established two years earlier.[1] More than four centuries later in 2017, there were over 50,600 M&A transactions worldwide with a total value of more than US$3.5 trillion.[2] The large number of M&A transactions undertaken or proposed worldwide and the steady, yearly increase in the number of such transactions (an increase of more than 25% from 2000 to 2017)[3] suggests that undertaking a M&A is a widely accepted business strategy and that its usage by business enterprises will continue to increase.

As to why companies engage in M&A there is no single, universal reason applicable to all instances, and for each M&A there are motives that are specific to each transaction. Some generic reasons for a company to undertake M&A have been described as follows, using an analytical framework called the Ansoff growth vector matrix developed by the business scholar and strategist H. Igor Ansoff for categorizing different basic types of business portfolio strategy.[4]

First, a company may engage in M&A to achieve market penetration, that is, to further increase its presence in a market that it is currently in by expanding the production output of products it already sells, using new manufacturing capabilities and facilities acquired from another company. Second, a company may do M&A to achieve market expansion for its current products through the acquisition of another company with distribution and/or sales capabilities in new markets not yet penetrated by the acquiring company. Third, a company may do M&A to achieve the development, or its acceleration, of new products to be sold in its existing markets by acquiring a company that manufactures or develops products or technologies not yet developed by the acquiring company. And fourth, a company may do M&A to achieve business diversification by selling new products into new markets by acquiring an enterprise that has products and is in a market that the acquiring company does not currently have and is not presently in. In addition to the above four reasons of M&A based on the Ansoff matrix, some companies aim to achieve vertical integration, that is, acquire resources held by another company for undertaking distinct value-adding activities internally within the acquiring company such as designing, manufacturing, and marketing.

Many companies that do M&A also state that they aim to realize synergy, which accelerates output, revenues, profits, and the creation of new businesses as a result of combining or rationalizing resources and operations. Companies may also justify M&A with motives that do not have much to do with business but are more based on emotion; that is, M&A can be done for the same reasons that the empire builders of world history such as Genghis Khan and Cecil Rhodes built their global empires: for gold, God, and glory.

Finally, we cannot exclude the possibility that companies may undertake M&A simply to eliminate a competitor within an industry sector, as was the case with what happened in the United States (US) railroad and oil industries in the late 19th century.[5] In this case companies undertake a M&A for anticompetitive reasons: to reduce the number of competitors and achieve economies of scale leading to greater market power for companies, with the results of lesser product choices, higher prices for consumers, and greater profits for companies. M&A may thus be viewed as a strategy that, on the one hand, through the process of elimination promotes economic efficiencies and innovation necessary for invigorating competition and capitalism. On the other hand, M&A may also lead to the elimination of competition and the creation of monopolies that are capable, through their size and economic resources, of deterring the entry of new competitors in the market. The incentive to drive innovation may decline as a result.

It goes without saying that when it comes to approving or rejecting a M&A transaction, the competition authorities that are responsible for enforcing competition laws will need to achieve a fine balance. Allowing too many M&A leading to the creation of huge oligopolies or monopolies may stifle innovation. Conversely, too much competition may promote a race to the bottom and prevent the accumulation of profits and capital by any company to allow the long-term investment necessary for promoting innovation. Excessive competition may also hamper the pooling of large amounts of capital needed for investing in large-scale projects such as infrastructure development.

The primary concern of competition authorities in their assessment of a M&A transaction is the impact on competition and consumer welfare. There have, however, been several instances in which a government has refused approval of a cross-border M&A for reasons of national security or maintaining public order. Maintaining public order or the security of citizens is a core, fundamental national interest of all states and taking measures for these purposes is considered by such organizations as the Organisation for Economic Co-operation and Development (OECD) to be a state prerogative. In the M&A cases that I will examine in this chapter, however, I will argue that, while states may have genuine concerns of national security or public order, there are also instances where states have used the guise of national security to cloak another agenda associated with furthering the national interest consistent with an outlook rooted in a Realist view of the condition of international relations.

National security, public order, and M&A

The US and national security

As mentioned above, governments have in the past intervened in blocking an essentially private M&A for the ostensible reason that the transaction would have some detrimental impact on a state's national security. A case in point is the 1987 opposition of the US Department of Defense (DoD) to the proposed sale of 80% of a US-based semiconductor maker, Fairchild Semiconductor Co. (Fairchild), by its owner, Schlumberger Ltd., of France, to the Japanese electronics and information technology company, Fujitsu Ltd. (Fujitsu), for over US$200 million.[6] According to congressional researcher James Jackson, the DoD opposed the acquisition as some officials believed that if the deal was consummated, the acquisition would give Japan control over a major supplier of computer chips for the military and would have made US defense industries more dependent on foreign suppliers for sophisticated high technology products.[7] This opposition by the DoD existed despite 1) there having been friendly relations between Japan and the US for more than 40 years since the end of World War II (WWII), 2) the US having a military/security alliance with Japan, and 3) from the perspective of competition policy and national defense concerns, the lack of any evidence that Fujitsu would restrict or discontinue production of critical semiconductor components used for US national defense purposes.[8] Congress for its part was concerned about the proposed Fairchild acquisition because of 1) the US trade deficit with Japan and other trade-related disputes, and 2) a view shared by some Americans at the time that the US was in decline while Japan was in the ascendant, clawing its way up to challenge US hegemony as the dominant power of the post-WWII international order.[9] Amid such growing concern and opposition in the US, Fujitsu called off the deal and Fairchild was acquired some months later by National Semiconductor Corp., an American semiconductor company headquartered in California.[10]

The acquisition attempt by Fujitsu was de facto blocked by the US government, not on grounds of possible violation of antitrust laws or out of concerns on the possible impact on consumers, but arguably because of increasing tensions emanating from growing US fears of a rising Japan.[11] This Fairchild acquisition proposal in 1987 generated enough anxiety in Congress for it to approve the Exon–Florio Amendment[12] to Section 721 of the Defense Production Act of 1950. According to co-sponsor Congressman James J. Florio, when "this whole Fujitsu situation evolved...there was a deficiency in authority in the Government" to take appropriate control if an acquisition "was a problem for national security." A situation could arise, Florio continued, where one might talk about an acquisition that did not involve a situation of monopoly or for that matter "even a restraint on trade." Yet such an acquisition "would still constitute a potential detriment" to areas of US commerce that "might be related to national security."[13] As a result of this amendment which passed into law under the Omnibus Trade and Competitiveness Act on August 23, 1988, Congress granted authority to the US president to "take such action...as the President considers appropriate to suspend or prohibit any acquisition, merger, or takeover...by or with foreign persons so that such control will not threaten to impair the national security."[14] The amendment also led to the strengthening of the Committee on Foreign Investment in the United States (CFIUS), an inter-agency cabinet level committee chaired by the Secretary of the Treasury and including representatives from 16 US government departments and agencies, first created in 1975 and charged with monitoring the impact of foreign investment in the US.[15] Initially, the powers of CFIUS were limited to requesting foreign governments to file reports about their foreign investment activities and to monitor such investments.[16] With the Exon–Florio Amendment, the subsequently passed Byrd Amendment of 1992, and the Foreign Investment and National Security Act of 2007 (FINSA), which established a statutory basis for CFIUS, however, CFIUS subsequently received authority from the president to review "covered transactions," defined as a foreign person or entity's acquisition of control of a US business with products, services, or intellectual property that present a "national security" concern.[17] If CFIUS determines during its reviews (which are confidential) that there is a threat to national security arising out of an acquisition, merger, or takeover by a foreigner, it can recommend that the president block the acquisition or, if the transaction is already executed, order divesture.[18]

According to a study published by the Fletcher School of Tufts University, the "overwhelming majority" of acquisitions have been approved by CFIUS after its 30-day preliminary review of a voluntarily filed acquisition proposal.[19] Indeed, of the 925 notices sent by foreign investors to CFIUS of plans to acquire, takeover, or merge with US companies during the eight year period from 2008 to 2015, 822 transactions, or 89% were completed.[20] CFIUS has emphasized that it "focuses solely on any genuine national security concerns raised by a covered transaction" and not political or other "national interests."[21]

What would arguably be of concern to foreign enterprises and governments, however, is ambiguity in the wording of the Exon–Florio Amendment, particularly concerning the term "national security." Nowhere in the amendment is this defined. According to legal scholar Marc Greidinger, Congress had intentionally left "national security" undefined in order to provide the president with broad discretion to evaluate threats and to take the necessary responsive measures.[22] In hearings before the Subcommittee on Economic Stabilization of the House Committee on Banking, Finance, and Urban Affairs,[23] the sponsors of the amendment freely admitted that national security was left undefined so that "national security should be looked in a broad sense."[24] In line with this the amendment's sponsors had both indicated that the concept of national security extends beyond defense industries and would cover, for example, new and emerging technologies such as in biomedical and health-related innovations.[25]

One may argue that leaving "national security" undefined in the amendment leaves open the possibility that the US government may block a M&A proposal in accordance with what it arbitrarily determines to be for the purposes of maintaining "national security." Indeed, some US government officials have indicated "national security" should also include national economic interests. In support of this view, Commerce Secretary Wilbur Ross, who was instructed by President Trump to conduct a probe that would determine whether imported cars caused a threat to national security, conceded that national security "is broadly defined to include the economy, to include the impact on employment, to include a very big variety of things."[26] Other officials including US senators Chuck Grassley, Joni Ernst, and Debbie Stabenow have proposed legislation calling for CFIUS to consider proposed transactions relating to US food and agricultural systems as national security risks.[27] CFIUS was in fact reported to have investigated a transaction between a Chinese and an American food company, an indication that even the meat industry is a part of national security.[28] Meanwhile, in reaction to the acquisition of the Hollywood movie studio Legendary Entertainment by a Chinese conglomerate, the Wanda Group, for US$3.5 billion in 2016, some other US legislators have been pushing for the definition of "national security" to include aspects of the media and "soft power," a development reminiscent of the attempts contemplated by certain members of Congress to block the acquisition of the US movie studio Columbia Pictures by the Japanese electronics company, the Sony Corporation, in 1989.[29]

In the US, the antitrust provision most frequently used to regulate M&A and takeovers is the Clayton Act, which prohibits the acquisitions of stock or assets where "the effect of such acquisition may be to substantially lessen competition."[30] The government may also use the Sherman Act to challenge a merger as either restraining trade or becoming a monopoly. The Federal Trade Commission Act may also be invoked to challenge a merger as an unfair method of competition. The existence of such laws for the purposes of protecting the values of competition and consumer welfare and a long history of past judicial antitrust cases have arguably provided the domestic and foreign business community with a general understanding of what they will need to do to overcome any legal hurdles when undertaking long-term investments and a M&A in the US. As a result of the Exon–Florio Amendment, however, a foreign enterprise will not only have to evaluate the anticompetitive impact of its M&A plans in the US, but it may also need to evaluate whether its plans may be perceived by the US government to have an impact on US national security and to make the necessary contingency plans for addressing the topic of national security concerns. This additional work is not made easier when, as mentioned before, "national security" is not defined in the Exon–Florio Amendment. While foreign enterprises may find the amendment in this respect a source of consternation and an unwelcome extra burden, it is perhaps interesting to note that the Antitrust Division of the DoJ initially opposed the Exon–Florio Amendment as it was perceived by them to be a threat to competition values as enshrined in the antitrust laws which should be the only legitimate basis for preventing a merger affecting the commerce of the US.[31]

What is perhaps the major concern with regards to the ambiguity surrounding the definition of "national security" in the context of M&A transactions by foreign companies in the US is that it may give rise to circumstances where a M&A or a takeover is blocked by a US president not out of concerns for protecting "national security" (in the narrow sense of protecting the sovereignty of the state), but rather as a protectionist tool for shielding certain domestic businesses from foreign competition or for purely political reasons. Indeed, it is interesting to note that within the context of rising rivalry and tensions in US–China relations, which arguably became a growing concern for Americans from the early 1990s, four out of the five M&A transactions which CFIUS, in its over 40 years of existence, had recommended the President to block, all involved Chinese companies. The first was in 1990 when then President George H.W. Bush ordered the China National Aero-Technology Import and Export Corporation (CATIC), a company that had strong ties to the People's Liberation Army (PLA) of the People's Republic of China (PRC), to divest its acquisition of MAMCO Manufacturing, an American aircraft parts manufacturer based in Seattle, Washington.[32] Of the remaining three,[33] one was blocked by Donald Trump, who became President in January 2017, eight months into his presidency; this was the acquisition of the Portland Oregon-based Lattice Semiconductor Corp. for US$1.3 billion by Canyon Bridge Capital Partners, a Chinese investment company.[34]

It is not only, however, towards companies originating in a state that is viewed as a strategic rival[35] or a threat to the US (i.e., China)[36] that a US president has used the recommendations of CFIUS in blocking a M&A transaction. In 2018, CFIUS had recommended another M&A attempt to be blocked by the president, the attempted hostile takeover of the US San Diego-based semiconductor maker Qualcomm by semiconductor maker Broadcom. Broadcom was founded in Singapore in 1961 as the semiconductor division of the American technology company Hewlett-Packard (HP). Over the years following its carve out from HP in 1999 the company had become a manufacturer and supplier of digital and analog semiconductor technologies and equipment. The company moved its headquarters from Singapore to San Jose, California, in 2018 after it had acquired an American technology company specializing in data and storage network systems, Brocade Communications Systems.

Broadcom's acquisition target, Qualcomm, was founded in San Diego in 1985 and became a major developer of wireless technology and producer of semiconductor chips. Among the many types of semiconductor chips that Qualcomm develops and produces are those that will be used in the next generation 5G wireless systems. 5G is envisioned by its developers and proponents as a network of sensors that will allow control of the functions of a vast array of products from autonomous vehicles to smart power grids.[37] National security concerns were raised by Qualcomm, which requested CFIUS to act in effect as a white knight and intervene in Broadcom's hostile takeover attempt.[38] While the details behind the arguments for national security put forth by Qualcomm are not known, the *New York Times* speculated about the possible scenario that since the 5G chips could allow companies to collect vast amounts of data that control critical infrastructure and give information about the location of people and objects in real time, foreign ownership of the technology and supply of such chips may pose a threat to national security.[39] Interestingly, CFIUS was reportedly split on whether or not to intervene when Qualcomm notified CFIUS of its national security concerns. The Treasury Department (Treasury), which chairs CFIUS, had pushed back. DoD officials, however, insisted on a review.[40] The Broadcom board, on its part, had not yet reached an internal consensus whether to acquire Qualcomm. Broadcom's management, led by Malaysian chief executive officer Tan Hock Eng, was attempting to win the support of Qualcomm shareholders to gain control of Qualcomm's board and move forward with its offer.[41] The Trump administration, perhaps swayed by the arguments of Qualcomm, became interested in the security implications of 5G technology and made it clear that it would support the efforts of Qualcomm to thwart the hostile takeover attempt by Broadcom. On March 4, 2018, the Treasury ordered Qualcomm to postpone its shareholder vote by 30 days, saying that a takeover by Broadcom threatened Qualcomm's leadership in developing the next generation of wireless technology.[42] On the next day, March 5, CFIUS disclosed in a letter that the Treasury had initiated another review by filing "an agency notice" to broaden "the scope of review to cover the proposed hostile takeover of Qualcomm." The March 5 CFIUS letter further stated that CFIUS "has identified potential national security concerns that warrant a full investigation of the proposed transaction." These concerns included: 1) "risks associated with Broadcom's relationships with third party foreign entities", 2) "the national security effects" of Broadcom's "'private equity'-style direction", "reducing long-term investment, such as R&D, and focusing on short-term profitability" as a result of the large "debt financing to support the Qualcomm acquisition," 3) risks associated with losing US-controlled Qualcomm's technology leadership and standard setting, particularly as to the developing 5G telecommunications technology, and 4) loss of Qualcomm as a trusted supplier to the defense industry.[43] More to the point, the letter emphasized that a possible outcome from Broadcom's acquisition of Qualcomm would be that "China would likely compete robustly to fill any void left by Qualcomm as result of this hostile takeover."[44] In response, Tan attempted to allay the fears and concern of the US by meeting with CFIUS officials after Treasury's March 4 order had been issued and argued using what would be the efficiency assertions of the so-called Chicago School that combining Broadcom and Qualcomm would essentially be in line with US interests by accelerating the development of 5G technology.[45] Tan's arguments, however, proved ineffective in convincing CFIUS.

On March 12, President Trump, acting on the recommendation of CFIUS, issued an executive order blocking Qualcomm from pursuing its hostile takeover of Broadcom. In issuing the order Trump announced that by acquiring Qualcomm, there "is credible evidence that leads me to believe that Broadcom Ltd.

might take action that threatens to impair the national security of the United States."[46] In response, on March 14, Broadcom announced that it had "terminated and withdrawn its offer to acquire Qualcomm Incorporated and withdrawn its nominations to the board of directors of Qualcomm Incorporated."[47]

When issuing his executive order, Trump did not provide details on the "credible evidence" in his possession. Neither was any statement given by the Trump administration with regards to protecting competition or on whether any consideration had been given by CFIUS to the pro-economic efficiency arguments presented by Tan. What is interesting and a bit of a puzzle is that the action taken by the US in the name of ensuring national security was against a company originally based not in a state that was perceived by the US as posing a threat, but in a close ally, in this case, Singapore.[48] Unlike the case of CATIC mentioned earlier, which was known to have ties with the PLA so that an acquisition by it of a US company may have arguably presented a genuine national security concern to the US government, Broadcom had no ties with any foreign military. Nor did its original home country, Singapore, at any time threaten the national security of the US. Unlike Japan or China, Singapore has arguably also never been perceived by the US as a competitor or "strategic rival" vying to become the leader of the post-WWII international order. Accordingly, it would be difficult for anyone to determine what those national security concerns were which Broadcom's takeover proposal of Qualcomm presented to the US government, in order to avoid similar difficulties in the future.

Given this opaqueness and the past example of Fujitsu which had given rise to the Exon–Florio Amendment, however, what may be suggested is that the US had used the reason of national security in the case of Broadcom for promoting another cause that has more to do with another national interest, namely maintaining its position as the preeminent power of the post-WWII international economic order and preventing or preempting any attempt from any country, whether it be China, Japan, or Singapore, to threaten to displace it. As the letter from CFIUS and statement from the Trump Administration suggests, the main driver for blocking the Qualcomm acquisition had to do with the growing preoccupation of Americans viewing China as a threat to American dominance. The *New York Times* noted "a cold war" is emerging between the US and China that is increasingly becoming centered on the advanced computer chips that Qualcomm manufactures.[49] In this regard, there is perhaps consistency in US behavior that ultimately places a higher priority on protecting its perceived national interest of maintaining its dominance of the post-WWII international economic order than on protecting competition and consumer welfare. In the 1980s when the Fairchild acquisition was in effect blocked by the US government, Japan was perceived by the US as the rising power attempting to displace it as the dominant power of the US-crafted post-WWII international economic order. Thirty years later the Qualcomm takeover attempt as well as the proposed acquisitions by China that were blocked by CFIUS are taking place at a time when it is China, the "strategic competitor" of the US, that is seen by Americans as threatening their dominance of the international economic order. Indeed, as the US DoD put it in its Summary of the 2018 Defense Strategy of the United States of America, China (along with Russia) is a "revisionist power" seeking to undermine the "resilient but weakening post-WWII international order" constructed by the US "to better safeguard" the US and its allies "from aggression and coercion," and intends to displace the US to "achieve global preeminence in the future."[50] On this last point, Defense Secretary Jim Mattis further elaborated that China is seeking to establish a "world consistent with" its "authoritarian" model,[51] a comment that brings to mind a parallel with the negative perception of Japan by many Americans during the 1980s and early 1990s as demonstrated in both fiction and non-fiction books and articles.[52]

Although it seems unlikely that the Fujitsu and Broadcom proposals posed genuine threats to US national security, as legal scholar Douglas Rosenthal and economist Phedon Nicolaides pointed out, there are legitimate national security reasons for a government to restrict business activity by blocking the sales of biological weapons or preventing the acquisition of know-how associated with producing weapons of mass destruction.[53] A government may also sacrifice the promotion of competition to protect the health and safety of the public. In the 1978 Supreme Court case, National Society of Professional Engineers v. United States,[54] the Court ruled (citing a 1970 Third Circuit decision in Tripoli Co. v. Wella Corp.)[55] that marketing restraints that did not necessarily enhance competition may be permitted if such restraints were for the purpose of protecting the public or shielding a company from product liability.[56]

For a nation to place priority on protecting its sovereignty or protecting the safety of the public over protecting competition and consumer welfare is also tolerated by the international community. In the OECD Code of Liberalisation of Capital Movements, member states are allowed to take what they deem to be the action necessary to protect essential security interests, public order, safety, health, and morals.[57]

What may be of concern to those who have an interest in protecting competition and consumer welfare, however, is that by allowing leeway as to what constitutes "national security" and permitting various parties with their respective vested interests to arbitrarily define it, it is possible that a future administration hostile to foreign investment in general or with a nationalistic bent would block a M&A deal on the grounds of "national security" and in effect impede competition, the optimal use of economic resources, and the protection of consumer welfare. We should also consider the possibility that a trade and investment war may erupt if other foreign governments retaliate against the US by blocking American companies from undertaking M&A in their country using "national security" as an excuse while overlooking the possible merits with regard to competition or consumer welfare that such a transaction may bring. As Rufus Yerxa, the president of the National Foreign Trade Council and a former deputy director general of the World Trade Organization (WTO), stated, "[i]f the United States has rewritten the rules of the WTO system to say you can do anything you want if it's in your national security interests, be prepared for every country in the world to come up with a new definition of what is its critical national security interest."[58]

China, the European Union (EU), and national security

In 2011 the Chinese Ministry of Commerce (MOFCOM) established a panel to conduct national security reviews of foreign investments in Chinese companies. The MOFCOM panel, similar to CFIUS, has the authority to investigate M&A deals undertaken by foreign companies and then to recommend that the M&A be blocked or revised so as to make it compliant with national security regulations.[59] To date, the MOFCOM panel has not moved to block any foreign M&A deal. However, considering that the panel was set up immediately after the Chinese telecommunications company Huawei had backed off from its proposed acquisition of the assets of an American server technology company 3Leaf as a result of CFIUS' recommendation that the Chinese company voluntarily divest its assets (over concerns of Huawei's links with the Chinese government, especially with China's security services),[60] the timing suggests that the panel was a politically influenced reaction by the Chinese government and raises the possibility of future retaliatory moves by the MOFCOM panel to block acquisitions of Chinese companies. A case in point is the position of Chinese competition authorities in refusing in substance an approval of the proposed acquisition of the Dutch company NXP Semiconductors by Qualcomm of the US.[61] Although the Chinese authorities issued a statement claiming that it was "regrettable" that Qualcomm withdrew their acquisition proposal before the authorities actually issued any decision, as one IT specialist saw it, for the competition authorities to extend the deadline for the decision by two months "practically amounts to a refusal for granting an approval."[62]

Although countries such as the US and Japan may block a foreign M&A deal on the grounds of national security, as Japanese lawyer Fujii Kojiro noted, China's use of its competition laws in blocking a foreign M&A deal such as in the above Qualcomm case may infringe upon the WTO ban against discriminatory treatment for non-domestic companies.[63]

In the EU, while several member states have implemented measures that may restrict the movement of capital between member states and between member states and third countries on grounds of public policy or public/national security,[64] up until 2018 the EU did not have a comprehensive framework for screening foreign direct investment (FDI) at the EU level on the grounds of maintaining national security or public order.[65] Rather, FDI screening was essentially a decentralized process and the exclusive responsibility of the EU member states.[66] One factor that had prevented the formation of an EU-level screening process was the existence of different concepts of "national security," with some states taking the view that national security would include economic security.[67] The EU, however, announced in 2017 a proposal for a new EU framework for screening FDI that might raise security or public order concerns for the EU or its member states. In his annual State of the Union address, on September 13, 2017, the President of the European Commission,[68] Jean-Claude Juncker, stated that the member states of the EU "are not naïve free traders. Europe must always defend its national interests. This is why we are proposing a new EU framework for investment screening… . It is a political responsibility to know what is going on in our backyard so that we can protect our collective security if needed."[69]

The EU FDI screening regulation came into effect on April 10, 2019. While this does not confer power upon the EU to block specific FDI, it does intend to harmonize the FDI screening mechanisms currently in use by some member states such as Germany, to enhance cooperation on FDI screening between the Commission and member states, and to ensure that the member states that already have a screening mechanism comply with the proposed EU requirements. Essentially, the regulation will allow the EU to carry out its own review of FDI that affects a project of interest to the EU.[70] The implementation of the regulation will likely be of concern to enterprises from non-EU states, especially with regard to the wide screening of a FDI on the grounds of its "potential effects" on security or public order which covers, inter alia: "critical infrastructure; including energy, transport, communications, data storage, space or financial infrastructure, critical technologies; including artificial intelligence, robotics, semiconductors, technologies with potential dual use applications, cybersecurity, space or nuclear technology, potential effects on the security of supply or critical inputs, or effects on access to sensitive information or the ability to control it."[71] The security and public order concerns captured in the EU regulation are, accordingly, wide-ranging, and the regulation leaves open the possibility that the EU may further broaden the scope of security and public order as it sees fit.

Japan and public order

In Japan, under the Foreign Exchange and Foreign Trade Act (FEFTA),[72] the Ministry of Finance (MOF) and the relevant ministries with jurisdiction over an investment transaction will review foreign investments including acquisitions of Japanese businesses by foreign persons or businesses. Through various amendments to the FEFTA most of the requirements for prior notification and government approval or licenses for inbound direct investment[73] and for specified acquisitions[74] had been abolished and replaced with a post facto reporting system in 1992.[75] Under this system, a foreign investor[76] has the obligation to report to the Minister of Finance and the relevant ministers the content and the time of making the investment after the transaction had been completed.[77] In some limited cases, however, prior notification is required for both. Inbound direct investments requiring advance notification and approval are those that are deemed to be related to national security, public order, public health and safety. Cabinet and ministerial orders have also identified the business sectors of agriculture, forestry and fisheries, the oil industry, leather and leather product manufacturing, and air and water transport as requiring advanced notification in the case of a foreign investor making an investment in Japan.[78] The prior notification requirements are in accordance with what is allowed in Article 3 ("Public Order and Safety") of the OECD Code of Liberalisation of Capital Movements.[79] Article 27 of the FEFTA states that the Minister of Finance and the competent minister for a particular business sector may prohibit an inbound direct investment by a foreign investor for up to four months from receiving the foreign investor's notification if the investment is likely to cause the impairment of national security, the disturbance of public order, or to hinder the protection of public safety. If, during that period, the Minister of Finance and the competent minister find that the inbound investment proposal in question will impact national security, public order, etc., the Minister of Finance may recommend the investor who gave the notification to change the content of the investment or to abandon the proposal.[80] Likewise, for specified acquisitions, advanced notification for those transactions relating to national security, public order, and public health and safety is required with the same timeframe as those for inbound direct investment.[81]

As with the Exon–Florio Amendment, Article 27 of FEFTA does not give a clear definition of national security. Partly in response to this ambiguity, on August 2, 2017 the MOF, the Ministry of Economics, Trade and Industry (METI), and the relevant ministries issued a public announcement in which they stated factors to consider from a national security perspective for approving an inbound direct investment including: whether the production base and technology infrastructure in Japan can be maintained vis-à-vis Japan's security-related industries (e.g., airplanes, weapons, nuclear power, and space development) and whether the outflow of sensitive technology important for security can be prevented. The announcement also suggested examining the past investment behavior of the foreign investors and their financial attributes.[82]

In contrast to the US, there has so far been no case where an inbound direct investment or specified acquisition had been blocked by the Japanese government on the grounds of national security. It may be that the government announcement of August 2, 2017 identifying security-related industries has had some effect in limiting the possibility of the government arbitrarily expanding the definition of national security.

This is not to say, however, that Article 27 has never been invoked. Aside from national security, Article 27(3)(a) allows the government to block an inbound direct investment if it "is likely to cause" disturbance to the maintenance of public order or hinder "the protection of public safety." In this regard, the only known instance to date of a transaction blocked under Article 27 for reasons of creating a possible obstruction to the maintenance of public order in Japan occurred in 2008. A London-based investment fund established in 2003, the Children's Investment Fund (TCI), made investments in global infrastructure assets, including airports, shipping facilities, and utilities throughout Asia.[83] The fund had a war chest of US$8 billion to support its investment activities and donated a portion of its investment proceeds to charity.[84] As part of its initiative in investing in infrastructure, in 2005 TCI started to build its stake in J-Power. This was a time when foreign investors had begun to step up their investment activities in Japan with expectations of economic reforms and growth.[85] J-Power was a Japanese power company established in 1952 as a government "special legal enterprise." As Japan's largest wholesaler of electricity, the company counted Japan's ten electric companies among its major customers.[86] In addition to J-Power's assets of coal-fired and hydroelectric power plants located all over Japan, the company owned a nuclear power plant located in Oma, Aomori Prefecture. Upon its privatization with its listing in the First Section of the Tokyo Stock Exchange (TSE) in October 2004, all of the company's shares owned by the Japanese government were sold off, making it at the time a prominent example of privatization of a government "special legal enterprise."[87]

TCI's initial investment in J-Power gave it 5.1% of the total shares.[88] By March 2007, TCI had acquired a 9.9% stake in TCI. With its increase in the ownership of J-Power shares, TCI sent a letter in November 2007 to the management of J-Power demanding managerial changes such as increasing shareholder dividends, disposing cross-shareholdings, and appointing independent members to the J-Power board with the view to improving the performance of the company, especially with regard to the company's return on equity (ROE) and operating profits, which had been in decline since 2004.[89] J-Power management rejected all of TCI's demands, countering TCI's arguments about declining performance by pointing out that operating profits were in fact exceeding original budget plan forecasts.[90] The rejection by J-Power's board of TCI's demand to boost dividends was confirmed at J-Power's 2007 shareholder meeting with its defeat by an undisclosed margin.[91] In response, TCI, in accordance with Article 27 of the FEFTA, notified the Japanese government in early 2008 of its intention to increase its 9.9% stake in J-Power to 20% with the objective of gaining a greater say over the management of the company.[92]

In response to the advance notification given by TCI, the Japanese government extended the period during which TCI was blocked from carrying out its investment plan to May 14, 2008. On April 16, 2008, the Special Task Force on Foreign Investment of the Council on Customs, Tariffs, Foreign Exchange and Other Transactions of MOF issued a recommendation that the acquisition of shares should not be permitted as "there is a likelihood that the maintenance of public order may be obstructed" since "it cannot be denied that if a foreign investor increases its share [in J-Power], there may be the possibility of an unforeseeable impact on the planning, operations, and maintenance of the basic equipment of electric power such as electric power lines and on the implementation of [the country's] nuclear energy policy."[93] The foreign response was, not surprisingly, critical. EU trade commissioner Peter Mandelson remarked that the response by the Japanese government confirmed that Japan was "the most closed investment market in the developed world."[94]

On April 25 TCI responded with a refusal to follow the government recommendation. In their response on May 13, MOF and METI ordered the fund to cease its acquisition of shares.[95] In a last-ditch effort, at the J-Power shareholder meeting held on June 26, TCI submitted five proposals for a vote including demands for higher dividends (to JP¥120 per share) and to appoint at least three outside directors.[96] All of the 700 other shareholders at the meeting rejected the demands. Upon the announcement of this development, J-Power's shares fell almost 7% to close at JP¥3,810.[97] With this defeat, on July 2008, amid rumors that TCI was planning to contest the order before a Japanese court, TCI announced that it would accept the government order to cease its pursuit of increasing its share in J-Power as it felt that it was "not in the interests of any of the parties to pursue an appeal or a lengthy judicial process."[98] On October 31, TCI sold back to J-Power all of its shares at JP¥3,830 per share, about a 30% premium compared to the market price.[99]

In rejecting TCI's bid for increasing its share in J-Power, no consideration was seemingly given by the Japanese government to the interests of shareholders who would have arguably benefited from TCI's demands for an increase in dividends or to whether TCI's action would have rejuvenated J-Power's management. Nor was any explanation given as to why in the case of a foreign investor making an inbound investment "there is a likelihood that the maintenance of public order may be obstructed." In any event, this outcome suggests that ambiguity with regard to what constitutes risks to public order had allowed the Japanese government to sacrifice consumer welfare, a possible improvement in corporate governance practices, and competition for reasons that reflect an arguably fundamental national interest of Japan as perceived by its predominantly male political and economic elite: prevent the weakening of Japanese economic power by keeping out obstreperous foreigners as far as possible. As lawyer Nagasawa Toru wrote in *Diamond* business magazine, the government's recommendation in the TCI case was in effect a statement calling for the "Black Ships" (referring to Commodore Perry's so-called Black Ships that approached the shores of a semi-isolated Japan in 1853) to cease their attack upon Japan and leave for good.[100]

Encouraging M&A and the formation of monopolies for the national interest

In contrast to the above cases where cross-border M&A and business transactions have been rejected for reasons ostensibly pertaining to defending national interests or maintaining public order, there have also been examples where a government has encouraged M&A among domestic companies leading to the formation of large, market-dominating enterprises or even monopolies with the view that such transactions would be in the national interest or in support of national security since their large size would deter an acquisition or hostile takeover attempt by other foreign enterprises. For example, regarding a merger between two French oil companies Elf and Total Fina, the former president of the IMF Dominique Strauss-Kahn unabashedly stated that the merger will create a "French oil group that is almost at the level of the three world leaders and therefore really protected from any takeover attempt by an Anglo-Saxon or American" company.[101]

A government may also encourage a merger among its homegrown companies if it felt that this would ensure having an enterprise that could become a national champion able to compete internationally, or for nationalistic reasons it wanted to avoid its domestic markets being dominated by foreign business players on its home turf. In February 2019 the German government issued a manifesto which endorsed the idea of a merger between two of the largest banks of Germany, Deutsche Bank and its rival Commerzbank, so that the country would have a bank that "can stand up to competitors from the United States and China."[102] While the German banking market is competitive with consumer and small business lending dominated by many semi-public savings banks, the stance of the German government in backing a merger reflects a fear among German political officials of being dominated by big and more powerful American investment banks and also reflects a need for a big German bank with an international presence that can provide German companies with a stable credit line.[103] As with the view of Dominque Strauss-Kahn mentioned earlier, what is conspicuously lacking in the arguments of the German government is any apprehension around what this merger between the two largest banks of Germany may do to competition or consumer welfare even though concern had been raised that this merger could prove ultimately costly to consumers.[104]

A state may also encourage the formation of large-size domestic enterprises through M&A that could dominate or monopolize an industry and indirectly allow a state to enhance its power vis-à-vis other states. In the US, government authorities for several years have taken a hands-off stance regarding the arguably anticompetitive M&A activities of the US Internet platform companies of Apple, Amazon, Facebook, Alphabet (Google), and Microsoft, leading to a situation where the US currently controls 92% of the worldwide Internet search market through Google and 70% of the social media market through Facebook.[105] And along with allowing the growth of these companies through M&A which has arguably resulted in damaging competition (see Chapter 1) a case in point where the US had seemed to look the other way on monopolistic behavior by one of the US Internet platform companies is what happened on June 27, 2017 when the EU slapped a record US$2.7 billion fine on the US-headquartered Alphabet (Google) on charges that it had abused its dominant market position in general Internet search markets by giving its own comparison price shopping service an illegal disadvantage over those of other companies through inferior placement and demotion in search results. Despite the fact that the companies that raised the complaints against Alphabet such as Microsoft, Oracle, and TripAdvisor were largely US-based companies and that they had brought up their case to the US Federal Trade Commission (FTC) as well, the latter, while finding evidence that Alphabet had indeed harmed competitors, decided not to prosecute as they found no harm done to either competition or to consumers in the form of increased consumer prices.[106] Although two years later on June 3, 2019, the US House Judiciary Committee announced that it planned to establish a bipartisan investigation of the digital platform companies such as Alphabet, Amazon, and Facebook, with the FTC undertaking an antitrust probe of Facebook and Amazon, and the Department of Justice (DoJ) opening an investigation of Alphabet towards allegations of unfair competition, the global dominance of these companies had already been established.[107]

The conflict in national interests between the EU and the US that became apparent from the different positions taken towards Google, however, was not something new or a recent phenomenon. An earlier major example of a point of contention between the EU and the US was the 2001 blocking of a merger between the US industrial and financial conglomerate General Electric (GE) and the aerospace and engineering conglomerate Honeywell by the EU.[108] Both companies were US corporations with headquarters in the US. American antitrust authorities had approved the merger and accepted the argument of both companies that the merger would be conducive to achieving efficiencies in the production of aircraft engines and expansion in avionic product offerings, resulting in the reduction of prices and the enhancement of consumer welfare. The EU, however, had blocked the merger with the reason that it would significantly reduce competition as GE's financial strength would enable Honeywell to invest more in R&D and offer its customers lower prices than its rivals who would as a result be eventually forced to exit the market. The EU decision led to the abandonment of the merger proposal.[109] While the economist Joseph Stiglitz commended the EU competition commissioner Mario Monti for standing up to the US and fulfilling his obligation to enforce EU competition laws,[110] the decision of the EU, as recounted by legal scholar David Gerber, evoked outrage among many Americans with some asking how a foreign authority could effectively squash a M&A deal that involved only US companies and was approved not only by the DoJ but also (with certain concessions) by some dozen other foreign competition authorities. More to the point, there was a view among Americans that the decision was motivated by supra-nationalist considerations, namely a pan-European desire to protect European industries although there was no evidence to substantiate this claim.[111]

Conclusion

According to a survey undertaken by the American financial services company J.P. Morgan, in 2017 the total transaction volume of global M&A reached US$3.7 trillion, making 2017 the fifth most active year on record for M&A activity.[112] A majority of these deals have been approved by governments. This indicates that, overall, political leaders are favorable to cross-border investments and fairly assess a M&A deal on its potential merits to enhance and protect consumer welfare and competition. The examples of cross-border M&A or investment deals that have been rejected by governments that we have looked at in the previous chapter seem to be a minority.

However, as an increasing number of countries enact legislation allowing them to block M&A transactions and other foreign direct investment (FDI) on the grounds of "national security" or in the name of "public order," there may be a concern that consumers around the world may end up as losers as a M&A or other international business transactions get blocked, not on the grounds of protecting competition or consumer welfare, but for political reasons that are conveniently cloaked in opaque national security and public order concerns. Indeed, on May 23, 2018, US President Trump launched an investigation into whether automobile imports have caused threats to national security. This may lead to the slapping of tariffs as high as 25% on automobile imports.[113] As the *New York Times* noted, many have found the national security argument behind Trump's decision specious as 98% of car imports come from major allies such as Canada, the EU, Japan, Mexico, and South Korea.[114] Such a move arguably opens up the possibility of other nations retaliating by imposing trade and investment restrictions on the grounds of national security. Georgetown University Law Center professor Jennifer Hillman notes that if the US is able to justify tariffs on cars as a threat to national security, what is to prevent every other country in the world from justifying restrictions to trade and investment on "almost any product" with a similar claim.[115] In such a situation, not only would consumers lose out from the increasing use of national security reasons for blocking or impeding international business transactions, but advocates of a global competition law or policies that enshrine the principles of protecting competition and consumer welfare may also lose out as countries may increasingly resort to using the reason of national security and public order as a political and protectionist tool. And quite possibly another major loser in the long run may turn out to be capitalism as competition that drives innovation or the forces of creative destruction may become increasingly sacrificed for political reasons.

Notes

1 Unoki, Ko, *Mergers, Acquisitions, and Global Empires*, Routledge, 2012, pp.34–35.
2 Institute for Mergers, Acquisitions, and Alliances, M&A Statistics, Online. Available https://imaa-institute.org/mergers-and-acquisitions-statistics/ (accessed June 29, 2019).
3 Ibid.
4 Ansoff, Igor, *Corporate Strategy*, Penguin Books, 1985, pp.108–111; Unoki, op.cit., p.34.
5 Christophers, Brett, *The Great Leveler*, Harvard University Press, 2016, p.149; Gellhorn, Ernest, Kovacic, William E., *Antitrust Law and Economics*, West Group, 1994, pp.15–20.
6 Husby, Christian, CFIUS: The Little Known Multi-Billion-Dollar Killer, *MJIL*, Vol.37, Online. Available http://www.mjilonline.org/cfius-the-little-known-multi-billion-dollar-deal-killer/ (accessed June 29, 2019).
7 Jackson, James K., The Committee on Foreign Investment in the United States (CFIUS), Congressional Research Service Report, July 3, 2018, p.5, Online. Available https://fas.org/sgp/crs/natsec/RL33388.pdf (accessed June 29, 2019).
8 Greidinger, Marc, The Exon-Florio Amendment: A Solution in Search of a Problem, *American University Law Review*, Vol. 6, 1991, p.134, Online. Available https://digitalcommons.wcl.american.edu/cgi/viewcontent.cgi?referer=&httpsredir=1&article=1553&context=auilr (accessed June 29, 2019).
9 Ibid.
10 *The New York Times*, Fairchild Being Sold to National, September 1, 1987, Online. Available https://www.nytimes.com/1987/09/01/business/fairchild-being-sold-to-national.html (accessed June 29, 2019).
11 *The New York Times*, C.I.A. Report on Japan Economy Creates Furor at Institute, June 5,1991, Online. Available https://www.nytimes.com/1991/06/05/news/cia-report-on-japan-economy-creates-furor-at-institute.html (accessed June 29, 2019).
12 50 U.S.C. app. Sec. 2170, Jackson, op.cit., p.5.
13 Greidinger, op.cit., p.130.
14 Exon–Florio Amendment, Section 2170(c).
15 Jackson, op.cit., p.3.
16 Husby, op.cit.
17 Ibid.
18 According to Section 2170 (b), "[a]ny information or documentary material filed with the President or the President's designee pursuant to this section shall be exempt from disclosure under section 552 of title 5, United States Code, and no such

information or documentary material may be made public, except as may be relevant to any administration or judicial action or proceeding...."

19 Greguras, Fred M., O'Neil, Michael J., Zhu, Chenhao, M&A in the United States: What Chinese Companies Need to Know about Exon-Florio Review in the Clean Technology and Other Business Sectors, Fletcher School of Law & Diplomacy, April 2012, Online. Available http://fletcher.tufts.edu/~/media/Fletcher/Microsites/swfi/pdfs/2012/Updated_Exon-Florio.pdf (accessed June 29, 2019). Unlike the Hart–Scott–Rodino Act antitrust review, formal review of a transaction is triggered by the voluntary filing of a notice of a transaction by both parties involved. CFIUS, however, has the authority to review a transaction even when the parties have not voluntarily filed a notice if it believes that a transaction may raise national security concerns, or a member of CFIUS has reason to believe that a particular transaction is a covered transaction and may therefore raise national security concerns.

20 Jackson, op.cit., p.21.

21 Husby, op.cit.

22 Greidinger, op.cit., p.121.

23 102d Cong. 2d Sess., 1992.

24 Husby, op.cit.

25 Greidinger, op.cit., p.130.

26 *Japan Times*, As U.S. Eyes Hike in Tariffs, Toyota Pushes Free Trade, May 26, 2018.

27 Bodansky, Robert L., Dyer, Jospeh J., "America First" and its Impact on Cross-Border, M&A, Association for Corporate Growth, August 7, 2017, Online. Available http://middlemarketgrowth.org/america-first-impact-cross-border-ma/ (accessed June 29, 2019).

28 Husby op.cit.

29 Ng, Julian, Foreign Investments: What Developments in the US and China Mean, National Security Reviews of Foreign Investment, October 23, 2017, Online. Available https://themarketmogul.com/national-security-review-us-china/ (accessed June 29, 2019); Spar, Debora L., Kou, Julia, Being There: Sony Corporation and Columbia Pictures, Harvard Business School Case, 795-025, December 8, 1994.

30 15 U.S.C. Ch.1 Sec.18.

31 Rosenthal, Douglas E., Nicolaides, Phedon, Harmonizing Antitrust: The Less Effective Way to Promote International Competition, Institute of International Economics, December 1997, p.379, Online. Available https://piie.com/publications/chapters_preview/56/11ie1664.pdf (accessed June 29, 2019).

32 Byrne, Mathew R., Protecting National Security and Promoting Foreign Investment: Maintaining the Exon-Florio Balance, *Ohio State Law Journal*, Vol. 67, No. 849, 2006, p.871, Online. Available https://kb.osu.edu/bitstream/handle/1811/71053/OSLJ_V67N4_0849.pdf;sequence=1 (accessed June 29, 2019), Greidinger, op.cit., pp.158–159. Greidinger asserts that, although President Bush blocked the sale of MAMCO ostensibly on the grounds of maintaining technology security, the timing of his decision suggests that the Exon–Florio Amendment provided the Bush administration with a mechanism to convey its dissatisfaction with China's policies pertaining to the Tiananmen Square incident of June 4, 1989 and to quell domestic dissatisfaction towards what was perceived to be Bush's weak response to China's human rights abuses towards its citizens thus making the amendment a means for the US to pressure other governments to modify their policies that concern the US.

33 Jackson, op.cit., p.7. The other four transactions blocked by the president based on a recommendation from CFIUS are as follows: the Chinese-owned Ralls Corporation acquisition of an Oregon wind farm project whose divestiture President Obama ordered in 2012, the Chinese company Fujian Grand Chip Investment Fund's proposed acquisition of Aixtron, a German semiconductor maker with assets based in the US, which was blocked by President Obama in 2016, the proposed acquisition of Portland Oregon-based Lattice Semiconductor Corporation by the Chinese

investment company Canyon Bridge Capital which was blocked by President Trump in 2017, and the 2018 proposed takeover of San Diego-based Qualcomm by Singapore-based Broadcom mentioned below.

34 Jackson, op.cit., p.7.

35 Stevenson, Alexandra, Hitting the Breaks of Chinese Deal Making, *The New York Times*, February 28, 2018.

36 Kang, Cecilia, Rappeport, Alan, U.S. and China Battle for Edge in Technology, *The New York Times*, March 8, 2018.

37 Swanson, Ana, Stevenson, Alexandra, Collateral Damage from a Trade Fight, *The New York Times*, April 20, 2018.

38 Ibid.

39 Ibid.

40 Bloomberg, Trump Blocks Broadcom Takeover of Qualcomm on Security Risks, March 13, 2018, Online. Available https://www.bloomberg.com/news/articles/2018-03-12/trump-issues-order-to-block-broadcom-s-takeover-of-qualcomm-jeoszwnt (accessed June 29, 2019).

41 Ibid.

42 Greguras, O'Neil, Zhu, op.cit. According to the Exon–Florio Amendment, Section 2170, the CFIUS review process has four steps: 1) a voluntary filing, 2) a 30-day preliminary review of the transaction, 3) a potential additional 45-day full investigation, and 4) a potential 15-day period during which the President decides to clear, suspend, or deny the transaction.

43 *The National Law Review*, CFIUS Deal Abandoned, Presidential Order: Broadcom and Qualcomm, May 3, 2018, Online. Available https://www.natlawreview.com/article/cfius-deal-abandoned-presidential-order-broadcom-and-qualcomm (accessed June 29, 2019).

44 Kang, Rappeport, op.cit.

45 Bloomberg, op.cit.; *The Economist*, Crony Capitalism, April 15, 2017; Gerber, David J., *Global Competition*, Oxford University Press, 2012, pp.141, 143; Stewart, James B., Antitrust Law is Overdue for an Upgrade, *The New York Times International Edition*, June 15, 2018; Mathews, Dylan, Antitrust was Defined by Robert Bork. I Cannot Overstate his Influence, *The Washington Post*, December 20, 2012; Gellhorn, Kovacic, op.cit., p.36.

46 Bloomberg, op.cit.

47 *The National Law Review*, op.cit.

48 From the Trump Administration's announcement that suggested that Broadcom's acquisition proposal might lead to the dominance in 5G technology by Chinese companies such as Huawei, it can be inferred that the US fear factor towards China was present in the background to the decision to block this proposal.

49 Swanson, Stevenson, op.cit.

50 US Department of Defense, Summary of the 2018 National Defense Strategy of the United States of America, 2018, pp.1–2. Online. Available https://www.defense.gov/Portals/1/Documents/pubs/2018-National-Defense-Strategy-Summary.pdf (accessed August 2, 2019).

51 Radio Free Europe, Pentagon Chief Calls Russia, China, "Revisionist Powers," January 19, 2018, Online. Available https://www.rferl.org/a/pentagon-mattis-calls-russia-china-revisionist-powers/28985632.html (accessed June 29, 2019).

52 Reich, Robert, Is Japan Out to Get US?, *The New York Times*, February 9, 1992.

53 Rosenthal, Nicolaides, op.cit., p.375.

54 435 U.S. 679; Gellhorn, Kovacic, op.cit., p.190.

55 425F.2d 932, 3rd Cir.; Gellhorn, Kovacic, op.cit., p.190.

56 Ibid.

57 Article 3 of Code. OECD, OECD Code of Liberalisation of Capital Movements, 2018, p.10. Online. Available http://www.oecd.org/investment/investment-policy/codes.htm (accessed June 29, 2019).

58 *The New York Times*, Tariff Battle Puts W.T.O. in Dicey Spot, August 13, 2018.

59 Ng, op.cit.

60 Reuters, Huawei backs away from 3Leaf acquisition, February 19, 2011, Online. Available https://www.reuters.com/article/us-huawei-3leaf/huawei-backs-away-from-3leaf-acquisition-idUSTRE71I38920110219 (accessed June 29, 2019).

61 Reuters, Qualcomm says China comment will not revive NXP deal, December 3, 2018, Online. Available https://www.reuters.com/article/us-nxp-semicondtrs-m-a-qualcomm/qualcomm-says-china-comment-will-not-revive-nxp-deal-idUSKBN1O20BG (accessed June 29, 2019). Multinational companies that do business in China need to get regulatory approval for a M&A from Chinese competition authorities regardless of whether the company they are acquiring or merging with is Chinese or not or whether the M&A is undertaken in or outside of China. Other major economies such as the EU, Japan, and the US also have similar approval requirements, ostensibly to ensure that a M&A does not lead to excessive market concentration in their markets. A similar case mentioned later in this chapter is the proposed merger between the two US companies of General Electric and Honeywell which collapsed after failing to receive approval by the European Commission.

62 *Nihon Keizai Shimbun*, Kokusai M&A chugoku no kabe (The wall of China facing international M&A), July 28, 2018.

63 Ng, op.cit.; *Nihon Keizai Shimbun*, Chugoku dokkinho gaishi Nakase (China's anti-monopoly law gives foreign investors headaches), August 2, 2018; *Nihon Keizai Shimbun*, Kokusai M&A chugoku no kabe (The wall of China facing international M&A), July 28, 2018. China's first competition law was enacted on August 1, 2008. According to one American lawyer based in a Chinese law firm in China interviewed on an anonymous basis by the *Nihon Keizai Shinbun* (op.cit.), "the law from the very start of its inception was designed to hamper the business activities of rival foreign companies."

64 Barbaglia, Pamela, Wagner, Rene, Schuetze, Arno, Germany sets EU tone with tighter curbs on foreign takeovers, Reuters, July 12, 2017. Online. Available https://www.reuters.com/article/us-germany-m-a/germany-sets-eu-tone-with-tighter-curbs-on-foreign-takeovers-idUSKBN19W2R6 (accessed June 29, 2019).

65 European Commission, Proposal for a Regulation of the European Parliament and of the Council: establishing a framework for screening of foreign direct investments into the European Union, Brussels, September 13, 2017, p.16, Online. Available https://ec.europa.eu/transparency/regdoc/rep/1/2017/EN/COM-2017-487-F1-EN-MAIN-PART-1.PDF (accessed June 29, 2019); European Parliamentary Research Service, EU framework for FDI Screening, January 2018, Online. Available https://epthinktank.eu/2018/01/22/eu-framework-for-fdi-screening-eu-legislation-in-progress/ (accessed June 29, 2019). As of January 2018, 12 EU member states have legislation in place which allows them to review FDI for reasons of security or public order.

66 K&L Gates, Screening of FDI in the EU, March 7, 2018, Online. https://www.lexology.com/library/detail.aspx?g=5cd76838-4d08-4b69-84dd-9befc0f0ea06 (accessed June 29, 2019).

67 Ibid.

68 European Union, Online. Available https://europa.eu/european-union/about-eu/institutions-bodies/european-commission_en (accessed June 29, 2019). The European Commission is the executive arm of the EU and is solely responsible for drawing up proposals for new European legislation. The EC also implements decisions of the European Parliament and the Council of the EU.

69 European Commission, State of the Union 2017-Trade Package: European Commission proposes framework for screening of foreign direct investments, Brussels, September 14,

2017, Online. Available http://europa.eu/rapid/press-release_IP-17-3183_en.htm (accessed June 29, 2019).

70 Regulation (EU) 2019/452 of the European Parliament and of the Council of March 19, 2019, Article 3, Online. Available https://eur-lex.europa.eu/eli/reg/2019/452/oj (accessed June 29, 2019).

71 Ibid., Article 4.

72 Act no. 228, December 1, 1949, Online. Available http://www.japaneselawtranslation.go.jp/law/detail_main?vm=&id=21 (accessed June 29, 2019).

73 As defined in Article 26(2) as including the acquisition of shares of a Japanese company, loans to a Japanese company, and the acquisition of company bonds of a Japanese company.

74 As defined in Article 26(3) as a transaction where a foreign investor acquires shares of a non-listed Japanese company from other foreign investors.

75 Uematsu, Takafumi, Japan, *The Foreign Investment Regulation Review*, Edition 5, October 5, 2017, Online. Available https://thelawreviews.co.uk/chapter/1149290/japan (accessed June 29, 2019); Usami, Jun, Moran, William, Cho, Fumiko, National Security Reviews 2017: A Global Perspective: Japan, Online. Available https://www.whitecase.com/publications/insight/national-security-reviews-global-perspective-japan (accessed June 29, 2019).

76 As defined in Article 26(2) and (3) as being any person who makes an inward direct investment or a specified acquisition.

77 Financial Worldwide, New regulations on foreign investors' acquisition of Japanese companies, September 2017, Online. Available https://www.financierworldwide.com/new-regulations-on-foreign-investors-acquisition-of-japanese-companies/#.WvJrC7lPr3g (accessed June 29, 2019).

78 Ibid. Such sectors are listed in the OECD Code of Liberalisation of Capital Movementsfor avoiding possible adverse effects on the Japanese economy.

79 OECD, op.cit., pp.10, 74.

80 Ministry of Justice, Japanese Law Translation, Foreign Exchange and Foreign Trade Act, Online. Available http://www.japaneselawtranslation.go.jp/law/detail/?id=21&vm=04&re=02 (accessed June 29, 2019).

81 Ibid., Article 28.

82 Usami, Moran, Cho, op.cit.

83 Daiwa Institute of Research (Daiwa), TCI no J Power kabu kaimashi ni chushi meirei, Daiwa Souken, July 10, 2008, Online. Available https://www.dir.co.jp/report/research/capital-mkt/esg/08071001strategy.pdf (accessed August 2, 2019).

84 Yamazaki, Tomoko, Sato, Shigeru, TCI learned the hard way via J-Power play, *Japan Times*, July 31, 2009. Online. Available https://www.japantimes.co.jp/news/2009/07/31/business/tci-learned-the-hard-way-via-j-power-play/#.XURHaPZuIgA (accessed August 2, 2019).

85 Nakamoto, Michiyo, TCI sells out of Power at a loss, *Financial Times*, October 31, 2008. Online. Available https://www.ft.com/content/f2028abe-a745-11dd-865e-000077b07658 (accessed August 2, 2019).

86 Ibid.

87 Daiwa, op.cit.

88 Ibid.

89 Ibid.; Yamazaki, Sato, op.cit.; Nakamoto, op.cit.

90 Daiwa, op.cit.

91 Yamazaki, Sato, op.cit.

92 Ibid.

93 Nagasawa, Toru, "J Power mondai" ga shocho suru keisanshou kanryo no gaishi arerugi, *Diamond* online, April 4, 2008. Online. Available http://diamond.jp/articles/-/6317 (accessed June 29, 2019).

94 McCurry, Justin, TCI's J-Power bid fails, *The Guardian*, June 26, 2008, Online. Available https://www.theguardian.com/business/2008/jun/26/tci.jpower.japan (accessed June 29, 2019).
95 Daiwa, op.cit.
96 McCurry, op.cit.
97 Ibid.
98 Uematsu, op.cit.
99 Yamazaki, Sato, op.cit.
100 Nagasawa, op.cit.
101 Dinc, Serdac, Erel, Isil, Economic Nationalism in Mergers and Acquisitions, *Journal of Finance*, Wiley, August 2013, p.1. Available, Online https://papers.ssrn.com/sol3/papers.cfm?abstract_id=1361107 (accessed June 29, 2019). What is notable in Strauss-Kahn's statement is that it does not address the concerns that consumers may have over possible monopoly pricing that such a merger may entail.
102 *The New York Times*, A Merger to Broaden Problems or Solve Them?, February 25, 2019.
103 Ibid.
104 Ibid.
105 *The New York Times*, Taking on the Tech Giants, June 24, 2019.
106 *The Economist*, Crony Capitalism, op.cit; European Commission Press Release, Antitrust: Commission fines Google €2.42 billion for abusing dominance as search engine by giving illegal advantage to own comparison shopping service, June 27, 2017, Online. Available http://europa.eu/rapid/press-release_IP-17-1784_en.htm (accessed July 7, 2017); Davidson, Adam, Teddy Roosevelt Would Not Understand the E.U.'s Antitrust Fine Against Google, *The New Yorker*, June 28, 2017, Online. Available http://www.newyorker.com/business/adam-davidson/teddy-roosevelt-wouldnt-understand-the-eus-antitrust-fine-against-google (accessed July 7, 2017); *The New York Times*, Google Fined Record $2.7 billion in E.U. Antitrust Ruling, June 27, 2017.
107 *Japan Times*, Washington Turns Up Antitrust Heat on Silicon Valley, June 5, 2019.
108 GE/Honeywell, Case no. COMP/M2220, July 3, 2001.
109 Europa EU, COMP/M.2220 GE/Honeywell Case, Online. Available http://ec.europa.eu/competition/mergers/cases/decisions/m2220_en.pdf (accessed July 2, 2017); Stiglitz, Joseph E., *Making Globalization Work*, Norton, 2006, p.201; Haucap, Justus, Muller, Florian, Wey, Christian, How to Reduce Conflicts over International Antitrust?, DIW Berlin, December 2004, pp.33–34.
110 Stiglitz, op.cit., p.201.
111 Gerber, op.cit., p.97.
112 J.P. Morgan, 2018 Global M&A Outlook, p.2, Online. Available https://www.jpmorgan.com/jpmpdf/1320744801603.pdf (accessed June 29, 2019).
113 *Japan Times*, Trump looks to up tariff ante as U.S. launches auto import probe, putting Asian carmakers on defensive, May 25, 2018, Online. Available https://www.japantimes.co.jp/news/2018/05/25/business/trump-looks-tariff-ante-u-s-launches-auto-import-probe-putting-asian-carmakers-defensive/#.W7lUNvZuKqk (accessed June 29, 2019).
114 *The New York Times International Edition*, Automotive Industry Winces, May 26–27, 2018.
115 Hillman, Jennifer A., New Tariffs a Danger to U.S. Security, *The New York Times International Edition*, June 2–3, 2018.

7 Conclusion

The arguments for a global competition law and Realism-inspired obstacles

As I have mentioned previously, rationally behaving consumers wherever they may be share a general, common interest in being able to buy the best possible products and services at the lowest possible price and at the greatest possible convenience. For consumers to be able to have this interest fulfilled, the protection of competition becomes essential in order for markets in which businesses freely compete for the attention of consumers to be established and maintained. To this end, it would seem to be a no-brainer for states to agree to have a common, global competition law that aims to protect competition and consumer welfare. For businesses, a major merit of a global competition law would be for them to have the possibility of alleviating their level of uncertainty when engaging in cross-border investment or commercial activities, which may realize a lowering of transaction and other related business costs.

There is perhaps another crucial argument in favor of having a global competition law or at least a common approach to protecting competition in the marketplace and consumer welfare. As we have mentioned in the previous chapters, since the advent of digital technologies and the Internet, the world economy has seen growing economic concentration centered around Internet platform companies such as Apple and Microsoft for operating software, Alphabet (Google) and Alibaba for search services, Facebook and Tencent for social networking services, and Amazon for Internet retail services. These companies have created positions of dominance in most industrialized economies (and in China), through their strong returns to scale and network effects (where goods and services become more valuable as usage increases), which are the core tenets of their business models, and by the acquisition of rival embryonic companies before they are able to fully establish themselves.[1] That the growth of such market concentration with the potential of arguably threatening the functioning of innovation-inducing competition has gone by largely unchecked suggests that the competition laws of certain states are either partially ineffective or are not being fully enforced, and therefore a more concerted global approach in dealing with excessive market concentration may be needed.[2]

While it may be that, given the positions of dominance some of these IT platform companies have established for themselves, it would be these companies in particular that would have the most to lose from any potential concerted global effort to stem the tide of market concentration and therefore the most against such an endeavor, a major factor hindering such a global effort (including the development of a global competition law) are states. Despite legislating for laws to protect competition and consumer welfare and despite high-flying statements coming from certain state leaders such as that delivered by Japanese prime minister Abe Shinzo at the G20 Osaka Summit held in June 2019 declaring the adherence of Japan and the other G20 states to "free, fair, non-discriminatory, open markets," and a "level playing field" for business,[3] as I have shown in the previous chapters, when it comes to some private international business transactions, states have found it expedient to interfere and arbitrarily interpret their competition laws or even outright ignore those laws when the transaction is deemed by them to be impacting their so-called "national interest."[4]

As mentioned earlier, at its most basic level, the national interest of all sovereign nations is the survival or the maintenance of sovereignty. Beyond this fundamental interest, however, each state's other national interests will be determined by the views of its leaders, which in turn will be shaped or influenced by how they view the condition of international relations. For the leaders of a state that adheres to the Realist school of thought, the condition of international relations is anarchical. Accordingly, they view international relations as a zero-sum game that is "won" at the expense of other states by capturing and amassing as much power as possible, be it political, economic, or military. In such circumstances, the interests of individual consumers and protecting competition are of secondary importance. Regardless of the impact on consumers and competition, leaders with a Realist outlook on international relations will have little or no compunction in blocking a foreign-originating merger and/or acquisition (M&A) investment transaction if they view it as detrimental to their state's power. The United States' (US) blocking of Fujitsu's attempted acquisition of Fairchild Semiconductor, or of Broadcom's attempted takeover of Qualcomm, or the hold up of TCI's attempt to acquire greater control over J-Power by the Japanese government, are all arguably examples in which a Realist outlook of international relations had induced national leaders to compromise on protecting consumers or competition in order to achieve, under the guise of national security and public order, what they perceive to be their greater cause, the amassing of more power at the expense of the power of other states.[5] Dominique Strauss-Kahn's comment mentioned in the previous chapter approving the merger of two French oil companies to prevent their acquisition by foreign investors or the backing of the German government for the merger of two leading German banks in the hopes of creating a national champion that can compete against US and Chinese banks are both also arguably reflections of a Realist perspective of the condition of international relations, held by state leaders, which is driven by an aspiration fueled in part by a nationalist search for more power which comes at the expense of protecting competition and consumer welfare.[6]

An earlier, perhaps more egregious example of a state leader who took the view that the protection of competition and consumer welfare was of lesser importance than the promotion of a state's power was US president Theodore Roosevelt's call for the US economy to be dominated by monopolies that were to be under the control of the government. Despite having the reputation of being the original "trustbuster" by successfully challenging and inducing the breakup of the monopolies of Standard Oil and J.P. Morgan, in 1912 Roosevelt campaigned for president on a platform which he called "New Nationalism" where he promised not to break up the monopolies but instead to nationalize them, "so as to give the National Government complete power over the organization and capitalization of all business concerns."[7] As he put it in a speech delivered on August 31, 1910, monopolies or combinations which controlled the daily necessities of life such as meat, oil, and coal, were the results "of an imperative economic law which cannot be repealed by legislation."[8] For Roosevelt, as with Karl Marx, capitalism contained an inexorable tendency towards becoming a monopoly economy. Accordingly, the measure to be taken was not to prevent such combinations as it would be a futile attempt, but "in completely controlling them in the interest of the public welfare."[9] In effect, Roosevelt (who also believed that "barbaric peoples" such as Native Americans and Aborigines had to be wiped out so that white people could monopolize their lands, and was an advocate of expanding the overseas US empire which by his time included Cuba, Hawaii, the Philippines, and a string of Pacific islands)[10] was proposing the abandonment of a decentralized, competition-based economy in favor of the creation of a corporation-state alliance state (which at the time the Germans had been building as we have seen earlier through encouraging cartelization of various industries) that would propel the US to achieving global economic and political primacy over its rivals. As policy advocate Tim Wu put it, if Roosevelt had had his way, all commerce would be controlled by a small group of monopolists who in turn would be controlled by the government, leading to a union of political and economic power unknown to even the most powerful rulers of history.[11] And if this state-corporate monopolist empire had been realized, Wu asserts that the US would have had a profoundly different and "far darker" history, given that similar empires were linked with fascist and totalitarian regimes including Nazi Germany, Fascist Italy, and Imperial Japan.[12]

Times have changed and the US is certainly in many ways a different country from what it used to be at the beginning of the 20th century when Roosevelt was president. Nevertheless, the fact that for several decades the US government had essentially looked the other way with regard to the activities and growth of US-based Internet platform companies such as Alphabet (Google) and Amazon, and allowed them to dominate their respective fields of search services and social networking, may make some wonder whether there are those in the US government who in this day and age either agree, sympathize, or empathize with the assertions of Roosevelt.

Strategies for dealing with Realists, Liberals, and followers of Power Transition theory

Given the views on the state of international relations held by Realists, a global investor who wants to receive the blessing of Realist-minded political leaders for an investment proposal including a M&A would be well advised to convince such leaders that approving the investment is in the interests of expanding the relative power of the state. For example, the investor could demonstrate that a certain merger proposal would lead to the state becoming the leading global provider of a certain product or technology, thereby increasing its leverage over other states. A case in point is the US Department of Justice's (DoJ) approval in July 2019 of the merger between the No.3 wireless carrier in the US, T-Mobile, with the No.4 carrier, Sprint Corporation. Germany's Deutsche Telekom owns T-Mobile while Japanese technology conglomerate Softbank owns Sprint. With this merger T-Mobile and Sprint's combined market share would be close to 30%, making it the third largest carrier in the US after the leader Verizon and second place AT&T. Just three carriers would be the provider of 95% of wireless services to customers in the US.[13] The DoJ had earlier under the Obama administration rejected the merger proposal stating that the reduction from four to three national wireless providers was uncompetitive. The DoJ under the Trump administration, however, consented and essentially reversed its earlier stance despite the vocal concerns that were registered that the merger would lead to higher prices, job cuts, and harm to consumers nationwide.[14] What made the DoJ change its mind is not known, but there have been reports that in having the DoJ reverse its stance the Japanese and German companies appealed to Donald Trump's arguably Realist worldview and his desire for the US to "win" the global next-generation 5G network race with China.[15] Ajit Pai, chairman of the Federal Communications Commission, also backed the deal with the Realist-inspired comment that the merger would advance the leadership of the US in rolling out the 5G networks.[16] In this case, unlike Broadcom in its attempt to acquire Qualcomm, the two foreign-owned wireless carriers were successful in tapping the Realist nerve of the Trump administration and its interest to enhance the relative power of the US especially vis-à-vis China, the perceived number one strategic rival to the US. And as such, the Trump administration's Realist-inspired drive for more power had arguably superseded the concerns held by the Obama administration and by fair competition advocates about the possible harm to consumers and competition that may arise as a result of this merger.

As for Liberals, they, like Realists, share the view that the condition of the state of international relations is a state of anarchy. Where Liberals depart from Realists is that Liberals maintain that the co-existence of various societal groups both within and among states creates incentives for deepening cross-border economic, social, and cultural interactions. State preferences or national interests cannot therefore be reduced to a simple metric such as security or power. Liberals do not assume, as Realists do, that each state pursues the specific goal of amassing power for the sake of increasing security. For Liberals, it is not the balance of power that will determine state behavior and maintain peace but rather the alignment of conflicting interests and goals held by states and the interdependence that is created from the interactions of various societal groups in and among states. Accordingly, if an inbound investment or a business merger or acquisition proposal was brought to the attention of government leaders with a Liberal view of the world, they would, like Realists, have concerns about the possible impact an investment or a M&A would have on their state's national security. They would also, however, be more likely than Realists to take into consideration the possible impact on competition and consumer welfare if such a proposal was approved or rejected, as well as to appraise the implications of either decision on bilateral relations with the country from which the M&A or investment proposal originated.

Hence, for a global investor to receive the blessing of Liberal-minded political leaders for its proposal, the investor may need to convince such leaders that approving the M&A or inbound investment is in the interests of promoting competition, increasing the welfare of individual consumers in the target state, and contributing to the growth of global wealth. The investor may also want to emphasize that approving the inbound investment will be in the interests of promoting peaceful international relations through greater economic interdependence arising out of the investment. Accordingly, had T-Mobile and Sprint taken this approach in pitching their merger proposal to the liberal-minded Obama administration which had rejected it out of concerns about its impact on competition, they might have been successful and would not have had to wait until several years later for the Realist Trump administration to bless the merger proposal.

Which goes to say, if there are any potential lessons to be learned from the Sprint-T-Mobile merger as well as from the other examples mentioned previously for global investors or business people who may face issues of competition law when undertaking an international business transaction such as when attempting to undertake a M&A, they are as follows:

- Be aware of the views held by state leaders about the condition of international relations (e.g., are they looking at international relations through the lens of anarchical Realism, International Liberalism, or do they perceive state-to-state relations to be shaped within the existence of an international order?).
- Understand what state leaders perceive to be their national interests beyond that of defending their sovereignty (e.g., do they prefer guns or butter? Do they highly care about improving the welfare of their citizens?)
- Adjust your business or sales "pitch" to state leaders such that would enable you to accommodate their view of international relations and their national interests (e.g., if the main interest of the state leaders is to grow the power of the state or to be "No.1" in the world, seeking approval from them for a merger or acquisition proposal by emphasizing its advantages or merits to efficiency, competition, or consumer welfare may not be wholly effective in garnering their sympathy for your proposal. Instead, frame your "pitch" from a perspective that would allow you to highlight to the state leaders why approving your merger or acquisition proposal would allow their state to

become a world leader or "No.1" in a certain field or industry or what approval would mean in terms of the state's power-relationship vis-à-vis states that it considers to be its competitors. Conversely, it would be recommended to emphasize to those state leaders that take a liberal internationalist view of the world the merits that your merger or acquisition proposal would bring to their *people* such as, improvements to consumer welfare, stable foreign relations, and more inbound foreign investment).

Finally, in taking into consideration the views of Power Transition (PT) theory followers who believe that instead of anarchy there is an international hierarchical order consisting of a Dominant Power and a group of Great Powers, global investors will need to be aware of how their investment in a foreign state may impact the relative standing of that state within the order, i.e., the most prominent one being that of the international liberal economic order established after World War II (WWII) and dominated since then by the US. For example, a M&A transaction in a Great Power state may significantly boost its economy to the extent that the Dominant Power may begin to feel threatened. This possible outcome may thus induce the Great Power state to either welcome the investment as they see it as an opportunity to challenge the Dominant Power for becoming the leader of the order or they may choose to deny approval of the transaction as they fear provoking the Dominant Power into undertaking some economic or political measure to keep the Great Power in its subordinate position. The Dominant Power on its part may apply pressure on the Great Power to refuse approving the foreign investment as they may view the transaction a potential threat towards its dominant position. An example of such a case is arguably the pressure that the US is applying on its European and Japanese allies in having them refuse equipment and services for their respective 5G high-speed communications infrastructure provided by the Chinese telecommunications company Huawei, which the US sees as an extended arm of the Chinese government and thus a challenge to its national security and to its position as the Dominant Power of the international order.[17] In effect, the US attempt to blackball Huawei, without any consideration of the impact on global consumer welfare, is arguably undertaken within the context of a geopolitical power struggle between the US and China over who gets to be the Dominant Power in the international economic order for the years to come.

Seen from this perspective, it appears that in the third decade of the 21st century we may have a situation where businesses and global investors may need to design their investment and commercial strategies within a liberal international economic order that is now facing a Realist-inspired, winner-take-all power struggle for the top position of Dominant Power. Who gets to be on top may entail substantial changes in the nature of the international economic order (thereby affecting among other things, the global enforcement of competition laws) and accordingly determine how business enterprises and global investors may need to adjust their commercial practices on an international level.

In the meantime

There have been episodes in world history when a wave of Liberalism has led to states making concessions of sovereignty for the goal of concluding global trade agreements. The General Agreement on Tariffs and Trade (GATT) and the establishment of the World Trade Organization (WTO) suggest that not all states have an insatiable appetite for power or take the view that maximizing power accumulation is essential for survival. Yet the past and recent behavior of states (including in the M&A examples detailed in the previous chapter), and particularly of the so-called Great Powers[18] which have had the greatest impact on world affairs, suggests that their leaders have held, and still do hold, a fundamentally Realist outlook on international relations that has manifested itself in tariff wars, political disputes, cancellation of trade agreements, border disputes, and armed conflicts. For the leaders of states who view international relations through a Realist framework, that is, a constant zero-sum struggle for power in a condition of anarchy, their national economies, spearheaded by their companies, are engaged in fierce competition to increase their market share of global economic power.[19] Such leaders see little incentive to agree with each other to enact a global competition law that will in effect force them to restrict their sovereignty and sacrifice their ability to protect what they perceive to be their national interests for the sake of increased global wealth and protecting business competition. The uptake in nationalist and exclusivist movements in the US and Europe, in no small part fueled by Donald Trump's call for "America first," will likely make the possibility of states agreeing on a global competition law even more remote.

In the meantime, what liberal-minded leaders in the international community could possibly work towards is agreement to the idea that respective competition laws and policies should be applied with consistency and fairness to cross-border M&A and other competition-related issues such as export cartels, regardless of whether the companies involved are domestic or international.[20] The Organisation for Economic Co-operation and Development (OECD) recommends that states work together in agreeing to observe the concept of comity or the voluntary policy of giving full consideration to another nation's important interests when enforcing a state's own competition law.[21] To this end, the building of better cooperation and understanding of best practices among the competition authorities of each nation may perhaps be accomplished by states working (as previously and currently undertaken) through avenues such as the International Competition Network (ICN).[22]

Ultimately, however, for there to be an agreement on a global competition law or policy, political and economic leaders of states may need to remind themselves that the protection of competition using competition laws is for the purposes of encouraging innovation and promoting the welfare of consumers everywhere, which in the end benefits the peoples of their own countries. State leaders may also consider that in taking a concerted approach towards protecting competition that would prevent excessive market concentration and the formation of monopolies a broader goal of a global competition policy and laws would be to reduce domestic and global wealth inequality, an objective that would probably have the support of most of the states that already have their own competition laws.

Finally, state leaders may need to recognize that competition is a private activity that takes place between companies and not states. Companies generally compete in a winner-takes-all struggle for profits and market share, and some with the hopes of becoming a monopoly. States on the other hand, as pointed out by the economist Paul Krugman, do not compete in this sense, although they may be rivals for prestige and power.[23] International trade between states, for example, is not a zero-sum game where one country amassing a trade surplus against another is deemed a "winner" and the quality of life of its people is necessarily better than that in other states. A prominent case in point is the US which has been having a large current account deficit towards China for several years. Despite this situation, the majority of Americans have been able to continue to buy low-priced mass consumer products from China, leading to a rise in the overall purchasing power and quality of life of Americans. The trade deficit with China has also not stopped the majority of Americans from continuing to enjoy having living standards far surpassing that of the majority of the citizens of China.

In short, states, unlike companies, do not have a "bottom line." States also do not go out of business (with the arguable exception of so-called failed states and states that have been conquered). What states may have to face, however, is the prospect of their companies failing to produce goods and services that meet the test of international competition and of resultant falling living standards for their citizens if their leaders, regardless of whether they are of the Realist, Liberal, or Power Transitionist mode, are not perspicacious enough to realize that the protection of competition is in effect in their national interest.

Notes

1 *The Economist*, Crony Capitalism, April 15, 2017, *The Economist*, Second Time, Farce, May 5, 2018, *The Economist*, The Economist at 175, September 15–21 2018, The Japan News, JFTC May Launch Investigation into IT Giants' Transactions, October 13, 2018.

2 *The Economist*, The Economist at 175, September 15–21 2018, p.44; Wu, Tim, Be afraid of economic "bigness." Be very afraid, *New York Times*, November 14, 2018.

3 Office of the Prime Minister, Presidency Press Conference by Prime Minister Shinzo Abe Following the G20 Osaka Summit, June 29, 2019, Online. Available https://japan.kantei.go.jp/98_abe/statement/201906/_00002.html (accessed August 3, 2019).

4 *Financial Times*, Chinese claims of chipmakers market abuse raise stakes in the trade war with the U.S., Nov. 20, 2018, Forbes, Class Action Suit Alleges Samsung, Micron, and Hynix Colluded on DRAM Supply Causing Price Inflation, April 27, 2018. Online, Available https://www.forbes.com/sites/davealtavilla/2018/04/27/class-action-suit-alleges-samsung-micron-and-hynix-colluded-on-dram-supply-causing-price-inflation/#683d1d1217ce (accessed June 29, 2019).

5 Given the political context surrounding these cases, i.e., rising rivalry between the US and China and a preoccupation with eliminating as much as possible foreign control in Japan, anti-Chinese and anti-foreign nationalism may also have been at play in the decisions behind the Broadcom and J-Power cases.

6 Dinc, Serdac, Erel, Isil, *Economic Nationalism in Mergers and Acquisitions*, Wiley, August 2013, p.1. Available, Online https://papers.ssrn.com/sol3/papers.cfm?abstract_id=1361107 (accessed June 29, 2019).

7 Wu, Tim, The Curse of Bigness, *Columbia Global Reports*, 2018, p.75.
8 Roosevelt, Theodore, New Nationalism Speech, August 31, 1910, Online. Available https://obamawhitehouse.archives.gov/blog/2011/12/06/archives-president-teddy-roosevelts-new-nationalism-speech (accessed June 29, 2019).
9 Ibid.
10 Unoki, Ko, Mergers, *Acquisitions, and Global Empires*, Routledge, 2012, pp.19–20.
11 Wu, The Curse of Bigness, op.cit., p.76.
12 Ibid.
13 *Wall Street Journal*, U.S. Approves T-Mobile-Sprint Merger, July 26, 2019, Online. Available https://www.wsj.com/articles/justice-department-approves-merger-of-t-mobile-us-and-sprint-11564155026 (accessed July 29, 2019).
14 *The Mainichi*, T-Mobile's $26.5B Sprint deal OK'd despite competition fears, July 27, 2019, Online. Available https://mainichi.jp/english/articles/20190727/p2g/00m/0bu/038000c (accessed July 29, 2019).
15 Ibid.
16 *Wall Street Journal*, op.cit.
17 *Japan Times*, Trump Losing Fight to Keep Huawei Out of Global Networks, May 15, 2019. Despite President Trump's worldwide campaign to keep Huawei out of global markets, not a single European state has heeded his call, while in Asia only Japan and Australia had joined the boycott (as of May 2019). Aside from not viewing Huawei as a threat in the way that the US does, the refusal of the Europeans to join the US could also mean from a Power Transition perspective that by refusing the Europeans in effect intend to challenge the US position as the Dominant Power of the International Liberal Economic Order, or that they no longer see the US as being able to continue in its position as the Dominant Power, and that by welcoming Huawei they are in effect placing their bets on the possibility that China may replace the US as the Dominant Power of a new international order.
18 That is, China, France, Germany, India, Italy, Japan, Russia, the UK, and the US.
19 Gilpin, Robert, *Global Political Economy*, Princeton University Press, 2001, p.181.
20 Reuters, Asia Pacific Nations Sign Sweeping Trade Deal Without U.S., March 8, 2018, Online. Available https://www.reuters.com/article/us-trade-tpp/asia-pacific-nations-sign-sweeping-trade-deal-without-u-s-idUSKCN1GK0JM (accessed August 3, 2019); Shiraishi, Takashi, The Geostrategic Significance of the TPP Agreement for the Asia Pacific, Nippon.com, January 28, 2016, Online. Available http://www.nippon.com/en/column/g00338/ (accessed August 3, 2019); United States Trade Representative, TPP Treaty, Online. Available https://ustr.gov/sites/default/files/TPP-Final-Text-Competition.pdf (accessed August 3, 2019); Bishop, William W., *International Law*, Little, Brown and Company, 1971, p.559; Gerber, David J., *Global Competition*, Oxford University Press, 2012, p.61.
21 Kojima, Takaaki, International Conflicts over the Extraterritorial Application of Competition Law in a Borderless Economy, Weatherhead Center for International Affairs, 2002, p.25; Concurrences, Glossary of Competition Terms, Online. Available http://www.concurrences.com/en/droit-de-la-concurrence/glossary-of-competition-terms/Comity (accessed June 25, 2017).
22 The ICN was launched in 2001 and provides a venue for competition agencies to deal with competition policy and enforcement issues.
23 Krugman, Paul, Competitiveness: A Dangerous Obsession, *Foreign Affairs*, Vol. 73, No. 2, March/April 1994, pp.28–44.

Suggested further reading

Allen, James S., *The Cartel System*, International Publishers, 1946.

American Antitrust Institute (AAI), How Mergers Can Harm Consumers, AAI Public Interest Advocacy Workshop on Mergers, October 11, 2013, Online. Available http://www.antitrustinstitute.org/sites/default/files/Overview_1.pdf.

Angell, Norman, *The Great Illusion*, Cosmo Inc., 2007.

Ansoff, Igor, *Corporate Strategy*, Penguin Books, 1985.

Barone, Charles A., *Marxist Thought on Imperialism*, M.E. Sharpe Inc., 1985.

Beckler, Richard W., Kirtland, Mathew H., Extraterritorial Application of U.S. Antitrust Law, *Texas International Law Journal*, Vol. 38, No. 11/Winter, 2003, Online. Available http://www.tilj.org/content/journal/38/num1/Beckler-Kirtland11.pdf.

Bishop, William W., *International Law*, Little, Brown and Company, 1971.

Bodansky, Robert L., Dyer, Jospeh J., "America First" and its Impact on Cross-Border M&A, Association for Corporate Growth, August 7, 2017, Online. Available http://middlemarketgrowth.org/america-first-impact-cross-border-ma/.

Bradford, Anu, International Antitrust Negotiations and the False Hope of the WTO, *Harvard International Law Journal*, Vol. 48, No. 2/Summer, 2007, Online. Available http://www.harvardilj.org/wp-content/uploads/2010/09/HILJ_48-2_Bradford.pdf.

Brooks, Douglas H., Competition Policy and Development, Asian Development Bank, October, 2005, Online. Available https://www.adb.org/sites/default/files/publication/28098/pb039.pdf.

Brown, Chris, Nardin, Terry, Rengger, Nicholas, eds, *International Relations in Political Thought*, Cambridge University Press, 2010.

Burchill, Scott, *The National Interest in International Relations Theory*, Palgrave Macmillan, 2005.

Byrne, Mathew R., Protecting National Security and Promoting Foreign Investment, *Ohio State Law Journal*, Vol. 67, No. 849, 2006, Online. Available http://moritzlaw.osu.edu/students/groups/oslj/files/2012/04/67.4.byrne_.pdf.

Calster, Geert van, International Law and Sovereignty in the Age of Globalization, *Encyclopedia of Life Support Systems*, Online. Available http://www.eolss.net/sample-chapters/c14/e1-36-01-04.pdf.

Carr, Edward Hallett, *The Twenty Years' Crisis 1919–1939*, Harper Torchbooks, 1964.

Christophers, Brett, *The Great Leveler*, Harvard University Press, 2016.

Cutts, Robert L., Capitalism in Japan: Cartels and Keiretsu, *Harvard Business Review*, July–August, 1992, Online. Available https://hbr.org/1992/07/capitalism-in-japan-cartels-and-keiretsu.

Daddow, Oliver, *International Relations Theory*, Sage Publications Ltd., 2013.

Davidson, Adam, Teddy Roosevelt Would Not Understand the E.U.'s Antitrust Fine Against Google, *The New Yorker*, June 28, 2017, Online. Available http://www.newyorker.com/business/adam-davidson/teddy-roosevelt-wouldnt-understand-the-eus-antitrust-fine-against-google.

de Bary, Wm. Theodore, Keene, Donald, Tanabe, George, Varley, Paul, *Sources of Japanese Tradition*, Vol. 1, Columbia University Press, 2001.

Dinc, Serdac, Erel, Isil, *Economic Nationalism in Mergers and Acquisitions*, Wiley, August, 2013, Online. Available https://papers.ssrn.com/sol3/papers.cfm?abstract_id=1361107.

Dougherty, James E., PfaltzgraffJr., Robert L., *Contending Theories of International Relations*, Addison Wesley Longman Inc., 2001.

Epstein, Julian, The Other Side of Harmony: Can Trade and Competition Laws Together in the International Marketplace?, *American University International Law Review*, January, 2002, Online. Available http://digitalcommons.wcl.american.edu/auilr/vol17/iss2/2/.

Fear, Jeffrey, *Cartels and Competition: Neither Markets nor Hierarchies*, Harvard Business School, 2006, Online. Available https://www.hbs.edu/faculty/Publication%20Files/07-011.pdf.

Fidler, David P., *Competition Law and International Relations*, Maurer School of Law, Indiana University, 1992, Online. Available https://www.repository.law.indiana.edu/cgi/viewcontent.cgi?article=3129&context=facpub.

Foster, John Bellamy, McChesney, Robert W., Jonna, Jamil R., Monopoly and Competition in Twenty-First Century Capitalism, *Monthly Review*, Vol. 62, No. 11, 2011, Online. Available https://www.researchgate.net/publication/275600503_Monopoly_and_Competition_in_Twenty-First_Century_Capitalism.

Friedman, Thomas, *The Lexus and the Olive Tree*, Thorndike Press, 1999.

Fukuyama, Francis, *The End of History and the Last Man*, Free Press, 2006.

Gellhorn, Ernest, Kovacic, William E., *Antitrust and Economics*, West Group, 1994.

Gerber, David J., *Global Competition*, Oxford University Press, 2012.

Gifford, Daniel J., *Antitrust and Trade Issues, University of Minnesota Law School DePaul Law Review*, Vol. 44, 1995, Online. Available https://scholarship.law.umn.edu/faculty_articles/318.

Graham, Edward M., Richardson, J. David., eds, *Global Competition Policy*, Peterson Institute of International Economics, 1997.

Greguras, Fred M., O'Neil, Michael J., Zhu, Chenhao, M&A in the United States: What Chinese Companies Need to Know about Exon-Florio Review in the Clean Technology and Other Business Sectors, Fletcher School of Law & Diplomacy, April, 2012, Online. Available http://fletcher.tufts.edu/~/media/Fletcher/Microsites/swfi/pdfs/2012/Updated_Exon-Florio.pdf.

Greidinger, Marc, The Exon-Florio Amendment: A Solution in Search of a Problem, *American University Law Review*, Vol. 6, 1991, Online. Available http://digitalcommons.wcl.american.edu/cgi/viewcontent.cgi?article=1553&context=auilr.

Haley, John Owen, *Authority Without Power*, Oxford University Press, 1991.

Hobbes, Thomas, *Leviathan*, Encyclopedia Britannica, 1982.

Hufbauer, Gary, Kim, Jisun, International Competition Policy and the WTO, Peterson Institute for International Economics, April 11, 2008, Online. Available https://piie.com/commentary/speeches-papers/international-competition-policy-and-wto.

Husby, Christian, CFIUS: The Little Known Multi-Billion Dollar Deal Killer, *The Michigan Journal of International Law*, Vol. 37, Online. Available http://www.mjilononline.org/cfius-the-little-known-multi-billion-dollar-deal-killer/.

Immenga, Ulrich, Export Cartels and Voluntary Export Restraints Between Trade and Competition Policy, Pacific Rim Law & Policy Association, 1995, Online. Available https://digital.lib.washington.edu/dspace-law/bitstream/handle/1773.1/932/4PacRimLPolyJ093.pdf?sequence=1&isAllowed=y.

Joll, James, *The Origins of the First World War*, Longman, 1992.

Kamenka, Eugene, ed., *The Portable Karl Marx*, Viking Penguin Inc., 1983.

Kang, David C., *East Asia Before the West*, Columbia University Press, 2010.

Kearns, Jason E., International Competition Policy and the GATS: A Proposal to Address Market Access Limitations in the Distribution Services Sector, *University of Pennsylvania Journal of International Law*, Vol. 22, No. 2, 2014, Online. Available https://scholarship.law.upenn.edu/cgi/viewcontent.cgi?article=1297&context=jil.

Keynes, John Maynard, *The Economic Consequences of the Peace*, Chapter 2, Online. Available http://www.econlib.org/library/YPDBooks/Keynes/kynsCP2.html.

Klein, Julius, International Cartels, *Foreign Affairs*, April, 1928.

Kojima, Takaaki, International Conflicts over the Extraterritorial Application of Competition Law in a Borderless Economy, Weatherhead Center for International Affairs, 2002, Online. Available https://programs.wcfia.harvard.edu/files/fellows/files/kojima.pdf.

Kokkoris, Ioannis, Should Crisis Cartels Exist Amidst Crises?, December 1, 2010, Sage Publications, Online. Available https://www.antitrustinstitute.org/sites/default/files/Financial%20Crisis.pdf.

Kugler, Jacek, Organski, A.F.K., *The Power Transition: A Retrospective and Prospective Evaluation, Handbook of War Studies*, Routledge, 1989.

Lee, J.S., *Strategies to Achieve a Binding International Agreement on Regulating Cartels*, Springer Nature, Singapore, 2016.

Machiavelli, Niccolò, *The Prince*, Encyclopedia Britannica, Inc., 1982.

Manne, Geoffrey A., Weinberger, Seth, International Signals: The political dimension of international competition law, *The Antitrust Bulletin*, Vol. 57, No. 3/Fall, 2012, Online. Available https://papers.ssrn.com/sol3/papers.cfm?abstract_id=1448223.

Martin, Stephen, The Goal of Antitrust and Competition Policy, Purdue University, July, 2007, Online. Available ftp://ftp.zew.de/pub/zew-docs/veranstaltungen/rnic/papers/StephenMartin.pdf.

Martyniszyn, Marek, Export Cartels: Is it Legal to Target Your Neighbor?, *Journal of International Economic Law*, 181–222, 2012, Online. Available https://pure.qub.ac.uk/portal/files/13701517/SSRN_id2012838_1.pdf.

Martyniszyn, Marek, Japanese Approaches to Extraterritoriality in Competition Law, Cambridge Core, 2017, Online. Available https://pure.qub.ac.uk/portal/files/125650658/JAPANESE_APPROACHES_TO_EXTRATERRITORIALITY_IN_COMPETITION_LAW.pdf.

Marx, Karl, Engels, Friedrich, *Capital*, Encyclopedia Britannica Inc., 1980.

Marx, Karl, A Contribution to the Critique of Political Economy (in Kamenka, *The Portable Karl Marx*, Viking Penguin Inc., 1983).

Marx, Karl, Manifesto of the Communist Party (in Kamenka, *The Portable Karl Marx*, Viking Penguin Inc., 1983).

Ministry of Economy, Trade and Industry (METI), Excessive Extraterritorial Application of Competition Laws, Online. Available http://www.meti.go.jp/english/report/downloadfiles/2008WTO/2-14-2ExcessiveExtraterritorial.pdf.

Moravcsik, Andrew, *Liberal Theories of International Relations: A Primer*, Princeton University, 2010.

Morgenthau, Hans J., *Politics Among Nations*, McGraw Hill, Inc., 1985.

Morris, Ian, *War: What Good is it for?*, Profile Books, 2015.

Nagasawa, Toru, "J Power mondai" ga shocho suru keisanshou kanryo no gaishi arerugi, *Diamond Online*, April 4, 2008, Online. Available http://diamond.jp/articles/-/6317.

Ng, Julian, Foreign Investments: What Developments in the US and China Mean, *National Security Reviews of Foreign Investment*, October 23, 2017, Online. Available https://themarketmogul.com/national-security-review-us-china/.

Noonan, Chris, *Emerging Principles of International Competition Law*, Oxford University Press, 2008.

Organisation for Economic Co-operation and Development (OECD), *OECD Code of Liberalisation of Capital Movements*, 2018, Online. Available http://www.oecd.org/investment/investment-policy/codes.htm.

Organski, A.F.K., *World Politics*, Alfred A. Knopf Inc., 1968.

Porter, Michael, *Competition and Anti-trust: A Productivity-Based Approach*, Harvard Business School, 2002, Online. Available https://www.isc.hbs.edu/Documents/pdf/053002antitrust.pdf.

Quigley, Carroll, *Tragedy and Hope*, The Macmillan Company, 1966.

Rifkin, Jeremy, *The Zero Marginal Cost Society*, Palgrave Macmillan, 2015.

Roddy, Peter, *The International Tin Trade*, Woodhead Publishing, 1995.

Rosenthal, Douglas E., Nicolaides, Phedon, Harmonizing Antitrust, Peterson Institute of International Economics, December, 1997, Online. Available https://piie.com/publica tions/chapters_preview/56/11ie1664.pdf.

Rosseau, Jean Jacques, *On Political Economy*, Encyclopedia Britannica Inc., 1982.

Saul, John Ralston, *The Collapse of Globalism*, Atlantic Books, 2018.

Schaede, Ulrike, *Cooperative Capitalism*, Oxford University Press, 2000.

Schumpeter, Joseph A., International Cartels and their Relation to World Trade, *Proceedings of the Academy of Political Science in the City of New York*, Vol. 12, No. 4, America as a Creditor Nation, The Academy of Political Science, Jan., 1928, Online. Available https://www.jstor.org/stable/1180285?seq=1#page_scan_tab_contents.

Schumpeter, Joseph A., *Capitalism, Socialism and Democracy*, Harper & Row Publishers, 1975.

Shiraishi, Takashi, The Geostrategic Significance of the TPP Agreement for the Asia Pacific, *Nippon.com*, January 28, 2016, Online. Available http://www.nippon.com/en/colum n/g00338/.

Shukan Diamond, Mokaru Nogyo 2018 (Profits from Agriculture in 2018), Diamond-sha, February 24, 2018.

Slaughter, Anne Marie, Liberal International Relations Theory and International Economic Law, *American University International Law Review*, Vol. 10, No. 2, 1995, Online. Available http://digitalcommons.wcl.american.edu/cgi/viewcontent.cgi?article=1432&context=auilr.

Smith, Adam, *An Inquiry into the Causes of the Wealth of Nations*, Encyclopedia Britannica Inc., 1982.

Sokol, D. Daniel, Monopolists Without Borders, University of Wisconsin Law School, Legal Studies Research Paper Series, Paper No. 1034, February, 2007, Online. Available https://papers.ssrn.com/sol3/papers.cfm?abstract_id=988381.

Starkey, David J., Harlaftis, Gelinda, eds, *Global Markets: The Internationalization of the Sea Transport Industries Since 1850*, St. John's, 1998.

Stiglitz, Joseph E., *Making Globalization Work*, Norton, 2006.

Stucke, Maurice E., Is Competition Always Good?, *Journal of Antitrust Enforcement*, Vol. 1, No. 1, 2013, Online. Available https://papers.ssrn.com/sol3/papers.cfm?abstract_id=215719.

Suzumura, Kotaro, Competition, Welfare, and Competition Policy, *CPRC*, December, 2005, Online. Available http://www.jftc.go.jp/cprc/koukai/sympo/2003symposium/2003agenda.files/agenda2.pdf.
Takahashi, Iwakazu, Anti-Monopoly Exemptions in Japan, The Specific Workshop between the Drafting Committee on Competition Law of Vietnam and the Japan Fair Trade Commission, August 8, 2003, Online. Available http://www.jftc.go.jp/eacpf/05/hanoiTaka.pdf.
Tammen, Ronald L., Kugler, Jacek, Lemke, Douglas, StamIII, Allan C., Alsharabati, Carole, Abdollahian, Mark Andrew, Efrid, Brian, Organski, A.F.K., *Power Transitions*, CQ Press, 2000.
Taylor, Martyn, *International Competition Law*, Cambridge University Press, 2006.
Teichova, Alice, *An Economic Background to Munich*, Cambridge University Press, 1974.
Uematsu, Takafumi, Japan, *The Foreign Investment Regulation Review*, Edition 5, The Law Reviews, September, 2017, Online. Available https://www.uria.com/documentos/publicaciones/5425/colaboraciones/2094/documento/Spain_tfirr.pdf?id=7095.
United States Department of Justice (USDJ), Federal Trade Commission (FTC), Antitrust Guidelines for International Enforcement and Cooperation, U.S. Department of Justice and Federal Trade Commission, January 30, 2017, Online. Available https://www.justice.gov/atr/internationalguidelines/download.
Unoki, Ko, *Mergers, Acquisitions, and Global Empires*, Routledge, 2012.
Usami, Jun, Moran, William, Cho, Fumiko, National Security Reviews 2017: A Global Perspective: Japan, Online. Available https://www.whitecase.com/publications/insight/national-security-reviews-global-perspective-japan.
Vesey, Caleb, Per se Rules in U.S. and EU Antitrust/Competition Law, New York Law School, Online. Available http://www.eucomplaw.com/comparing-eu-and-us-competition-law/per-se-rules/.
Waltz, Kenneth N., *Theory of International Politics*, McGraw-Hill Inc., 1979.
Weber, Cynthia, *International Relations Theory*, Routledge, 2001.
White, Lawrence J., The Role of Competition Policy in the Promotion of Economic Growth, CPRC Discussion Paper Series, May, 2008, Online. Available http://lsr.nellco.org/cgi/viewcontent.cgi?article=1136&context=nyu_lewp.
Wu, Tim, The Curse of Bigness, *Columbia Global Reports*, 2018.

Index

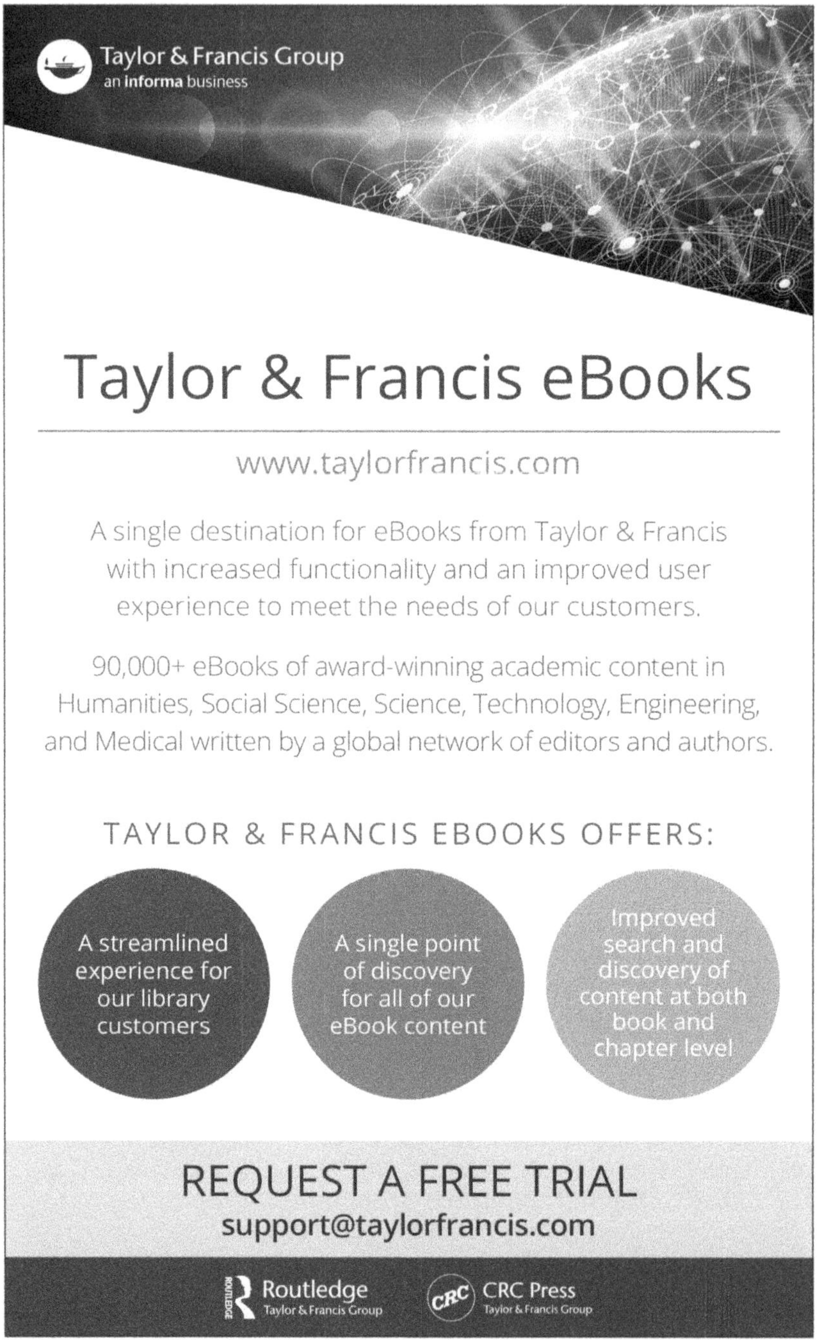
Taylor & Francis Group
an informa business
Taylor & Francis eBooks
www.taylorfrancis.com
A single destination for eBooks from Taylor & Francis with increased functionality and an improved user experience to meet the needs of our customers.
90,000+ eBooks of award-winning academic content in Humanities, Social Science, Science, Technology, Engineering, and Medical written by a global network of editors and authors.
TAYLOR & FRANCIS EBOOKS OFFERS:
A streamlined experience for our library customers
A single point of discovery for all of our eBook content
Improved search and discovery of content at both book and chapter level
REQUEST A FREE TRIAL
support@taylorfrancis.com
Routledge
Taylor & Francis Group
CRC Press
Taylor & Francis Group

For Product Safety Concerns and Information please contact our EU
representative GPSR@taylorandfrancis.com
Taylor & Francis Verlag GmbH, Kaufingerstraße 24, 80331 München, Germany

www.ingramcontent.com/pod-product-compliance
Ingram Content Group UK Ltd.
Pitfield, Milton Keynes, MK11 3LW, UK
UKHW022122190926
475702UK00013B/1593

* 9 7 8 1 0 3 2 0 8 6 9 3 4 *